An Essay on Theology and History

ÆR

American Academy of Religion
Studies in Religion

Editor
Lawrence S. Cunningham

Number 61
AN ESSAY ON THEOLOGY AND HISTORY

by
J. A. Colombo

AN ESSAY ON THEOLOGY AND HISTORY
Studies in Pannenberg, Metz,
and the Frankfurt School

by
J. A. Colombo

Scholars Press
Atlanta, Georgia

AN ESSAY ON THEOLOGY AND HISTORY

by
J. A. Colombo

© 1990
The American Academy of Religion

Library of Congress Cataloging in Publication Data
Colombo, Joseph A., 1954-
    An essay on theology and history : studies in Pannenberg, Metz,
    and the Frankfurt School / by J. A. Colombo.
    p. cm. — (American Academy of Religion studies in religion ;
    no. 61)
    Includes bibliographical references and index.
    ISBN 1-55540-540-1 (alk. paper). — ISBN 1-55540-541-X (pbk.)
    1. History (Theology)—History of doctrines—20th century.
2. Pannenberg, Wolfhart, 1928-   . 3. Horkheimer, Max, 1895-1973.
4. Adorno, Theodor W., 1903-1969. 5. Metz, Johannes Baptist, 1928-
I. Title. II. Series: AAR studies in religion ; no. 61.
BR115.H5C58 1990
230'.0943—dc20

                                              90-24042
                                            CIP

Printed in the United States of America
on acid-free paper

CONTENTS

INTRODUCTION

Christianity is a "historical religion." What appears clear at first glance, however, becomes opaque upon reflection. A number of distinct meanings are potentially included within this phrase. First, it may mean that the origin and norm of Christianity is a historical person, Jesus of Nazareth. Christianity is a historical religion then insofar as the referent of its affirmations is the action of God in that historical person. Needless to say, the emergence of the historical sciences has rendered such a position problematic as "quests" and "new quests" of the historical Jesus demonstrate.

Second, the assertion that Christianity is a historical religion may refer to its mediation by its historical situation, i.e., its boundedness by a social and cultural milieu which enter into its language and symbols. Contemporary hermeneutics, further, has raised to a reflective level the "historicity" of the process of *traditio*: the handing-on through interpretation of the *tradita* which bridges the distance between past and present in a "fusion of horizons." In this, there is nothing peculiar about Christianity as a historical religion. It is a characteristic which it shares with other religions as well as paradigms of science, organizations of political life, aesthetic styles etc..

Third, to call Christianity a historical religion sometimes refers to the "sort" of religion which Christianity is. Schleiermacher's definition of Christianity as a "monotheistic faith belonging to the teleological type of religion,"[1] Weber's designation of Christian piety as "inner-worldly asceticism,"[2] Farley's of "ecclesiality" as a "world-transforming reli-

---

[1] Schleiermacher, *The Christian Faith*, eds. H. R. Mackintosh and J. S. Stewart, with an introduction by Richard R. Niebuhr (New York: Harper and Row, 1963), p. 52.

[2] Max Weber, "The Social Psychology of the World Religions" and "Religious Rejections of the World and Their Directions," in *From Max Weber: Essays in Sociology*,

gion"[3] or Heiler's of Christianity as a "prophetic religion,"[4] to name a few, point to a particular relation between Christianity and the world: a referencing of Christianity's meaning and truth claim to the world understood as history. To be sure, such designations are peculiarly "modern" and thus appear at odds with the classical theology of the patristic, medieval and protestant-orthodoxy periods. But that such descriptions are not exclusively modern and draw upon the deep-structure of Christian symbols is suggested by the dialectic of creation and fall in the history of Christian theology—the orthodox church's rejection of an explicit ontological dualism between the world and salvation—and the affirmation of an hope in the resurrection of the dead and the advent of the Kingdom of God. It remains a further question to what degree classical theology and its paradigm of transcendence as spatially-vertical[5] implicitly internalized what it explicitly anathematized and effectively suppressed as apocalyptic "heresy" what it publicly affirmed. If each paradigm of theology must rewrite the history of Christianity from its own perspective, then it still remains a task to retrieve that history from the perspective of Christianity as a historical religion in this third sense.

It is important to note at this juncture a relation between Christianity as a historical religion in the first and third sense which is found in some theologians. A statement by Eduard Schillebeeckx is representative:

> First of all, I want to secure the openness of our developing history and therefore the reality of ongoing history even after the advent of Jesus. . . . Of course the Christian believes, in and through Jesus, that despite everything the Kingdom of God, as salvation for mankind, is still coming and will come; what has been achieved in Jesus Christ is the guarantee of this.[6]

What is interesting is neither Schillebeeckx' affirmation of the openness of history nor his assertion of Christianity's hope for an eschatological salvation and the redemption of history. What is interesting is his grounding of the "certainty" of the latter on a particular piece of history,

---

trans., ed. and with an introduction by H. H. Gerth and C. Wright Mills (New York: Oxford University Press, 1946), pp. 267-301, 323-59.

[3] Edward Farley, *Ecclesial Reflection* (Philadelphia: Fortress Press, 1982).

[4] Freidrich Heiler, *Prayer: A Study in the History and Psychology of Religion* (Oxford: Oxford University Press, 1932).

[5] Jürgen Moltmann, "The Future as a New Paradigm of Transcendence," in *The Future of Creation*, trans. Margaret Kohl (Philadelphia: Fortress Press, 1979), pp. 1-17.

[6] Eduard Schillebeeckx, *Interim Report on the Books "Jesus" and "Christ,"* trans. John Bowden (New York: Crossroad Publishing Co., 1981), p. 101.

Jesus of Nazareth. That piece of history is the bulwark against all subsequent history and guarantees it as a whole, all appearances to the contrary notwithstanding. The world-transforming quality of Christianity in its essential reference to history is not matched by any reciprocal relation whereby the events of history raise a fist against faith. Is it too much of an overstatement to suggest that here history as the history of suffering which has an ultimate if not final claim on humanity's attention is occluded and hence prevented from questioning the foundations of Christian belief and praxis?[7] Is not Christian theology thereby immunized in its noetic self-identity from the nonidentity of history as suffering and optimistically allowed to continue "business as usual" without being thrown back to reflect on its own foundations and fragility, or better, its foundations as fragile? Is the world as history "irredeemably redeemed" with the advent, death and resurrection of the Christ and does the *truth* of the Christian witness of faith have any essential relation to the events of this "open" history?

It is with Christianity as a "historical" religion in this third sense and these questions that I am concerned. This essay is a tentative way-marker more than a finished work. This is reflected in the structure of the expository portion of the essay: a chapter on Wolfhart Pannenberg, a chapter on Max Horkheimer and Theodor Adorno, and a chapter on Johann Metz. While one might think these men to be strange bedfellows, the choice was not arbitrary. Each addresses in an exemplary way some facet of the questions raised above.

Wolfhart Pannenberg has addressed the question of the meaning and truth of Christian faith and history in his "hermeneutics of universal history." Johann Metz has addressed the issue of the social mediation of the Christian tradition in his attempt to articulate a political theology in the context of the first-world. It is not misleading, I think, to observe that the reflections of Theodor Adorno and Max Horkheimer revolve around the reality of history as a history of suffering. In charting the "dialectic of Enlightenment" they attempted to restore to thought the nonidentity of reason and freedom in history as well as to advocate the necessity of a post-Enlightenment transition to the primacy of practical reason through a critical theory of society oriented to the good, the true and the beautiful as historical and therefore social exigencies.

---

[7] On the distinction between "finality" and "ultimacy," see Arthur Cohen, *The Tremendum: A Theological Interpretation of the Holocaust* (New York: Crossroad Publishing Co., 1981), p. 49-52.

The thesis of this essay is that there is a correlation between a theology of (universal) history and political theology. This relationship may be specified with two further assertions. First, a theology of (universal) history is the implied horizon of political theology. Second, political theology represents the most appropriate actualization of a theology of (universal) history. Lest I be misunderstood, the phrase "theology of (universal) history" always refers to a horizon. It is a horizon because it involves a fundamental reference of the meaning and truth claims of Christian faith to history "as a whole and eschatologically valorized." It also denotes a horizon because the attempt to write a theologically coherent narrative of history shatters on the events of public suffering which is the text of history. I have also bracketed the term "universal" in the sentences above. A *Christian* theology of (universal) *history* is a Christian *theology* of (*universal*) history because religion concerns, to use Pannenberg's phrase, a "totality of meaning." Yet insofar as that anticipation of meaning is confronted by the nonidentity of history in the surd of suffering, the project of "universal history" is ruptured.

As noted above, there is a separate chapter on each figure. Each figure is used to get at a particular set of issues. Yet this does not mean that there is a disjunctive relationship between the figures examined. The theological question is "What is the relation of the meaning and truth claims of the Christian witness of faith to history?" Implicitly, this question rejects the position which correlates the abstract historicity of the individual "hearer of the Word" with an equally time-less, i.e., kerygmatic, witness of faith which are bound together in a pure decision. Such positions unwittingly reduce history as the concrete nexus of socially-mediated events to a position of penultimacy or mere indifferent "matter" for faith. Increasingly these positions are themselves under suspicion of being ideological, a form of "false consciousness." The intersection of a "theology of history" as represented by Pannenberg and "political theology" as represented by Metz lies in their interpretation of the Christian tradition, especially the biblical witness: not in the context of the historicity of the subject of faith but in the context of history as a process of events within an eschatological horizon. The mediating link between Pannenberg and Metz is the work of Adorno and Horkheimer which exhibits the post-Enlightenment transition to the primacy of practical reason, an orientation to history as socially mediated and, hence, an orientation towards the nonidentity of reason and freedom in history as society. A more detailed outline of the argument follows.

The first chapter on Pannenberg focuses on his "foundational theology": anthropology and the question of God, the sense of religious language and its reality referent, the dialectic of religions and the construal of Christianity's anticipated totality of meaning. I try, however, to follow an immanent critique of this foundational theology in order, first, to identify those tendencies in Pannenberg's work where the "gap" between history as the determinate horizon of Christianity's totality of meaning and history as the open and indeterminate process of the transmission of traditions is attenuated. My aim here is to defend the claim to truth of other religious anticipated totalities of meaning. Second, I also question Pannenberg's defense of the resurrection as an historically verifiable event as a strategy for immunizing Christianity from the surd of history, suffering. In fact, these two lines of criticism overlap because his position on the resurrection functions both to veil the nonidentity of history as a history of suffering vis á vis Christianity as a totality of meaning and to negate the nonidentity of the truth claim of Christianity against those of other religions. If deprived of the certainty of the meaning of history as a whole through a reversal of his position on the resurrection, then the provisional and anticpative element of Christian faith becomes a focal point for theological reflection. The nonidentity of history with reason and freedom, i.e., history as the history of suffering, becomes relevant in understanding both the meaning and truth claims of Christianity.

Recourse is made to the work of Adorno and Horkheimer in the second chapter for two reasons. First, if for Pannenberg history is the transmission of traditions, Adorno's and Horkheimer's reflections demonstrate that an understanding of history as simply the transmission of traditions is an abstraction. The transmission of traditions has a context in which it is embedded, namely, the collective self-formation of men and women i.e., history as mediated by social totality. The assumption implicit in the "digressions" of the second chapter, i.e., on art, political economy, science, etc., is that she who wishes to speak of history concretely must simultaneously speak of society. The concept of history as the transmission of traditions is thus given a "materialist" twist and the work of Adorno and Horkheimer is important because of their explicit recognition of and reflection on the mediations of subject and object (as history/nature, individual/society, knowing subject/known object) which is history in its most concrete sense.

Second, the work of Adorno and Horkheimer exemplifies that interpretation of reality which is called post-Enlightenment because of their espousal of a "critical theory" which rejects both the notion of an "innocent criticism" and the myth of "pure reason." "The challenge of critical theory is to end innocent critique. By innocent criticism I mean that type of critical perspective so central in the development of modern culture: criticism unaware of its own presuppositions and thereby tending to erect itself as *the* criterion of all criticism."[8] Critical theory is a shorthand for "critical theory of society" with its exigency that "reason" and "freedom" are social-historical tasks.

Horkheimer and Adorno's thesis of the dialectic of enlightenment—in post-Enlightenment civilization "history is regressing to myth," regressing to an elimination of the objective conditions and subjective capacities for transcendence in history through the consolidation of the objective and subjective conditions for the automatic reproduction of the already existent—poses a challenge to Christian faith and theology. Theologians who cry "History, history!" in the name of Christianity and who overlook such conditions may no doubt register surprise at the cunning of a socially mediated history congealing upon itself. The most appropriate response of a Christian theology oriented to history as the horizon of its meaning and truth is an explicit "political theology" which raises to a reflective level the social-historical mediation of faith and reason.

The conclusion of this chapter explores the so-called "pessimism" and "resignation" in the works of both men. My argument is that phenomenon can be best analyzed into three converging themes: the method of determinate negation and the increasing precariousness of the critic qua academic to social praxis; an inversion of the "end of ideology" thesis; and, most importantly, a subtle shift in the work of both men from reification to alienation whereby critical theory of society becomes a philosophy of history: an identity-system of history as "catastrophe." Finally, I attempt to sketch the aporia of a critical theory of society which is unreflective of its own "religious" presuppositions.

Metz's "political theology" orients itself to the world as history, history as eschatologically valorized and history as socially mediated and hence brings forward the ideas in the first two chapters. His *Theology of the World* is a delineation and defense of this framework as appropriate to the Christian tradition and adequate to the situation of western, post-Enlightenment society. As Metz's latest work indicates, however, the

---

[8] Matthew Lamb, *Solidarity with Victims* (New York: Crossroad Publishing Co., 1982), p. 30.

turn to a political theology, to a theology of the world as history recoils on the foundations of theology itself—a fact which is witnessed in the change from "political theology" to "practical fundamental theology."

Metz's reflections in his latest work fall, I argue, in two major directions. First, in an attempt to defend political theology as *Christian* theology, Metz increasingly specifies the material content of the formal categories of political theology. Second, he endeavors to force a recognition of the practical mediation of faith and history as society which undercuts the original sin of theology to reconcile faith and history in thought as the "theological system." Here I argue that for Metz the primordial locus of Christianity's truth claim as well as the mediation of faith and history is the praxis of (Christian) conversion which is a practically-mediated (the categories of memory, narrative and solidarity) "mystical-political" (disclosive-transformative) appearance of truth.

While Metz preserves theology against the transformation of the nonidentity of history as suffering into a noetic reconciliation with faith, his reticence to consider those questions which have occupied Pannenberg occludes another "nonidentity," i.e., the nonidentity between Christianity and other religious totalities of meaning. By way of an immanent critique, I argue that even in Metz's latest work, the formation of subjective identity is coextensive with the formation of Christian identity as such and, further, that his silence regarding "truth," "history," "the future" and "God" also arise from his reticence to address those very questions raised by Pannenberg—questions which are unavoidable even for a practical fundamental theology.

The final chapter gathers together the reflections of the previous ones in order to bring the thesis into focus. There I attempt to state at what "cost" the thesis can be maintained. This demands a defense of nonidentity and the reversal of the "rage for identity" in much of contemporary theological reflection which often slips into the forgetful negation of nonidentity. More specifically, I argue that a Christian political theology must recognize a threefold nonidentity which like three overlapping transparencies defines its parameters.

The first nonidentity is the nonidentity of religion and its implication that Christian theological reflection is marked by a "confessional proviso." If religion concerns a totality of meaning and if the world's religions manifest a material conflict concerning this while raising an identical formal claim to truth and if this material conflict can be adjudicated no further than the dialectic of the history of religions, then the truth claim of religion is essentially a provisional and proleptic one.

Constructive theological reflection always already stands under the mark of a particular totality of meaning—even if only as a *vis a tergo*. Hence the "confessional proviso." Here I briefly relate the nonidentity of religion to a traditional Christian theological rubric: the theme of the hiddenness and manifestness of God.

If the first form of nonidentity deals with religion per se and religions in their difference as determinate totalities of meaning, the second form of nonidentity acknowledges that such totalities are not windowless monads. A totality of meaning is subject to both diachronic and synchronic pluralism. At stake here are the issues concerning the "essence of Christianity" (or Buddhism, Judaism or Islam etc.) and thus conflicting or nonidentical projections of the "point" of a specific religion. Political theology is a form of Christian theology and thus represents a way of construing the substance of Christian faith. Yet it is *a* form and not *the* form and hence stands under a "theological proviso." The question treated here concerns the adjudication of differences between nonidentical construals of Christian faith as manifested in different projections of the "essence of Christianity."

The final form of nonidentity is emphatic in "political theology" and constitutes its glowing core: the nonidentity of suffering which not only frustrates but forbids as blasphemous the articulation of a Christian theology of history which negates or reconciles noetically such suffering and Christian faith. The concrete mediation of the nonidentity of history as suffering and Christian faith is, as suggested by Metz, a practical one of mystical-political discipleship which is normed by the *memoria Jesu*, actualized in solidarity with past and present victims of suffering and oriented in hope to an eschatological horizon, the Kingdom of God. The proximate task of a Christian political theology today is to preserve without negation the reality of suffering in history which posits an ultimate if not final claim on Christianity's self-understanding and praxis. Christian theology as a political theology as a theology of history thus stands under an "eschatological proviso," that is, by abiding with suffering it witnesses to the hope of the redemption of history. At that point, I address the question of analogical versus dialectical speech about the God whose reality is at stake in history itself.

Finally, I would like to express my gratitude to Mr David Tracy who directed the original research at the Divinity School, University of Chicago. Thanks are also due to Ms Monica Wagner and Ms Juli Busse of the University of San Diego who spent many hours typing and correcting the manuscript.

CHAPTER I

Wolfhart Pannenberg: Religion and Religious Language

> Be ready at all times to answer anyone who asks you to explain the hope you have in you.
>
> 1 Peter 3.15

INTRODUCTION

Perhaps more than any other theologian in this century, Wolfhart Pannenberg has explicitly addressed over the course of his career—a career still "in progress"—the cluster of issues concerning Christian faith, theology and history. In his essay, "Redemptive Event and History," Pannenberg boldly articulated the standpoint which has been the hallmark of his theological program:

> History is the most comprehensive horizon of Christian theology. All theological questions are meaningful only within the framework of the history which God has with humanity and through humanity with his whole creation—the history moving toward a future still hidden from the world but already revealed in Jesus Christ.[1]

The theme of "Christian faith, theology and history" is not, however, all of the same piece of cloth. A number of distinct questions and lines of reflection constituted by differing focal problems are contained within this theme. This is reflected in the term "history" itself which can take on

---

[1] Wolfhart Pannenberg, "Redemptive Event and History," in *Basic Questions in Theology*, 2 vols., trans. George H. Kehm (Philadelphia: Fortress Press, 1970-71), 1: 15.

a spectrum of connotations along a subject-object continuum. On the one hand, history can refer to the "subject" enduring, forming and either prethematically or thematically "cognizing" his or her world. On the other hand, it can refer to the "object" endured, formed and "cognized" in its continuity and effects either thematically or unthematically. More specifically, under the rubric, "the question of history," are such diverse inquiries as: (1) the elaboration of the possibility and content of a "universal history" as in Kant, Herder and Hegel; (2) the specification of the canons and morality of historical inquiry, either with regard to the problem of religious assertions as in Strauss, Troeltsch, Bradley and Harvey, or with regard to a delimitation of historical inquiry from works of fiction as in Collingwood and Croce; (3) the attempt to differentiate the foundation of the *Geisteswissenschaften* from that of the natural sciences as in Dilthey, Simmel and Rickert; (4) the turn from history to "historicity" and "temporality" in the fundamental ontologies of Heidegger and Gadamer; (5) the attempt to clarify the logic of historical explanation and to bring it into correspondence with the understanding of explanation used in the "sciences" as in Popper, Hempel, M. White and Mandelbaum; (6) the attempt, largely in reaction to (5) to work out a narrative approach to the question of history in Danto, Minks, Gallie, H. White, Baumgartner and Ricoeur; or (7) the attempt to thematize different levels of historical time in Braundel or Kosolleck.[2] These

  2 Immanuel Kant, *On History*, ed. and with an introduction by Lewis White Beck (Indianapolis, Indiana: Library of Liberal Arts, The Bobbs-Merrill Co., 1963); Johann Gottfried Herder, *Reflections on the Philosophy of History of Mankind*, trans. T.O. Churchill, ed. Frank Manuel (Chicago: University of Chicago Press, 1968); G.W.F. Hegel, *The Philosophy of History*, trans. J. Sibree (New York: Dover Publications, 1956); Alfred Heuss, *Zur Theorie der Weltgeschichte* (Berlin: Walter de Gruyter, 1968); David Friedrich Strauss, *The Life of Jesus Critically Examined*, trans. George Eliot, ed. Peter Hodgson (Philadelphia: Fortress Press, 1972) and *The Christ of Faith and the Jesus of History*, trans. and with an introduction by Leander Keck (Philadelphia: Fortress Press, 1977); F.H. Bradley, *The Presuppositions of Critical History* ed. and with an introduction by Lionel Rubinoff (Chicago: Quadrangle Books, 1968); Ernst Troeltsch, "*Über historische und dogmatische Methöde in der Theologie*," in *Gesammelte Schriften*, 4 vols. (Tübingen: J.C.B. Mohr, 1913), 2:729-53; R.G. Collingwood, *The Idea of History* (Oxford: Oxford University Press, 1956); Benedetto Croce, *History: Its Theory and Method*, trans Douglas Ainslee (New York: Harcourt and Brace, 1923); Wilhelm Dilthey, *Selected Writings*, trans., ed. and with an introduction by H.P. Rickman (Cambridge: Cambridge University Press, 1976) and *Descriptive Psychology and Historical Understanding*, trans R.M. Zaner and K.L. Heiges, with an introduction by R.A. Makkreel (Hague: Martinus Nijhoff, 1977); Georg Simmel, *The Problems of the Philosophy of History*, trans., ed. and with an introduction by Guy Oakes (New York:

"paradigms" for raising the question of history (as historicity, universal history, the nature and status of historical explanation, the concept of history-writing, or historical inquiry) can no doubt be multiplied, differentiated and nuanced. This is neither to deny that there is certainly a great deal of diversity in each paradigm nor that any particular thinker will not to a greater or lesser extent take account of figures or ideas outside his or her own immediate context. However, what I wish to suggest is

---

The Free Press, 1977); Heinrich Rickert, *Die Grenzen der naturwissenschaflichen Begriffsbildung* (Tübingen: J.C.B. Mohr, 1913) and *Kulturwissenschaft und Naturwissenschaft* (Tübingen: J.C.B. Mohr, 1915); Martin Heidegger, *Being and Time*, trans, ed. and with an introduction by John Macquarrie and Edward Robinson (New York: Harper and Row, 1962); Hans Georg Gadamer, *Philosophical Hermeneutics*, trans., ed. and with an introduction by David Linge (Berkeley: University of California Press, 1976); Karl Popper, *The Poverty of Historicism* (London: Routledge, Kegan and Paul, 1961); Carl Hempel, "The Function of General Laws in History," in *Theories of History*, ed. and with introductions by Patrick Gardiner (New York: The Free Press, 1959), pp. 344-55 and "Explanation in Science and History," in *Philosophical Analysis and History*, ed. William Dray (New York: Harper and Row, 1966); Morton White, "Historical Explanation," in *Theories of History*, pp. 356-72 and *Foundations of Historical Knowledge* (New York: Harper and Row, 1965); Maurice Mandelbaum, *The Anatomy of Historical Knowledge* (Baltimore: Johns Hopkins University Press, 1977); Arthur Danto, *Analytic Philosophy of History* (Cambridge: Cambridge University Press, 1965); Louis Minks, "Philosophical Analysis and Historical Understanding," *Journal of Metaphysics* 21 (1968): 667-98, "History and Fiction as Modes of Comprehension," in *New Directions in Literary History*, ed. Ralph Cohen (Baltimore: Johns Hopkins University Press, 1974), pp. 107-24, "The Autonomy of Historical Understanding," in *Philosophical Analysis and History* and "Narrative Forms as a Cognitive Instrument," in *The Writing of History*, ed. Robert Canary and Henry Kozicki (Madison: University of Wisconsin Press, 1978), pp. 129-49; W.B. Gallie, *Philosophy and the Historical Understanding* (New York: Schocken Books, 1968); Hayden White, *Metahistory: The Historical Imagination in 19th Century Europe* (Baltimore: Johns Hopkins University Press, 1973); "The Burden of History," *History and Theory* 5 (1966): 111-34, "The Fiction of Factual Representation, " in *The Literature of Fact*, ed. Angus Fletcher (New York: Columbia University Press, 1976), pp. 21-44, "The Historical Text as Literary Artifact," in *The Writing of History*, pp. 41-62, and "The Value of Narrativity in the Representation of Reality, " in *On Narrative*, ed. W.J.T. Mitchell (Chicago: University of Chicago Press, 1981), pp. 1-23; Hans Michael Baumgartner, *Kontinuität und Geschichte* (Frankfurt: Suhrkamp, 1972); Paul Ricoeur, "The Narrative Form," *Semeia* 4 (1975): 37-73, "Narrative Time," in *On Narrative*, pp. 165-86, and *Time and Narrative*, 3 vols., trans. Kathleen McLaughlin and David Pellauer (Chicago: University of Chicago Press, 1984-88); Fernand Braudel, *On History*, trans. Arah Matthews (Chicago: University of Chicago Press, 1980); Emmanuel Le Roy Ladurie, *The Mind and Method of the Historian*, trans. Sian and Ben Reynolds (Chicago: University of Chicago Press, 1981); Reinhardt Koselleck, *Vergangene Zukunft* (Frankfurt: Suhrkamp Verlag, 1979).

that the history of reflection on history is not a continuous one but one characterized by disruptions in the placement of significant issues and questions.

This state of affairs is mirrored in the work of Pannenberg and is especially reflected in the essay-form of his *Grundfragen Systematischer Theologie* where the specific focus of each essay is always already set under the sign of a dialogue bounded by another specific figure or delimited *topos*. As of yet, there is in Pannenberg's corpus no "systematic theology" in a "systematic form" as in Aquinas, Calvin or Schleiermacher, only a systematic theology in an essay-form.[3] I make this observation only to suggest that Pannenberg means a number of possible things by the term "history": history as promise and fulfillment, i.e., as the horizon of reality which arises from Christianity's totality of meaning; history as the process of the transmission of traditions as the dialectic of the history of religions; history as universal history as a corollary to the hermeneutic circle regarding "meaning"; and history as a mode of inquiry bound by specific methodological canons. Which interpretive focus is selected in a specific essay is of great importance because by such a focus certain issues and questions proceed to the foreground while others recede to the background: a change of interpretive center changes the constellation of issues and questions which it gathers to itself as more or less proximate, more or less distant.

This chapter explores one aspect of Pannenberg's thought which may serve as such an interpretive center from which other aspects of his thought may be illuminated and criticized. No pretense is made, therefore, concerning a "comprehensive" interpretation of Pannenberg's thought. That interpretive center is Pannenberg's positions on "anthropology," "the nature of religious language and its reality-refer-

---

[3] My central texts are: "Toward a Theology of the History of Religions," in *Basic Questions* 2: 65-118; "Anthropology and the Question of God," in *The Idea of God and Human Freedom*, trans. R. A. Wilson (Philadelphia: Fortress Press, 1973), pp. 80-98; "Theology as the Science of God," in *Theology and the Philosophy of Science*, trans. F. McDonagh (Philadelphia: Fortress Press, 1976), pp. 297-345; and, *Anthropology in Theological Perspective*, trans. Matthew J. O'Connell (Philadelphia: Westminster Press, 1985). During the past year, Pannenberg has begun to publish his long-awaited *Dogmatics*. A fine (provisional) presentation of its contents based upon the volumes currently being published and Pannenberg's lectures in systematic theology can be found in Stanley Grenz, *Reason for Hope: The Systematic Theology of Wolfhart Pannenberg* (New York: Oxford University Press, 1990). Grenz' text is also indispensable as a guide to the secondary literature on Pannenberg.

ents" and the "dialectic of religions" where "history" in the first two senses in Pannenberg's usage come to the foreground.

The crux of Pannenberg's theological program which this chapter indirectly seeks to illuminate through such an interpretive center is that the most adequate form of a Christian theology is a theology of (universal) *history* because it is a *Christian* theology. "In principle" such a thesis appears theologically appropriate and adequate. My misgiving is whether that thesis is plausible today in the way that Pannenberg has construed it. The interpretive center of this chapter deliberately seeks to question the plausibility of such a thesis. As subsequent chapters argue, Christian theology as a theology of (universal) history is most appropriately realized today in an explicit political theology which attends to the (socially mediated) transmission of the Christian tradition. Further, because it attends to the tragic events of history as a history of suffering, Christian theology witnesses to "universal history" in an indirect manner.

This chapter is divided into six parts. First, there is an exposition of the specific interpretive center. Second, there is a summary of Pannenberg's argument regarding the resurrection as a historically verifiable event. The third and fourth sections describe various strategies by which the provisionality of Christianity is attenuated and immunized from history as a history of suffering and from the witness of other religious totalities of meaning. Finally, the fifth and sixth sections are postscripts which treat Pannenberg's understanding of the task of theology and his dispute with Gadamer with regard to the question "What is the foundation of the provisional claim to truth of religion?"

AN INTERPRETIVE CENTER: RELIGION, RELIGIONS, RELIGIOUS LANGUAGE AND HISTORY

Three positions form the background for Pannenberg's reflections on religion. First, there is his acknowledgement that the Copernican revolution of an anthropocentric turn is irreversibly effective in the sphere of theology. Negatively, this signifies that the time is past when one could appeal immediately from the world or nature as a whole or some part thereof to ground a sure or certain knowledge of the divine. Positively, this has led to an anthropologizing of the idea of the divine itself, that is, an attempt to situate the question of the nature and existence of the divine within the framework of the self-understanding of human being.[4]

Second, this anthropologization of the divine is the common ground of and provides the clue to the morphology of modern atheism.[5] What unites the great modern atheists i.e., Feuerbach, Marx, Freud and Nietzsche, despite the variety of their arguments, is the affirmation that religious consciousness is a "false consciousness," a development which does not belong to the essence of human being. It is a hypothesis which is dispensable. Further, because religious consciousness is a "projection," "ideology," "illusion" or "pathology," it must be dispensed with and eliminated in order to achieve an adequate self-understanding of human being. Meeting this challenge is, according to Pannenberg, the necessary condition of theology today.

> If it cannot be shown that the issues with which religion is concerned, the elevation of man above the finite content of human experience to the idea of an infinite reality which sustains everything finite, including man himself, are an essential of man's being, so that one is not really considering man if one ignores this dimension—if this cannot be shown with sufficient certainty, then every other viewpoint with which one may concern oneself in this field is an empty intellectual game, and what is said about God loses every claim to intellectual veracity.[6]

A third position is Pannenberg's consistent rejection of the strategy of immunizing Christian faith from modern atheism associated with "dialectical," "revelational," or "existential" theology. These forms of theological reflection only speciously internalize the critical impulses of modern atheism in order to make a distinction between "religion" and "revelation." Corresponding to this is a constriction of the anthropological focus in such theologies to the mathematical point of the ethical (existential) subject addressed by the sovereign Word of God—a subject created virtually *ex nihilo coram Deo.* The results of such a theology: the isolation of the self-understanding of the human subject from his or her understanding of the world even as the former is mediated through the latter; a spurious answer to the challenge of atheistic criticism which needs only to be reapplied to "revelation" as well as "religion" in order

---

[4]　Pannenberg, *The Idea of God and Human Freedom*, passim.

[5]　Idem, "Speaking about God in the Face of Atheist Criticism," in *The Idea of God*, pp. 95-115; "Types of Atheism and Their Theological Significance" and "The Question of God," in *Basic Question*, 2: 184-200, 201-34.

[6]　Idem, "Anthropology and the Question of God," p. 89.

to abolish the distinction between the two; and a retreat to decisionism or fideism regarding the truth of revelation vis-à-vis other "mere" religions. All of these corollaries are rejected by Pannenberg.[7]

In view of the above, Pannenberg asserts that reflection on "anthropology" is necessary for fundamental theology today. More specifically, an adequate theological anthropology which "attempts to identify an anthropological basis for the discussion of the question of God"[8] must include both empirical as well as philosophical reflection on subjectivity. While his 1960-61 radio lectures, *Was ist der Mensch?*, are schematic and confined to a relatively abstract level,[9] his later text, *Anthropology in Theological Perspective* (1985), is a detailed philosophical reflection on the natural, psychological, social, cultural and historical dimensions of human nature. Despite this difference between these two works, the outlines of his theological anthropology are constant and have remained consistent through the past 25 years.

That characteristic of men and women for the "elevation of man above the finite content of human experience to the idea of an infinite reality" is denoted by the phrase "openness to the world," *Weltoffenheit*. That power by which men and women can potentially surpass through questioning any personally achieved judgment or one received from tradition; that power by which we can envisage in anticipation a future distinct from the present or by which the mute present-at-hand becomes disclosed reality through language; that power by which we transform and, so to speak, push back the limits of nature and thus structure a distinctly human sphere of society, polity and culture; that power by which men and women "have a world" and are not merely "situated-in-an-environment" *is* human being's "openness to the world" or "exocentricity."

> . . . openness to the world must mean that man is completely directed into the "open." He is always open further, beyond every experience and beyond every given situation. He is also open beyond the world, that is, beyond the picture of the world at any given time. But in questioning and searching he also remains open beyond every possible picture of the world and beyond the search for pictures of the world as such, as essential as this search may

---

[7] See, for example, Idem, "Christian Theology and Philosophical Criticism," in *The Idea of God*, pp. 116-27; *Theology and the Philosophy of Science*, pp. 161-77, 265-76; and "Die Krise des Ethischen und die Theologie," in *Ethik und Ekklesiologie* (Gottingen: Vandenhoeck and Ruprecht, 1977), pp. 41-54.

[8] Idem, *The Idea of God*, p. vii.

[9] *What is Man?*, trans. D. A. Priebe (Philadelphia: Fortress Press, 1970).

be. Such openness beyond the world is even the condition for man's experience of the world.[10]

Like Karl Rahner in his discussion of *excessus ad esse* and Bernard
Lonergan in his discussion of "the pure and unrestricted desire to
know," Pannenberg grounds the religious dimension of human existence
in human-being's self-transcendence.[11] As self-transcending beings in
openness to the world, men and women are directed toward an infinite
horizon which is distinct from any particular world and even world as
such. It is this "openness" toward which men and women transcend
themselves and which surpasses all finite reality and upon which they
experience themselves as dependent that is the primordial signification
of the "sacred."[12]

This self-transcendence or being-in-the-open of human being can be
redescribed according to various interests (i.e., cognitive, ethical, aesthetic, etc.). In its thematically religious redescription, the openness to the
world of human being may be designated as the quest for *Heil*. This is
not to be understood in its restricted sense as concerning the salvation of
the "soul"; nor is it to be understood in its broader, yet still traditional
Christian terms as the dialectic of sin and grace. In its most fundamental
meaning, *Heil* is to be understood as a concern for the totality and integrity of life (*die Ganzheit des Lebens, die Unversehrheit des Lebens*), or as
Pannenberg more commonly expresses it, the totality of meaning, *die
Ganzheit des Sinns*.[13] It is this orientation to the question of meaning
which, for Pannenberg, constitutes the realm of religious discourse. More
specifically, it is the reference to and thematization of an *integral* and
comprehensive context of meaning which is the distinguishing characteristic of religious discourse: "all religious experience is concerned with
such a totality of existence."[14] Again, "the reality of God is always present only in subjective anticipations of the totality of reality, in models of

[10] Pannenberg, *What is Man?*, p. 8. See also, *Anthropology*, pp. 67-71.
[11] Karl Rahner, *Spirit in the World*, trans. William Dych (New York: Herder and
Herder, 1968) and Bernard Lonergan, *Insight: A Study of Human Understanding* (New
York: Philosophical Library, 1970).
[12] Pannenberg, "Anthropology and the Question of God," pp. 92-8. In what follows, I have substituted references to "God" with the circumlocutions, the "divine,"
in order not to prejudice the question in the direction of the monotheistic religions.
[13] Idem, "*Weltgeschichte und Heilsgeschichte*," in *Geschichte: Ereignis und Erzählung*,
ed. R. Kosolleck and W. D. Stempel (Munich: Wilhelm Fink Verlag, 1973), pp. 312-15.
[14] Idem, "Christian Theology and Philosophical Criticism," p. 133.

the totality of meaning presupposed in all particular existence."[15] What is at stake in religious discourse is the apprehension and description a totality of meaning—a totality which integrates individual meanings and experiences and realms of meanings into a whole according to the logic of the "part and the whole."

Pannenberg's understanding of "meaning" is most proximately drawn from Wilhelm Dilthey's formulation of the hermeneutic circle where the categories of "meaning" (*Sinn*) and "significance" (*Bedeutung*) are formal structures of human experience (*Erlebnis*) which are related as "part" and "whole."

> Even if we speak of the "significance" which is attributed to the individual phenomenon, though always in relation to a context, and of the "meaning" which the totality makes, but which can also be attributed to the individual phenomenon in its relationship to the whole, a strict distinction is difficult.[16]

What is clear, however, is that meaning and significance *is* the nexus between part and whole and is characteristic not only of the hermeneutic situation of language and texts (i.e., word/sentence, sentence/paragraph, etc.) but also of human experience where the meaning and significance of individual experiences stand at stake in the flux of the whole of an individual's life.

> Because of the historical nature of the experience of meaning, that is, because the whole of life is a historical process, the future, and particularly the ultimate future, has a decisive function in the question of the meaning of our life as a whole and of the final significance of individual experiences. The final significance, the real nature (*Wesen*) of the individual things that have happened to us, but also of our own actions, is decided only in the final future of our life, because only then does the whole of life, which forms the horizon for the meaning and significance of all the individual factors in it, at last take shape.[17]

Yet insofar as the individual subject is an abstraction, i.e., inasmuch as he or she is constituted by society, this too is implicated in the logic of the part and the whole:

> The anticipation of the totality of the individual life, which supplies the individual with confidence (*Selbstgewissheit*) in himself at any given moment, always extends, therefore, to the social unity in the context of which the in-

---

[15]   Idem, *Theology and the Philosophy of Science*, p. 310.
[16]   Idem, "Eschatology and the Experience of Meaning," in *The Idea of God*, p. 200.

dividual lives, and looks beyond his own particular society to its place in the life of mankind.[18]

The concept of a "totality of meaning" thus points to a comprehensive context "which apprehends in anticipation, in a still incomplete and contradictory reality, a wholeness of meaning which is not yet realized in all the relationships of meaning within that."[19]

Three points should be noted at this juncture. First, Pannenberg asserts that such a projection or anticipation of a total context of meaning is the condition of the possibility of the apprehension of the meaning and significance of any experience whatsoever.

> Such a totality of meaning is not a merely regulative idea of the unity of the whole content of experience. It is rather the whole unit of meaning which in any given case already constitutes the significance of the individual and the particular. It cannot therefore be claimed that it is a secondary and extrinsic principle of integration for a primary and prior diversity of experience.[20]

While the articulation of a totality of meaning may be more or less explicit for any given individual, it must be implicitly or indirectly apprehended for an individual to make any sense of his or her environment.

Second, through the temporalization of the question of meaning and the logic of part and whole, the epistemic status of both specific totalities of meaning and their apprehension is unavoidably hypothetical because it is an anticipation. Human being's knowledge of the world is anticipatory because the very identity of things is not yet completely present and is dependent upon "whatever future it is whose coming will bring about the wholeness of the whole"[21] in which things achieve their essence. From this follows the hypothetical character of a totality of meaning: since articulations of totality are anticipatory they are at stake in time and subject to confirmation or refutation in the ongoing temporal experience of men and women. What Pannenberg asserts regarding the identity and difference of "concept" and "thing" applies to totalities of meaning:

---

[17] Ibid., p. 201.

[18] Ibid., p. 202.

[19] Ibid., p. 203.

[20] Idem, "Christian Theology and Philosophical Criticism," p. 132. See, also, "Faith and Reason," in *Basic Questions*, 2: 62-4.

[21] Idem, *Metaphysics and the Idea of God*, trans. Philip Clayton (Grand Rapids,MI: Eerdmans Publishing Co., 1990), p. 87.

the anticipation is not yet identical in every respect with the anticipated thing; it remains exposed to the risk of untruth....Yet given the presupposition that the thing will appear in full form sometime in the future, in the anticipation the thing is already present.[22]

Third, religion is that human phenomenon explicitly concerned with the articulation of a "totality of meaning." This is the case "even where the saving totality of existence is contemplated not in the mode of 'not yet' and of promise, but as the archetypal and primeval order proclaimed in myth."[23] While the sort of totality of meaning articulated in Judaism and Christianity has a peculiar relation to the "historicality" of the apprehension of meaning, i.e., "anticipation" characterizes not only the formal mode of the appearance-apprehension but also the material content of its totality of meaning, this does not exclude the claim of "other" religions where the concrete, material content of these religion's totalities is ahistorical, fixed *in illo tempore*.

At this basic level of theological anthropology, Pannenberg appears to operate with two distinct lines of argument. One centers on *Weltoffenheit* as a description of the self-transcendence of human beings; the other centers on the "experience of meaning according to the logic of part/whole." The latter specifies the former and tends to dominate in the work of Pannenberg due to two factors. First, the logic of part and whole allows Pannenberg to introduce the concept of religion as "totality of meaning" with relative ease. Second, it allows him to "temporalize" the concept of totality—as distinct from i.e., Rahner—in a way that the rather abstract notion of *Weltoffenheit* would not allow—a factor which becomes significant given the "privileged" status which Pannenberg wishes to claim between the temporal process of the human experience of meaning and its correspondence with the content of the Christian faith.

Pannenberg's notion of religion as thematizing a totality of meaning is polemically related to what he regards as the strategy of immunization predominant in the "kerygmatic theology" which has dominated 20th century theology. This strategy amounts to a restriction of the question of the reality of God to an "in principle" nonobjectifiable realm of human self-understanding polarized and isolated from the self's understanding of the world—a strategy consistently formulated in W. Hermann's location of the believer's communion with God in the realm of "practical consciousness" and, through him, influencing Barth's "revelational posi-

---

[22] Ibid., p. 104.
[23] Idem, "Christian Theology and Philosophical Criticism," p. 133.

tivism," Bultmann's existential hermeneutic of authentic/inauthentic existence, and Ebeling's polarization of the informative and communicative aspects of language in his hermeneutic of the word-event.[24] This constriction of the sense of religious discourse to the realm of self-understanding—what Pannenberg often calls the "ethical"—is an abstraction because the authenticity of self-understanding cannot be separated from the understanding of the world which is implied therein.

> The outlines of ethical conduct are, at any given time, first given out of the understanding of reality as a whole.

> Nevertheless the shattering of the ethic of values by the aporia of the relation between value and being produced by this ethic shows the priority of ontological problems. It shows the foundational significance of how reality is understood for any attempt to establish a foundation for ethics which is demonstrated in the dependence at any given time of ethical convictions on worldview.[25]

If in their eccentric being men and women are open to an infinite horizon and if religious discourse renders explicit a totality of meaning, then I suggest that the latter term can be analyzed into three distinct "moments" which, though formally distinct, are not separate and mutually conditioning moments in any single concrete "totality of meaning." While the following suggestion goes beyond any explicit statements of Pannenberg, it appears justifiable by his *obiter dicta*.[26]

First, while the "sense" of religious discourse is not solely a possible existential self-understanding, it surely includes that. Religion articulates an "ethic" in the sense of an *ethos*. It describes a possible mode of being in the world (Ricoeur) and in that description asserts this mode of being as "authentic," that is, as warranted by the nature of the "world"[27] Second,

---

[24] Idem, *"Die Krise des Ethischen und die Theologie,"* pp. 39-54.

[25] Idem, *"Antwort an Gerhard Ebeling,"* in *Ethik und Ekklesiologie*, pp. 52, 59. [All translations from texts cited in German are my own.] See also "Faith and Reason," in *Basic Questions*, 2: 52.

[26] See, for example, Idem, "Hermeneutic and Universal History," pp. 110-11, *"Die Krise des Ethischen und die Theologie"* and *"Antwort an Gerhard Ebeling,"* passim., "Christian Theology and Philosophical Criticism," pp. 121-25, and "Faith and Reason," 2: 52.

[27] "It is the task of hermeneutics to disentangle from the 'world' of the texts, their implicit 'project' for existence, their indirect 'proposition' of new modes of being" [Paul Ricoeur, "The Specificity of Religious Language," *Semeia* (4): 144]. This is not to insinuate that Ricoeur's position on religious language focuses on its "ethical" sense in the narrow meaning of the term. On the contrary, central to his work is the argu-

religions also articulate a "worldview," "world-orientation" or "ontology" with which the first sense stands in correspondence.[28] In this sense, religious discourse offers a re-description of the world. It founds or opens up a world as of "such and such a type," produces an orientation to what is "real" and what is mere "appearance" thus providing a "deep-structure" for the subjective apprehension of reality. It differentiates and integrates "spheres" of reality (i.e., the relation between the "natural" and "social" realm) and it sets the parameters for raising questions such as the nature of the "good." Further, one may surmise from

---

ment that the distinction between "action" and "description" is sublated in the originating form of religious language as "limit-language" whose core is a metaphorical redescription of ordinary human experience. "But if we give to poetic language the function of redescription through fictions, then we can say that the logical space opened by Kant between *Denken* and *Erkennen*, between "thought" and "knowledge," is the place of indirect discourse, of symbol, parables, and myths, as the indirect presentation of the Unconditioned" (Ibid., p. 143). Ricoeur's position on religious language represents an intersection between his explorations of the metaphorical process and his retrieval (through Hegel) of Kant's notion of limit. The "referent" of religious language stands "before" the text in the redescription of ordinary human experience, that is, the unveiling of a possible mode-of-being-in-the-world which indirectly is a presentation of the Unconditioned—a position which in its "aesthetic moment avoids the decisionism of Bultmann and representatives of the "new hermeneutic." Yet it is here, in his "unpacking" of the referent of religious discourse, that there occurs a constriction of religious language, i.e., in discussing the referent of religious language Ricoeur in fact focuses on "mode-of-being" as existential possibility to the neglect of "in-the-world." Yet if in fact religious language involves a redescription of ordinary human experience, then it also ineluctably involves a redescription of the "world" and hence at least indirectly or implicitly a "worldview." Ricoeur's major writings on religious language can be found in a collection of essays published in *Semeia* 4 (1975) and his *Essays on Biblical Interpretation*, ed. Lewis S. Mudge (Philadelphia: Fortress Press, 1980). His fullest account of metaphor and the metaphorical process can be found in *The Rule of Metaphor*, trans. Robert Czerny with Kathleen McLaughlin and John Costello (Toronto: University of Toronto Press, 1977). On the distinction between "sense" and "referent," see *Interpretation Theory: Discourse and the Surplus of Meaning* (Fort Worth: The Texas Christian University Press, 1976), pp. 19-22.

[28] A terse description of "worldview" has been given by Patrick Burke: "World views, like portraits, are cases of 'seeing as'. We have a world view, when we succeed in seeing the sum total of things as something or other. It is not necessary that we give an account of all the items in the world individually, but of the whole as the whole. So in one sense, a world view must embrace everything, but in another sense not," cited by Jürgen Habermas, *Theorie des kommunikativen Handelns*, 2 vols. (Frankfurt: Suhrkamp, 1981), 1: 92. For an attempt to typologize world views, see Stephen Pepper, *World Hypothesis: A Study in Evidence* (Berkeley: University of California Press, 1966).

the work of Pannenberg, that there is a certain "priority" of the second moment of religious discourse over the first: a particular *ethos* or mode of being in the world is "authentic" insofar as it is entailed by and congruent with a particular ("true") worldview, not vice-versa.[29] Finally, religious discourse brings to speech the limit-to and limit-of all reality. It represents that infinite horizon which is the limit-to any particular world as that to which the eccentric being of men and women is oriented and as that which "founds," "grounds" or "embraces" the previous two "senses" as limit-of both worldview and ethos.[30] Again, it must be said that these three "senses" of religious discourse are only formally distinct and that concretely, in their mutual qualification, they constitute the single sense of religious discourse as a totality of meaning. Further, if this interpretation of religious discourse as a totality of meaning is appropriate, then in addition to an "external" limit to a particular religion's viability (i.e., its assimilative power in regard to the experience of reality), there is an "internal" limit to any particular religion: the congruence of each of its moments with one another.[31]

Given the this position on anthropology, religion and religious language, it must be recognized that there is a limit to such a procedure.

> A general theological anthropology cannot be expected to do more than demonstrate the religious dimension of man's being. . . . But it cannot be expected to supply a proof of the reality of God. . . . General anthropological considerations can never take us further than the assertion that when man's

[29] See Schubert Ogden, *The Point of Christology* (San Francisco: Harper and Row, 1982), pp. 30-34. It is this that I believe to be the fundamental point of Pannenberg's disagreement with the "neoorthodoxy" of Bultmann, Fuchs and Ebeling.

[30] On the distinction between "limit-to" and "limit-of," see Tracy, *The Analogical Imagination* (New York: Crossroad Publishing Co., 1981), pp. 159-67.

[31] If this explication of the *Sache* of religion as a "totality of meaning" is plausible, then I suggest that Pannenberg's concept bears a resemblance to concepts in i.e., the work of figures as Julian Hartt (religion as a way of construing the world), Ian Barbour (religion as paradigm), Giles Gunn's exposition of the category "hypothetical world," and John Cobb's portrayal of the structure of "axial existence." See Julian Hartt, *Theological Method and Imagination* (New York: The Seabury Press, 1977); Ian Barbour, *Myths, Models, and Paradigms* (New York: Harper and Row, 1974); Giles Gunn, *The Interpretation of Otherness* (New York: Oxford University Press, 1979); and John Cobb, *The Structure of Christian Existence* (New York: The Seabury Press, 1979). While Pannenberg's exposition of the *Sache* of religious discourse has focused on its logical status within the context of anthropology and ontology, these other authors have focused on the peculiarity of religious language, i.e., as metaphor, within the context of the aesthetic and scientific imagination. Curiously, sustained reflection on

being is fully aware, man is conscious that he is dependent upon a reality which surpasses and sustains everything finite and it is in this sense a divine reality.[32]

As long as this kind of argument deals only with statements about the structure of human existence, the question about the independently existing reality of God or of divine powers still remains open.[33]

What is the limit of theological anthropology? On the one hand, Pannenberg distinguishes his own project from e.g., Rahner's transcendental anthropology and Nygren's defense of a religious *a priori*. According to Pannenberg, these positions lead to a "leveling" of the concrete manifestations of the divine witnessed to in the multiplicity of religions which actually enters into the historical formation of the *Dasein* of men and women. On the other hand, Pannenberg maintains that there is a religious dimension constitutive of human existence in that being's eccentricity which always already relates it to an infinite horizon—a position which Pannenberg first formulated in an attempt to respond to the challenge of modern atheism.

Minimally, it can be asserted that for Pannenberg there is a "gap" between the level of anthropological reflection and the reality of the divine which is given in the "happening" (*Widerfahrnis*) of the appearance of the divine, in the actual association with the divine in the elevation of finite life to the infinite. A general phenomenological analysis of *Dasein* functions heuristically as the preparation for a "science of religion." He also seems to maintain, however, that the powerful appearances of the divine as culturally and historically embodied in the "positive religions" are not merely different categorial manifestations of an essential transcendental essence of *Dasein*, but are constitutive of that essence which is still in the process of formation. Transcendental analysis may thematize a "limit-to" dimension of human existence, but that very project is borne and grounded in a "prior" determinate powerful appearance of the divine as the "limit-of" human existence as manifest in the history of religions. An abstract concern with the structure of subjectivity cannot go as far as the reality of God, but only as far as to see the problematic nature of man's being as a question about God. "The reality of God, on which man is dependent in the structure of his subjectivity, is encountered only where, in

---

this issue is absent in Pannenberg's work and would be enhanced through its incorporation.

[32] Pannenberg, "Anthropology and the Question of God," p. 94.
[33] Idem, "Toward a Theology of the History of Religions," 2: 102-3.

the context of this world, he receives himself as a gift in the experience of freedom."[34] While anthropological analysis can point to the divine as the "whither" of self-transcendence, this analysis is an abstraction; the reality of the divine is given in the concrete religious experiences of specific men and women. The issue of the divine's reality-reference is thus inseparable from that concerning its appearance or "revelation."[35] Further, it is in this characteristic of religious experience, the experience of the appearance of the divine, that one may speak of the "self-evidence"[36] of religious experience: in the religious experience of the "significant particular"[37] is donated—always more or less clearly—a totality of meaning which through its power illuminates—again, always with more or less adequacy—one's experience of the self and the world.

> Where the gods transmitted by tradition from earlier generations, or remembered from one's own previous experience, or even as never before so conceived—or even the impersonal, hidden mystery of human existence—suddenly becomes relevant for the experience of human existence in a concrete situation, at that point there takes place a happening of *the* reality to which religious language, and implicitly, all human behavior is related in its transcending fore-conception beyond itself and everything finite.[38]

Thus the reality which religious language renders thematic is ultimately given in its disclosive and transformative appearance, which, in view of that reality's persuasive power, may be spoken of as that reality's "self-revelation."[39] At this juncture, Pannenberg's use of "revelation"

---

[34] Idem, "Anthropology and the Question of God," p. 96.

[35] Idem, "Toward a Theology of the History of Religions," 2: 104-12, and "Anthropology and the Question of God," pp. 94-98.

[36] Idem, "*Wahrheit, Geswissheit und Glaube*," in *Grundfragen systematischer Theologie: Gesammelte Aufsatze*, 2 vols. (Gottingen: Vandenhoeck and Ruprecht, 1967-80), 2: 259-64.

[37] Idem, "Christian Theology and Philosophical Criticism," p. 133. Implicitly in what follows here, I have assimilated Pannenberg's notion of the "significant particular" to Tracy's exposition of the "classic" as found in *The Analogical Imagination*, pp. 99-153.

[38] Idem, "Toward a Theology of the History of Religion," 2: 105.

[39] Further, Pannenberg "reduces" the concept of the "personal" character of the divine back to its "powerful" appearance because of its nonmanipulatedness, its impenetrability and its immediate claim to attention, which in turn grounds the notion of person as such. Thus the issue of the anthropomorphization of the divine is stood on its head. See, Idem, "Analogy and Doxology," and "The Question of God," in *Basic Questions*, 1: 231-33, 2: 226-33.

language appears to be grounded upon a self-acceptance of religious experience's own self-interpretation.

> Religious experience nevertheless understands itself, on the contrary, as a recognition of the appearance of the divine over which man has no power to dispose, so that it is a demonstration of the divine favor not only in its "that" but also in its content.[40]

Two further observations should be added at this juncture.

First, the exposition has moved from a consideration of the nature of religious discourse to a specification of the reality-referent of that discourse in the appearance of the divine reality, i.e., in the *event* of the disclosure of a totality of meaning. Now it must be added that particular, concrete appearances of the divine are usually mediated by the grammar of particular positive religions. Religion exists only in the concrete appearances of the divine which form the focal perceptions of the "positive" religions and thus in the intersubjective religious experiences of humanity which in turn instanciate, reduplicate or transform those same positive religions.[41]

> . . . therefore, it is the historical religions rather than individual religious experiences which must be regarded as the expressions of the experience of divine reality within the totality of meaning of experienced reality.[42]

Perhaps to restate Pannenberg's assertion that today anthropology has assumed the form of a fundamental theology, it may be said that together anthropology and the science of religion constitute that discipline with the former constituting an abstract heuristic and the latter, the concrete material.

---

[40] Idem, "Towards a Theology of the History of Religions," 2: 100 n.47

[41] Idem, *Theology and the Philosophy of Science*, pp. 301, 313-15. See, also, Edward Farley, *Ecclesial Man* (Philadelphia: Fortress Press, 1975), pp. 92-105, 186-234, and *Ecclesial Reflection*, pp. 217-41.

[42] Pannenberg, *Theology and the Philosophy of Science*, p. 313. Pannenberg's reflections here parallel, as with his concept of "totality," those of Schleiermacher and, more specifically, the qualification of the second of his "speeches" on religion by the fifth. See Friedrich Schleiermacher, *On Religion*, trans. John Oman and with an introduction by Rudolph Otto (New York: Harper and Row, 1958), pp. 26-118, 210-65. On Pannenberg's transformation qua temporalization of Schleiermacher's concept of the "whole" ("totality"), see "Eschatology and the Experience of Meaning." pp. 204-7 and "Meaning, Religion, and the Question of God," in *Metaphysics and the Idea of God*, pp. 162-8.

Second, because Pannenberg connects the reality of the divine to its powerful appearance and that appearance has a "totality of meaning" as its proper subject-matter, the appearance itself is marked by "historicality" (*Geschichtlichkeit*), i.e., is hypothetical and anticipatory in its claim to truth. As human being's understanding of the world changes, so too, a particular appearance of the divine does not automatically retain its illuminating and persuasive power over the experience of men and women. If, earlier, it were asserted that in the appearance of the divine not only thematized a sense of the divine per se, but also an ethos and worldview, then here it must also be affirmed that these senses of religious discourse and experience are also provisional, subject to revision and discard. "Reality" whose limits and parameters are initially construed by a specific religious totality of meaning can, so to speak, escape and fracture the boundaries set by a particular religion and hence can "outstrip" any particular appearance of the divine encoded in a specific positive religion.[43]

If what is at stake in the powerful appearance of the divine as a totality of meaning is the *definitive* "arrival-in-preappearance (*Zumvorscheingekommensein*) of the ultimate"[44], then that appearance does not transcend time but takes the form of an "anticipation" which acknowledges both the finitude of the subject and the impossibility of an absolute knowledge concerning totality of meaning which is itself at stake in history as the process of the transmission of tradition.[45] "Anticipation" thus defines the "logical" status of both the act of apprehension and what is apprehended in religion.

[43] Idem, "Anthropology and the Idea of God," pp. 97-98, and *Theology and the Philosophy of Science*, pp. 319-21, 364-66.

[44] Idem, "On Historical and Theological Hermeneutic," 1: 173.

[45] "The totality of reality does not exist anywhere complete. It is only anticipated as a totality of meaning. The totality which is an essential framework for any item of experience to have a determinate meaning does not exist at any point as a totality; rather, it can only be imagined by transcending what exists at any point. This anticipation, without which, as we said above, no experience is possible at all, always involves an element of hypothesis, of subjective conjecture, which must be confirmed— or refuted—by subsequent experience. This has an important implication for the way in which within the context of human experience of reality God can become the theme of human experience. The reality of God is always present only in subjective anticipations of the totality of reality, in models of the totality of meaning presupposed in all particular experience. These models, however, are historic, which means that they are subject to confirmation or refutation by subsequent experience." Idem, *Theology and the Philosophy of Science*, p. 310. See, also, "Christian Theology and Philosophical Criticism," p. 132.

Since the individual man relates himself to the still outstanding wholeness of his existence, he relates himself to the whole of the world and its history. In this way he also relates himself to God as the mysterious power that constitutes this-absent-wholeness. Every such anticipation is conditioned by its standpoint, bound to its location in history. To this extent, it is a *mere* anticipation, and not the whole itself. . . . With the establishment of the point that all concepts of wholeness as well as all statements expressive of essence depend upon thought's fore-conception of not-yet-present wholeness and truth, post-Hegelian philosophy, with its insistence on the finitude of human thought, would receive its due without thereby surrendering the theme of wholeness or even that of absolute being. However, in distinction from the Hegelian philosophy of the concept, a type of thought that understands itself as anticipation, and thus as an intrinsically reflected anticipation, would not be able to be self-constituting. Rather, as anticipation, it would always refer to something preliminary, in relation to which all thought and knowledge prove also to be at once again *mere* anticipation, which can never be overtaken or superseded by means of a type of thought that itself has anticipatory structure. . . . A form of thought that understands itself as a mere fore-conception of the truth does not have the truth in itself but is rather the process that strives beyond itself toward it.[46]

With the transition to positive religions as the locus of the appearance of the divine which is constitutive for the intersubjective religious experiences of individual subjects, there arises the question concerning the "unity" of religions: religions raise a formally identical claim regarding the definitive totality of meaning but also exhibit material differences regarding how this totality is understood, i.e., nonidentical worldviews, ethoi and characterizations of the divine. In contrast to the universalism intended by specific religions, there stands a manifest plurality of religions. For Pannenberg, the unity of religions is to be found neither in an a priori periodization of the history of religions nor in the abstract identity of form supplied by the psychology, phenomenology or philosophy of religion.[47] Corresponding to what was said above regarding the historicality of the appearance of the divine, the unity of religions is to be found in that structure of historicality "writ large," i.e., in the history of

---

[46] Idem, "On Historical and Theological Hermeneutics," 1: 171-72.

[47] Idem, "Toward a Theology of the History of Religions," 2: 71-84. This is not to dismiss such endeavors, but to assert that the unity of a category, morphology or form is an abstract unity. To be sure such investigations may be quite important, especially as mediating between a general analysis of *Dasein* and research into determinate religious totalities of meaning and their vicissitudes, but to rest reflection in the unity of form(s) is to ignore—and thereby annul—the nonidentity of religions. Pannenberg, *Theology and the Philosophy of Science*, pp. 368-69.

religions as the transmission of traditions.[48] In the process of mutual and reciprocal interaction, confrontation and competition, assimilation and syncretism, and growth and decline of religions with one another—and at the limit, their disappearance and "death"—is given that unity of religions which can only be understood a posteriori as the reconstruction of the transmission of traditions.

> For all the special conditioning of a given historical situation by what are today called non-religious factors—e.g., of a political or cultural sort—the growth or fixation, retrogression or disappearance of religious motifs, the fate of God-figures and of whole religions is ultimately decided by their religious convincingness or lack of it; by the power over reality in relation to the horizon of experience of the current historical situation which either emanates from them or fails to appear.[49]

If in this process of the transformation of religions, the truth claim of a specific appearance of the divine as definitive is at stake, and if the unity-giving context of this appearance is that process itself, and if the definitiveness of a religion's provisional claim to truth is established in the "end" of the process understood in a regulative sense, then the history of religions as the transmission of traditions is an empty or purely formal concept which does not give a priviledged status to any specific religion.[50] This concept of "end" must be distinguished from the more concrete, specific and determined understanding of the "end" of history which constitutes the totality of meaning of Christianity , i.e., its specification of a particular kind of "end": the reconciliation of all things in the resurrection of the dead and the advent of the "kingdom of God." The latter must be distinguished from the former as the more concrete to the more abstract.

> If it is correct . . . that we have access to the truth only in anticipation, then the truth's presence can be conceived, from its side, only as an anticipation in the sense of a pre-appearance (*Vorschein*) of that which has ultimate validity and of the whole constituted by the end of all history. . . . Until then, the difference between a pre-appearance and the ultimate, which is inherent in the fact that the former is the appearance of the latter, will be mirrored by the anticipation of that which appears in a pre-appearance, in such a way that such anticipations will anticipate the ultimate truth of events as the

---

48 Ibid., pp. 84-96.
49 Ibid., p. 89.
50 Ibid., p. 94. See, also, Pannenberg, "What is Truth," in *Basic Questions*, 2: 20-23.

definitive *arrival*-in-pre-appearance (*Zum-Vorscheingekommensein*) of the ultimate.[51]

What then can be said about the totality of meaning of a particular positive religion, Christianity? My remarks fall into two parts: first, a characterization of the sort of totality of meaning which defines the specificity—or, if one prefers, the "essence"—of Christianity; and, second, a sketch of Pannenberg's understanding of the significance or "positional role" of Christianity in the process which is the unity of religions.[52]

The central innovation which characterizes Christianity is one which it inherited. The "futurization" of "experience" (Pannenberg) or the "rendering history historic" (Moltmann), of the religion of ancient Israel is forged in its confrontation with, partial assimilation of and delimitation from the mythic horizon of the ancient Near Eastern religions.[53] In the interaction of Canaanite myth and Hebrew epic emerges the sphere of history in its futurity which breaks the lockhold of myth and its interpretation of the real in terms of conformity to the archetypically real *in illo tempore*. The horizon of "myth" as a primordial and paradigmatically real history is sublated by an eschatologically-oriented one.[54]

In terms of the threefold sense of religious discourse, this innovation may be sketched as follows. The worldview which emerges in the Hebrew witness of faith has been indicated by the phrase "futurization of experience." If the tacit assumption conditioning Pannenberg's recon-

---

[51] Idem, "On Historical and Theological Hermeneutics," 1: 173.

[52] The turn to "eschatology" in the 1960's in an attempt to articulate the specificity and peculiarity of Christianity on the part of Pannenberg, Moltmann and Metz is the result of a complex prior development: the biblical recovery of eschatology and apocalyptic, the crisis of orthodoxy and neoorthodoxy in the twentieth century and a growing appreciation of the "modern age" as one of the "history of freedom." An exposition of this context can be found in Wayne Meeks, *Origins of the Theology of Hope* (Philadelphia: Fortress Press, 1974); Gerhard Sauter, *Zukunft und Verheissung* (Zurich: Theologischer Verlag Zurich, 1973); and Walter Jaeschke, *Die Suche nach den eschatologischen Wurzeln der Geschichtsphilosophie* (Munich: Chr. Kaiser Verlag, 1976).

[53] Pannenberg, "Redemptive Event and History," pp. 16-23, Wolfhart Pannenberg, et al., *Revelation as History*, trans. David Granskou, ed. Wolfhart Pannenberg (New York: The Macmillan Co., 1968), pp. 125-35; and Idem, "*Zeit und Ewigkeit in der religiosen Erfahrung Israels und des Christentums*," in *Grundfragen systematischer Theologie*, 2: 189-200; Jürgen Moltmann, *Theology of Hope*, trans. James Leitch (New York: Harper and Row, 1967), pp. 95-138.

[54] Pannenberg, "The Later Dimension of Myth in Biblical and Christian Traditions," in *The Idea of God*, pp. 1-80.

struction of the meaning or sense of religious discourse is that "the truth
is the whole," then the totality which emerges is one which explicitly and
reflectively recognizes that that whole is history eschatologically qualified. History in its futurity and hence partial indeterminacy becomes the
horizon of the real and "truth" may only be spoken of in relation to an
anticipation of the "end" of that process.[55] "History is reality in its totality."[56] What a thing is, is inseparable from what it is to become and what
it will be in the end: "essence" and "appearance" become categories refracted through history. In this perspective, history as eschatologically
valorized takes on an "ontological depth" as that within which all distinctions are made thus differentiating it from the formal notion of history as the transmission of traditions; what is real as distinct from mere
appearance and hence what is true is something at stake in this process,
anticipatorily construed in a *determinate manner* by the totality of meaning of Christianity.

The *ethos* which conforms to this is "faith" as trust insofar as the
sense of the whole may only now be possessed in anticipation and
"hope" in fidelity to the one who is firm and reliable in its dealings with
men and women and whose disclosure in the event of revelation evokes
and demands the response of love. Yet both "worldview" and "*ethos*" are
inseparable from and grounded in that characterization of the appearance of the divine which was the focal perception of the experience of
ancient Israel. YHWH was one who was experienced in historical change
itself; a "living God" who is creative in history and of history—not confined *in illo tempore*. Pannenberg therefore asserts that "(T)he presupposition of historical consciousness in Israel lies in its concept of God. . . .
History is event so suspended in tension between promise and fulfillment that through the promise it is irreversibly pointed toward the goal
of future fulfillment.[57] Thus in what follows, the phrase "history
eschatologically valorized" is a shorthand to name that thematic totality
of meaning which emerges in ancient Israel were (1) the totality of reality
is coextensive with history as a process; (2) it is asserted that there is a
unity to history determinately construed on the basis of the fidelity of the
divine; and (3) the dimension of time as "future," as the not-yet present
and partially indeterminate and thus only present in the mode of

[55] Idem, "What is Truth" and "Faith and Reason," in *Basic Questions*, 2: 1-27, 46-64.
[56] Idem, "Redemptive Event and History," in *Basic Questions*, p. 21.
[57] Ibid. p. 18.

anticipation, is accorded a primacy in that through it (1) and (2) receive their substantial content.[58]

[58] In his essay *"Erfordert die Einheit der Geschichte ein Subjekt?"* (*Geschichte: Ereignis und Erzählung*, pp. 478-90) Pannenberg argues that if "history" is to be conceived as a "unity," then such a unity cannot be conceived merely as the succession of events or structural epochs or particular "subjects of history" (such as the "proletariat"), but only on the postulate of a divine subject of history. Secularized versions of salvation-history collapse under their own weight insofar as the unity so conceived is an abstraction based either on a categorical unity or an hypostasization of inner-historical reality (i.e., "humanity). Second, in speaking of the primacy of the future, I want to distance myself from Pannenberg's rhetoric of the reality (*Wirklichkeit*) of the future and his identification of this reality with the reality of God. To be sure, the connection between the reality of the "divine" (both its "thatness" and its "character") and the "future" can be defended in a twofold sense. First and formally, the reality of the divine is at stake in the as yet open-ended process of the history of the transmissions of traditions given materially nonidentical anticipations of a totality of meaning. Second, given Pannenberg's turn to eschatology as the key to the "essence of Christianity," the understanding of Christianity's God construes history in a determinate fashion and anticipates a determinate consummation of history, where that consummation is constitutive of its construal of history as a whole or unity. In that sense, it can be said that the reality of the Christian concept of God is tied to the yet-outstanding reality of that anticipated future. Yet third, Pannenberg appears to want to claim more than this, i.e., that the specific anticipated future of Christian faith is already real in the eternal life of God and that such a "real" future already acts in a causal manner on the present. This claim raises questions of "systematic theology," that is, *within* the totality of meaning of Christianity, how is divine causality and worldly freedom to be understood and is therefore beyond the parameters of this chapter. My sole point here is that the connection between the reality of God and the future can and must be separated in the two previous senses from this last claim. I am persuaded by the criticisms of Langdon Gilkey that this last claim is not only far too fragmentary, but incoherent as it stands. For an example, see Wolfhart Pannenberg, *Theology and the Kingdom of God*, ed. Richard Neuhaus (Philadelphia: The Westminster Press, 1969), pp. 53-57, 61-64, 127-42. Pannenberg's most recent attempts to explicate his position, [*Metaphysics and the Idea of God*, pp. 43-90] through reflection on the relation between "time" and "eternity" are, in my estimate, still too schematic and fail to address crucial issues such as the relation between divine and human causality. Gilkey's critique may be found in Langdon Gilkey, *Reaping the Whirlwind* (New York: The Seabury Press, 1976), pp. 226-38. See also David Polk, "The All-Determining God and the Peril of Determinism," in *The Theology of Wolfhart Pannenberg* eds. Carl Braaten and Philip Clayton, (Minneapolis: Augsburg Publishing House, 1988), pp. 152-68. My distinction here corresponds to that of Philip Clayton's between "anticipation$_2$" (the first and second points above) and "anticipation$_1$" (the third point). I would add that Clayton's distinctions correspond with the immediate theological context: foundational theology and Christian systematic theology. See Philip Clayton, "Anticipation and Theological Method," *Theology of Wolfhart Pannenberg*, pp. 131, 178-8.

If Pannenberg is relatively clear concerning what occurs at the inter-face of Canaanite myth and Hebrew epic, he is less precise in his formu-lation of what occurs at the interface of Israelite faith and Christian faith. In this context, at least three considerations should be mentioned.

First, in Jesus' proclamation of the coming Kingdom of God, there occurred a "consolidation" and "universalization" of the eschatological horizon which emerged in Israel. Who or what God is, is now under-stood as inseparable from his coming in power such that trust in the coming God becomes the sole factor regarding participation in the Kingdom as distinct from fidelity to the Law and the religious traditions of Israel.[59] Second, and closely related to this consolidation of an eschato-logical horizon is that through this explicit temporalization of the divin-ity as the power of the future, there occurs a protest against the finitiza-tion of the divine in religions and against religions' closure to their own transformation.

> . . . just the appearance of the divine reality *as* infinite—if this can occur at all in the realm of finitude—is precisely the one thing that could have a defini-tive character because it would not displace but would instead *disclose* the openness of the future, the non-closeability of the knowledge of mankind *even with respect to its knowledge of God*.[60]

Here the infinity of the divine and the openness of the future—and hence the history of religions as the history of religious transformations—are intimately intertwined. Finally, it is the affirmation of the resurrection which allows Pannenberg to speak of history in more than a formal way because with the affirmation that the end of history is given in that event it becomes possible to speak of history with a specific content, meaning and integrity which already now is present and effective although not-yet consummated. Hence it is particularly with reference to Christianity that it may be said that the totality of meaning which it projects is an *anticipated* one in both a formal and material manner.[61]

Four comments must now briefly be added concerning the signifi-cance of Christianity for the history of religions. First, the historicality of the appearance of the divine which is a formal characteristic of the his-tory of the transmission of religious traditions is made explicit and reflex-ively incorporated into Christianity.[62] Second, Christianity, due to its

59   Pannenberg, "Toward a Theology of the History of Religions," 2: 113-14.
60   Ibid., 2: 110.
61   Idem, "Redemptive Event and History," 1: 36-8.
62   Idem, "Towards a Theology of the History of Religions," 2: 105-110.

syncretistic power—a power which arises from its recognition of the temporalization of the divine and its identification of this with its infinity—has led to a universal mission issuing in an unity in the religious world situation.

> ... by means of its thrust towards a universal mission, Christianity has become the ferment for the rise of a common religious situation of the whole of mankind. ... the history of Christianity is of special interest in the history or religions on account of its specific contribution to the rise of a worldwide religious situation.[63]

Thirdly, if it is argued that this unity among various cultures is the product of a "secular understanding" of existence, Pannenberg counters that this understanding itself is an "effect," a "product of Christianity."[64] Most important therein is the "historical understanding of reality": "Biblical faith is not only the temporary, accidental presupposition of the western consciousness of historical reality, but the origin to which the consciousness remains essentially bound."[65] Finally, the most explicit restatement of the horizon of Christian faith best takes the form of a discourse concerning "universal history." The following would minimally seem to be asserted in such a notion: history provides the comprehensive horizon within which all other aspects of reality receive their intelligibility; the unity of history may only be conceived on the basis of the unity of the divine working in it; as a form of *religious* discourse, Christian theology must have as its horizon history "as a whole"; as a form of discourse *within* the sphere of a specific religious horizon, Christianity offers an *interpretation* of history as a whole mediated by the specific material elements of the Christian totality of meaning; and finally, given the indeterminacy of the future and the absence of an absolute knowledge, such theological understanding also takes the form of "anticipation."

THE MITIGATION OF ANTICIPATION: THE RESURRECTION OF JESUS

To summarize the exposition thus far: religious discourse concerns a totality of meaning which receives its intersubjective embodiment in the

---

[63] Ibid., 2: 94.

[64] Idem, "Christianity as the Legitimacy of the Modern Age," in *The Idea of God*, pp. 178-91.

[65] Idem, "Redemptive Event and History," 1: 33.

various positive religions. These must continually "prove" their claim to truth through their illuminating power. Insofar as the ensemble of totalities of meaning raise an identical formal claim to truth yet exhibit nonidentical material understandings regarding what is the definitive totality of meaning, it is these which are at stake in the process of the transmission of traditions. This process includes not only the process of each religions' confrontation with one another, but also the ability of each religion to assimilate and "comprehend" those events or nonevents which might provoke a crisis of credibility in an anticipated totality of meaning.[66] Further, the process of the transmission of traditions is the provisional testing of the truth-claims of religion and is not susceptible to any a priori comprehension. Hence the faith in or allegiance to a particular totality of meaning takes the form of anticipation. Finally, the specificity of the Christian totality of meaning is one which refers the believer back into history as the arena of the actions of the divine resulting in an interpretive theology of history as the form of Christian theology. To state the point rather baldly, encoded within the "symbols" of the resurrection from the dead and the Kingdom of God in the context of "christology," the totality of meaning which is Christianity anticipates a redemption *of* history.

Over and against this position in Pannenberg's foundational theology, there is another which coalesces around the question of the resurrection and the canons of historical inquiry. The disjunction between these two positions may be initially illuminated by reference to his essay "Insight and Faith." Here, Pannenberg asserts:

> The discussion up to now has not aimed at disputing the fact that—not with respect to the truth of the contents of the Christian message, but certainly with respect to the psychological process of its apprehension—an illumina-

---

[66] While Pannenberg alludes to political and social changes which may provoke a crisis of credibility regarding a particular totality of meaning, these sorts of events are certainly not exhaustive. Natural events, such as the crisis provoked by the Lisbon earthquake are certainly relevant. So, too, in our own century have events as Auschwitz and Hiroshima provoked a profound crisis concerning Christianity's assertion of an already definitive redemption of men and women and the world accomplished in Christ. So also have nonevents as the emergence of the various natural sciences (physics, biology, geology and astrophysics) provoked crises in the credibility of Christianity. Perhaps most ominous is the "nonevent" as the real possibility of a nuclear holocaust which itself would be a decisive refutation of at least this particular construal of Christian faith. In short, the list of such occasions is only to be determined from a reconstruction of the tradition and history itself.

tion is necessary in order for that which is true in itself to appear evident in this character to a man.[67]

This illumination is needed

> . . . in order for the truth, which is clear in itself and demonstrable as true, to dawn upon the individual man . . . in order to clear away the prejudgements standing in the way of unencumbered perception of the event that reveals God thus, in the nature of the case, adds nothing substantive to the content of this event or to the content of the message that reports about it and its meaning.[68]

The context for these statements is the relation between historical inquiry and faith which Pannenberg compares to the Reformed discussion of the relation between *historica fides* and *fiducia*. The latter is grounded upon the former, *fiducia* upon *notitia*.[69] Thus the relation of illumination or disclosure appears extrinsic to the question of the *truth* of a (particular) faith. Yet, in the same essay, Pannenberg asserts that

> . . . the insight we may acquire into the revelation of God that occurred in Christ always presupposes a telescoping of vision that links the fate of Jesus with the end of the world that is still outstanding for us. To this extent, even talk about the revelation of God in Jesus Christ is proleptic.[70]

What is this "telescoping of vision?" If what is at stake in the question of revelation is the definitive appearance of the divine, and if this is given in the powerful appearance of the divine, and if this event must prove itself anew both with regard to other religious interpretations of reality and the ongoing events of history, and if what is at stake in the history of the transmission of traditions is a particular tradition's truth claim, then can the moment of "illumination"—a "telescoping of vision"—be extrinsic to those truth claims, rather than constitutive, if only in a provisional manner? After all, Pannenberg can also assert that the "truth of such an experience (of the gods) depends upon its power to illuminate the situation of men in their actual historical world."[71] There is, I think, a real ambiguity in Pannenberg's work regarding the relation between the religion's claim to truth and the powerful appearance of the divine. Further, this

67 Pannenberg, "Insight and Faith," in *Basic Questions in Theology*, 2: 40.
68 Ibid., 2: 42.
69 Ibid., 2: 35-37.
70 Ibid., 2: 44.
71 Idem, "Anthropology and the Question of God," in *The Idea of God*, p. 97.

disparity between two positions seems to be a function of the immediate context within which Pannenberg raises his questions: on the one hand, the context of Christian faith, historical inquiry and the historicality of events (primarily the resurrection) witnessed to in the gospels; and, on the other hand, the context of the nature of religion as situated between the poles of anthropology and the history of the transmission of religious traditions.

Without exaggeration, it may be asserted that as christology is the core of Pannenberg's theology *qua* christian theology, so the resurrection is the foundation of his christology. Jesus' revelational unity with God is not yet established by the claim implied in his pre-Easter appearance, but only by his resurrection from the dead as his vindication by God. In his revelational unity with God, which constitutes Jesus' own divinity, he at the same time remains distinct from God as his Father: the beginning of the doctrine of the Trinity lies in this. As God's revelation, Jesus is at the same time in his destiny of resurrection the revelation of the future essential determination (*Wesensbestimmung*) and destiny of all men and women. The office of Jesus was to call men and women into the Kingdom of God which appears in him and so the church today through the power of his spirit is the eschatological sacrament of witness to the Kingdom of God. Shown to be the Son of God by his dedication to his Father and his resurrection, Jesus is the eschatological ruler toward whom all things are, so that all things are also through him. As even this short list of theses culled from Pannenberg's *Jesus—God and Man* demonstrates, the resurrection is central to his construal of the material meaning of the Christian faith.[72]

Yet Pannenberg wishes to assert that the resurrection is also historically verifiable apart from the *fiducia* of Christian faith. While the meaning and significance of the affirmation of Jesus' resurrection from the dead falls beyond the scope of this chapter, the claim that the resurrection is historically verifiable to all who seek to investigate it, must be investigated inasmuch as the position regarding truth and the appearance of the divine implied in this line of argument appears incompatible with the position described in the preceding section. What I suggest in this section is that Pannenberg's arguments for the historical verifiability of the resurrection are implausible. Inasmuch as they appear to contradict positions concerning the truth and status of the religious apprehension of

---

[72] Pannenberg, *Jesus-God and Man*, trans. Lewis Wilkins and Duane Priebe (Philadelphia: The Westminster Press, 1968).

a totality of meaning detailed in the preceding section, the significance of this line of argument in Pannenberg's thought is to be sought in its functional role: as a "strategy of immunization" which attempts to attenuate the provisionality of Christianity in order to secure its truth vis-à-vis other anticipated totalities of meaning and the nonidentity of history as a history of suffering.

The first part of Pannenberg's argument concerns the intelligibility of the notion of a resurrection from the dead. Insofar as the meaning of an event is to be sought within its essential context or tradition, then the question of the intelligibility of the notion of a resurrection from the dead is inseparable from the question concerning the meaningfulness of its context, the expectation of the end of history rooted in apocalyptic thought.

> The expectation of resurrection must already be presupposed as a truth given by tradition or anthropologically or is established philosophically when one speaks about Jesus' resurrection. That this expectation has already become an event in Jesus can strengthen *ex post facto* the truth of the expectation, but cannot establish it for the first time. . . . The basis of the knowledge of Jesus' significance remains bound to the original apocalyptic horizon of Jesus' history, which at the same time has been modified by this history. If this horizon is eliminated, the basis of faith is lost . . . .[73]

For Pannenberg, the continuity of the apocalyptic tradition with the understanding of men and women in the modern world need not include all the details of the apocalyptic understanding of the end of the world, but must include enough to render intelligible the expectation of a resurrection from the dead. This condition is satisfied through reflection on the *Weltoffenheit* and *Umweltfreiheit* of men and women in the context of a phenomenology of hope "which indicates that it belongs to the essence of human existence to hope beyond death."[74] If this is so, then

> . . . (i)t is only necessary to say enough to indicate that the expectation of a resurrection from the dead need not appear meaningless from the presuppositions of modern thought, but rather is to be established as a philosophically appropriate expression for human destiny. Thus precisely today a continuity of our thought with the apocalyptic hope has become possible at

[73] Ibid., pp. 81, 84.
[74] Ibid., p. 85. See, also, *What is Man?*, pp. 41-67.

a decisive point, and with this also a continuity with the primitive Christian perception of the event of Jesus' resurrection.[75]

While this first line of argument can only secure the general intelligibility of the resurrection from the dead, Pannenberg's second line of argument secures a second necessary but not sufficient condition for the historical affirmation of Jesus' resurrection, i.e., the *possibility* of a resurrection against the "dogmatic" presupposition "that the dead do not rise."[76] The form of this argument is a critique of the canons of historical reason and insofar as that principle which is most frequently invoked in the "in principle" denial of the possibility of a resurrection from the dead is the principle of analogy, the argument is a critique of that principle. The use of the principle of analogy witnesses to the inescapable *methodological* anthropocentricity of inquiry.

> The analogies with which the historian understands the content of the tradition as an expression of possible human behavior always arise out of an already given world of expressions in which the historian is at home, and never from a value-free sense experience.[77]

In itself, this methodological anthropocentricity of historical inquiry is not to be objected to except when it is expanded and transformed from a formal heuristic structure into a material affirmation which postulates an inviolable homogeneity of events.

> A constriction of historical-critical inquiry, in the sense of domination by a biased world view, first occurs when, instead of pointing out analogies from case to case, one postulates a fundamental homogeneity of all reality with the current range of experience and research.[78]

Under such conditions, a methodological anthropocentricity becomes a substantive one and the principle of analogy whose limits might "in principle" be breached by a particular event are made absolute in a leveling of the particularity of historical phenomena which, ironically, it is the task of historical inquiry as an "idiographic" science (Dilthey) to uncover. To think historically becomes a form of "identity-thought."

---

[75] Ibid., p. 88.
[76] The following exposition is drawn from "Redemptive Events and History," in *Basic Questions in Theology*, 1: 38-53.
[77] Ibid., 1: 44-45.
[78] Ibid., 1: 45.

If this argument concerning the limits of the principle of analogy is acceptable and "the historian must also consider this possibility, resurrection, for a reconstruction of the course of events as long as no special circumstances in the tradition suggest another explanation,"[79] a third line of argument is necessary: one which turns to the "sources" of the tradition to examine the *plausibility* of their assertions concerning the destiny of Jesus.[80] It is important to note here, *what* is to be explained: the emergence of primitive Christianity and *therefore* the plausibility of the tradition's claims that the condition of its emergence lies in Jesus' resurrection from the dead. The details of Pannenberg's reconstruction of the history of the two major "resurrection traditions"—the "empty tomb tradition" of Mk.16 and the "appearance tradition" whose formulaic style in 1 Cor.15.1-11 points to a tradition antedating Paul—need not be addressed here. Positively, his task at this juncture is to defend the integrity and independence of the two traditions. Negatively, his task is to dispute the so-called "subjective vision hypothesis" against which he notes that "(t)he Easter appearances are not to be explained from the Easter faith of the disciples; rather, conversely, the Easter faith of the disciples is to be explained from the appearances"[81] and this from a commonsense "psychological" point of view. Further, the number of appearances and their disparity in time presents a further difficulty for such a hypothesis. Given the meaningfulness and the possibility of a resurrection from the dead, Pannenberg now concludes from the sources of the tradition:

> If the appearance tradition and the grave tradition came into existence independently, then by their mutually complementing each other they let the assertion of the reality of Jesus' resurrection . . . appear as historically very probable, and that always means in historical enquiry that it is to be presupposed until contrary evidence appears.[82]

In sum, Pannenberg's argument for the facticity of Jesus' resurrection is really *three* arguments: an argument concerning its intelligibility, an argument concerning its possibility as a historical fact, and an argument concerning the plausibility of the tradition's witness to that event which is the condition of that tradition's emergence.

My first criticism concerns Pannenberg's grounding of the intelligibility of the concept of a resurrection. As noted above, the proximate

---

79 Pannenberg, *Jesus-God and Man*, p. 98.
80 The following brief summary is drawn from *Jesus-God and Man*, pp. 88-106.
81 Ibid., p. 96.
82 Ibid., p. 105.

grounding of the meaningfulness of that concept is drawn from the ideas of *Weltoffenheit* and *Umweltfreiheit* of the being of human beings in general and from a phenomenology of human hope in particular. The question is, is there not a disparity between the former and the latter in that the former is more indeterminate and hence abstract than the latter? More exactly, a phenomenology of hope posits *Weltoffenheit* and *Umweltfreiheit* as construed in a particular manner through the determining force or effect of a particular tradition(s). This might be generalizable for the "West" through the effective history of the apocalyptic tradition and its merger with the Greek notion of the immortality of the soul in the Christian tradition; but, precisely in this "context dependence" is witnessed its own historicality qua provisionality. The intelligibility of such a notion cannot be drawn from an alleged "ontological" analysis of the condition of human existence as such, but always already presupposes its determination in a particular manner through an equally particular "traditioned" totality of meaning which valorizes history in the modality of the future. In short, Pannenberg seems to assume what is to be demonstrated: the truth of a particular religious totality of meaning.

My second criticism is based on the fact that although Pannenberg polemicizes against the constriction of the principle of analogy to the postulation of an "in principle fundamental homogeneity of events," he still allows that principle to operate within its proper place.

> That a reported event bursts analogies with otherwise usual or repeatedly attested events is still no ground for disputing its facticity. It is another matter when positive analogies to forms of tradition (such as myths and even legends) relating to unreal objects, phenomena referring to states of consciousness (like visions) may be found in the historical sources. In such cases historical understanding guided by analogy can lead to a negative judgement about the reality of the occurrences reported in the tradition. Such a judgement will be rendered not because of the unusualness of something reported about, but rather because it exhibits a positive analogy to some form of consciousness which has no objective referent.[83]

Cannot this same argument be directed against Christianity's claim about Jesus' resurrection from the dead? Could not a historian responsibly argue that insofar as that event is affirmed as a unique event and that such claims are found in other major religious traditions, Christianity's claim must be assimilated to those of other major religious traditions which stand in competition to one another? It does not appear to me that

---

[83] Idem, "Redemptive Event and History," 1: 48-49.

the historian shirks his or her professional responsibility by holding in abeyance historical judgment concerning the truth of the interpretations of the foundational events which stand at the root of particular religions.

Thirdly, it must be asked "Is what is to be explained the destiny of Jesus or the emergence of the primitive Christian kerygma?". In my estimation, the former is of significance only on the basis of the actuality of the latter and Pannenberg's argument for the historical facticity of Jesus' resurrection often takes the form of an argument from the "miracle of Christian faith," of which the resurrection-event is the objective condition. Yet in speech concerning a "resurrection from the dead," Pannenberg realizes that the limits of language are being broached.

> An important material consequence follows immediately from the observation of the metaphorical structure of language about the resurrection of the dead: the intended reality and the mode in which it is expressed in language are essentially different. The intended reality is beyond the experience of the man who lives on this side of death. Thus the only possible mode of speaking about it is metaphorical, using images of this-worldly occurrences. . . . Because the life of the resurrected Lord involves the reality of a new creation, the resurrected Lord is in fact not perceptible as one object among others in this world; therefore, he could be experienced and designated by an extra-ordinary mode of experience, vision, and only in metaphorical language.[84]

What does it mean to affirm a "metaphor" as an historical event? The historian, insofar as what is to be explained is the emergence of primitive Christianity and its kerygma, might well abjure as improbable the "subjective vision hypothesis" or the "hypothesis of fictive malicious deception" and assert that "something happened" between the event of the cross and the proclamation, but that the determination of what that "something" was, is not possible. There is no law of "excluded middle" in historical inquiry. Between affirmation and negation of a tradition's claims concerning its origins, there is the responsible path of "abstention" and I see no compelling historical—as distinct from theological—reason to force the historian into the position of either categorically affirming or denying the witness of the tradition. Indeed, the historian might well assert that the "truth" of a particular religious tradition's claims about itself and the historical assertions concerning the facticity of foundational events which are asserted as constitutive of the truth of a tradition—which is itself a *theological* judgment(!)—are at stake in the his-

---

[84] Pannenberg, *Jesus-God and Man*, pp. 77, 99.

tory of the transmission of traditions and hence abdicate historical judgment.

My last criticism is a coda to the first three and concerns that principle of historical understanding and judgment which Pannenberg does not take account of: what Van A. Harvey terms the "texture of historical assent."[85] Historical judgments are made along a "spectrum of assent." They are "qualified" in terms of the witness and disposition of the sources and the canon of analogies which obtain at any given time. Some judgments may warrant the assertion that they are "as good as certain"; others may be qualified as "highly hypothetical." Along this continuum of the texture of assent—highly probable/probable/improbable and the "limits" of "as good as certain" and "pure conjecture"—there is also the rare option of the suspending judgment. Pannenberg, unfortunately, seems to cast the role of the historian as having to, when put on the spot, cast his or her lot in a nay or yea with the tradition and misses the point that "perhaps," "maybe," "probably," "conceivably" etc., are irreducibly part of the professional vocabulary of the historian.

RESURRECTION AND THE NEGATION OF NONIDENTITY

What I wish to suggest at the end of this chapter is that there is a major dissonance or disjunction of perspectives throughout the work of Pannenberg: between truth as a proleptic and hence provisional disclosure of a totality of meaning within the context of history as the history of the transmission of traditions and truth as correspondence ("in the realm of history meaning must remain bound to facticity")[86] within the context of history as the object of methodical inquiry. More specifically, it is a disjunction between his fundamental theological perspective whose structure is formed by a consideration of fundamental anthropology, the specification of the meaning and status of religious language and the dialectic of religions, and his systematic theological perspective whose structure is formed by the claims of the historical facticity of the events witnessed to in the gospels and the public criteria of historical inquiry. It is the former, not the latter, which I find plausible in Pannenberg's work.

---

[85] Van A. Harvey, *The Historian and the Believer* (New York: Macmillan Co., 1974), pp. 59-64.

[86] Pannenberg, "On Historical and Theological Hermeneutic," 1: 149. See, also, his curious qualification of this in *Theology and Philosophy of Science*, pp. 338-39.

The question then arises "Why Pannenberg's defense of the historical verifiability of the facticity of the resurrection?" What follows is a theological hermeneutics of suspicion which seeks to uncover the dissonance of the two perspectives in the function of the affirmation of the facticity of the resurrection. First, Pannenberg's position on the resurrection functions to secure the claims of Christian faith as *the definitive* appearance of the divine. The historical public knowability of the facticity of the resurrection secures the proleptic appearance of the divine in Jesus Christ as definitive and thus "short-circuits" the claims to the truth of other extant religious totalities of meaning. *If* in the realm of history meaning must remain bound to "facticity" and *if* the resurrection can be affirmed as a historical event, then the truth of Christianity is guaranteed over and against other religious totalities of meaning whose horizons either are not claimed as grounded in historical facticity or being claimed as so grounded cannot be sustained by public historical inquiry. This constriction of perspectives and the paradigms of truth from proleptic disclosure to historical correspondence appears to be grounded not in fundamental theological considerations, but in systematic theological ones: the debate over the relationship of the historical Jesus to the Christ of faith and, more specifically, as polemically related to Protestant neoorthodoxy which grounded the historical facticity of the gospel reports in the privileged knowledge or belief of faith. While these issues remain beyond the scope of this chapter, what is interesting is Pannenberg's silence on those positions—most notably, that of Schubert Ogden—which disaffirm the intrinsic relevance of the historical Jesus to the truth of the Christ of faith: a position which might be more consonant with Pannenberg's foundational theological perspective.[87]

Second, at the close of the first section of this chapter, I suggested that the peculiarity of the sort of totality of meaning of Christianity lay in the fact that it refers the believer into history as a concrete nexus of events in anticipation of the redemption of history. The knowability and verification of the event of the resurrection not only grounds the certainty of the Christian faith and its claim to truth vis-à-vis other religions, but functions also to secure an "optimism" concerning the events of history whereby history in its nonidentity with faith as the interruption of suffering is occluded by the outstanding yet certain resurrection of the dead in the Kingdom of God. The verifiability of this piece of history

[87] Schubert Ogden, *The Point of Christology* (San Francisco: Harper and Row, 1982). See, also, David Tracy, *A Blessed Rage for Order* (New York: Seabury Press, 1975), pp. 204-36, and *The Analogical Imagination*, pp. 248-338.

leads to its nonfalsifiability by any other piece of history and its seeming "indifference" to any other piece of history. What Emil Fackenheim asserts concerning the resurrection in general, appears particularly applicable to Pannenberg: "Only the original Good Friday was before Easter. Every subsequent Good Friday, Auschwitz included, is after Easter overcome in advance."[88] What is remarkable is that Pannenberg appears theologically untroubled by the systematic distortions of the transmission of the Christian tradition (racism, sexism, anti-Semitism, imperialism) and the manner in which they have and continue to engender in the name of Christ Jesus an enduring witness of suffering, cruelty and horror. Indicative of this is Metz' characterization of the sort of eschatology in the work of Pannenberg. "Wolfhart Pannenberg's anticipation of a total meaning in history is not [sic] too little interrupted or irritated by what is described in the apocalyptic tradition as a universal catastrophe, in other words, the reign of the Antichrist."[89]

More specifically, Metz has sought to illuminate this situation through the German fairy-tale of the "hedgehog and the hare."[90] The hare challenges the bandy-legged hedgehog to a race, who then manages to excuse himself temporarily in order to go home. There, he arranges with his wife that each of them will stand at opposite ends of the furrow in the field during the time of the race. In the "running of the race," the hedgehog, through his cunning is always at both "ends" and seemingly ahead of the hare, who eventually dies of exhaustion. The hedgehog is always already at both "ends" and seemingly encompasses the whole without the risk of having to "run the race," i.e., participate in history as the nexus of concrete socially mediated events either in terms of being critical of the nexus or allowing such events to challenge the truth claims of the tradition. It is this "trick" of idealistic (i.e., transcendental or universal-historical) reflective groundings of the identity, truth and triumph of the Christian faith which Metz explicitly directs to Pannenberg.

> If we opt for the hare, we opt to enter the field of history, a field that can be measured in running the course of the race, in competition or in flight. . . . And this option for the hare also means that we must try to expose critically the idealistic guarantee of the threatened identity of Christianity. This guarantee leaves out of account the power of praxis to save the historical identity

[88] Emil L. Fackenheim, *To Mend the World* (New York: Schocken Books, 1982), p. 133.

[89] Johann Baptist Metz, *Faith in History and Society*, trans. D. Smith (New York: The Seabury Press, 1980), p. 55.

of Christianity and acts as a kind of theological hedgehog trick which aims to safeguard the identity and triumph of Christianity without the experience of the race (that is, without the experience of being threatened and possibly of being defeated).[91]

More specifically, Metz adds,

> The ultimately promised saving meaning of history is not disclosed as it were while the course of that history is being run. It is not evoked, narrated or remembered (for all men) as a practical experience of meaning in the middle of our historical life. It is, so to speak, rigidified into a definition for reflection that cannot be affected by the collective historical fears or threats of catastrophe and is therefore not in need of any hope provided with expectation. The present state of meaning has all its wrinkles ironed out and is free of all contradictions. It is, as it were, "hopelessly" total.[92]

I would add here that a "nodal point" for the hedgehog trick in Pannenberg's theology is his argument for and defense of the possibility and necessity of the affirmation of the resurrection as a historical event.

NONIDENTITY AND THE ANTICIPATORY STATUS OF RELIGIOUS TOTALITIES OF MEANING

I would like to begin this section by first commenting on Pannenberg's "Eurocentrism," a "Eurocentrism" which I do not believe derives from his foundational perspective, but from his specific construal of the concrete process of transmission of traditions. If one reads the work of Pannenberg, it is clear that his investigations into the history of the transmission of religious traditions has remained confined to the relatively brightly lit sphere of the "linear" progression of ancient Near Eastern religions—the faith of Israel—the rise of primitive Christianity—the confrontation of Christianity with Hellenism, i.e., to the progressive victory of an eschatological-historical horizon over a mythical-historical one.[93] In short, Pannenberg's investigations have been restricted to the area of reconstructing the religious archeology of Western civilization and, most particularly, the historical self-consciousness of Western civilization which arose in the late 17th century. This, in turn, is generalized

---

[90] Ibid., pp. 161-66.
[91] Ibid., p. 161.
[92] Ibid., p. 162.
[93] Pannenberg, "Toward a Theology of the History of Religions," 2: 84-92.

as a "world-historical" situation. While I tend to agree with Pannenberg that biblical faith is the origin of the Western consciousness of historical reality, I cannot comprehend any possible significant meaning concerning his assertion of the "rise of a worldwide religious situation." In the following lengthy quote, Pannenberg sketches "that presentation of the unity of the history of religions as a unity that proceeds from the processes of historical interaction between the different religions. . . ."

> It is not necessary to take as such a point the obscure, scarcely discoverable beginnings of religion. The path to the religious unity of mankind can be attacked from many points of departure, but the critical process of integration begins in the comparatively bright light of historical knowledge, with the religions of the ancient Mediterranean world and of the Near East, with the Egyptians in the Tigris-Euphrates valley, with the Persians and their Indian kin who then went their own way for quite a while. The overlapping and coalescence of the most varied religious traditions is evidenced with particular intensity in the history of Israel and then of the Greeks—and more than ever in primitive Christianity, in which the Jewish and the Greek heritages were united, and in the expansion of Christianity throughout the religious world, which was saturated with Hellenism. The process of religious integration was at first interrupted by the rise of Islam at the borders of the Christian world, only then to maintain a development that was nonetheless in many respects parallel to it. The process advanced farther in the outreach of the Christian missionary movement beyond the Hellenistic realm, especially by the conversion of the Slavic and Germanic peoples to the Christian faith, and then by the colonization of America, and finally by encountering the religions of the Far East and the illiterate cultures of Africa and Australia, which at that time along with their histories entered the stream of the world history of religion which the Christian mission had mediated. Finally, in this century, the diffusion of the secular culture of the West altered the traditional form of the Christian mission itself after this had led—not to the conversion of man, of course, but in another sense—to a common religious situation characterized, on the one hand, by the confrontation of all the religious traditions of mankind with the Christian tradition, and, on the other hand, by the secularized form of human existence in industrialized existence.[94]

If the transmission of religious traditions cannot be deduced from any sort of principle, but is to be understood only by reflecting upon the way it actually took place, is it not only lately that an "historical interaction" between other religions and Christianity can occur without recourse to the pogrom, auto-da-fé and the ghetto to coerce "a progressive religious

---

[94] Ibid., 2: 94-95.

integration of mankind?" Even more, have not only the events of the past few years provoked from the penumbra of a dull semiawareness the recognition of the existence of Islam? In short, even in a relatively homogenized West—homogenized only insofar as its three major religious traditions remain oriented, in some sense, to "history" as the horizon of reality—a plurality of anticipations of totality of meaning still remains and what "integration" obtains has, to the shame of the Christian mission, been forged over the corpses of those baptized in their own blood in the name of Christ Jesus. The "historical interaction" and "integration" of religions has proceeded less on the model of a seminar in München, than through the coercion of the sword, firebrand and bullet. An integration and consensus forged by coercion is one in name only. Rather than acknowledge an existent plurality of religious claims to truth, it seeks to negate them by smothering and stifling them.

Even to appeal in this context to a "secularized understanding of reality" is problematic. Insofar as it is assumed that a constitutive element of this understanding of reality is historical consciousness which recognizes that reality in its totality is historical and that there is a unity to reality so conceived, such a stance is "crisis-riddled" today. More precisely, there seems to be an ambiguity in the phrase "the Western consciousness of historical reality," because the term can refer to (1) the consciousness of the unity of history which is an "effect" of one or more religious totalities of meaning, or to (2) the consciousness of the historicity of events and significant continuities in history. Certainly in the sense of (1) Pannenberg wishes to argue that a dynamic unity of history which is more than a mere aggregate of events demands a (specific?) theistic interpretation of history where God is the "unity-giving subject of history." But that historical consciousness in sense (2) remains essentially bound to the Christian vision of reality as its origin does not seem to follow. Perhaps it can be argued that such a historical consciousness derives from or is an "effect" of its Christian origins, but that it is essentially bound to its origin seems unwarranted. One would further have to argue that (2) necessarily entails (1), and (1) further entails a specific theistic (i.e., Christian) interpretation.[95]

---

[95] Pannenberg himself appears to be aware of this ambiguity when he writes, "It must be asked, however, whether historicity rather is not grounded in the experience of reality as history, just as it is made accessible in the history of promise of God with Israel pointing towards the anticipated fulfillment in Jesus Christ. . . . The emancipation of historicity from history, the reversal of the relationship between the two so that history is grounded in the historicity of man—this seems to be the end of the

Undeniable today is the proliferation of modes of viewing reality which witness to an attenuation of a secular historical consciousness certainly in sense (1) and quite possibly in sense (2). Perhaps more important has been the waning of the belief in progress which was the glue of the modern historical self-consciousness.[96] Indeed, more plausible today appears the thesis of the integration of society and the extirpation of the subject announced in the works of Adorno and Horkheimer which will be the subject matter of the next chapter. The opacity of the societal totality has taken on the form of "fate" where men and women are reduced to the status of cogs in the machine for the reproduction of the "always the same," while the growing integration of the subject into a hegemonic totality has led to an erosion of memory, desire, imagination and anticipation and the rise of resignation and an impotent ennui. For Adorno and Horkheimer, "history" in the period of late capitalism and authoritarian state socialism has reverted to "myth." Perhaps this ironically confirms Pannenberg's conjunction of biblical faith and the secular understanding of reality as the historical consciousness of the West. Yet to appeal to the latter to support the former is like asking the blind to lead the lame.

Just as profound, I believe, are the problems and questions which arise from a consideration of the two other major world religions which fall outside the sphere of the West and which seemingly do not merit mention in Pannenberg's sketch quoted above: Buddhism and Hinduism. The challenge of a serious consideration of the non-Western religions is that they witness to anticipations of a totality of meaning in which "history" does not significantly enter as the comprehensive framework of meaning and reality. These same religions are powerful forces in history as the process of the transmission of religious traditions and cannot be dismissed inasmuch as the outcome of the process of the transmission of traditions cannot be deduced from any a priori principle. The question is: are Pannenberg's heuristic terms, "myth" as primordial history or an "eschatological valorization of history"—terms which are forged in an attempt to understand the interface of ancient Near Eastern religions and Yahwism—too narrow and too Eurocentric to comprehend the sorts of totality of meaning which are at stake in Buddhism and Hinduism and which are live options in the contemporary world?

---

way which began when modern man made man instead of God the one who bears history" ["Redemptive Event and History," 1: 35].

[96] For an exposition of the "idea" of progress in the West, see Robert Nisbet, *History of the Idea of Progress* (New York: Basic Books, 1980). See, also, Gilkey, *Reaping the Whirlwind*, pp. 8-14, 80-81, 202-7, 222-24.

If the thesis of the emergence of an integration and unity of the religious of humanity situation is premature and a pluralism of religious perspectives must be acknowledged, then there emerges a "gap" between two notions of history utilized by Pannenberg: history as the process of the transmission of traditions as the history of religions which is rendered thematically present to consciousness as the "reconstruction" of that process, and history as "promise and fulfillment" as a specification of the horizon of the totality of meaning of Israel which remains effective in Christianity. Regarding the former, Pannenberg asserts:

> The history of the transmission of tradition, including the origins of the traditions and the concrete occasions of their change, is itself treated as an historical object, and can be treated in hardly any other way. It is just the history of the transmission of tradition that has to be seen as a deeper concept of history generally.[97]

The religious traditions of Christianity and Israel bear a peculiar relation to history understood as the transmission of traditions. Insofar as they project the horizon of all reality as history eschatologically valorized, they raise to a self-reflexive level the historicality of the appearance of the divine which is witnessed to in the interactions and transmission of religious traditions. There is a self-referencing of these traditions to this process itself. Yet does not a gap emerge between the two conceptions of history when it is asserted by Pannenberg that "the mutual interaction of religious traditions which has resulted in the furthering of such competitive struggles among the gods over the nature of reality is not to be deduced from any sort of principle, but to be understood only by reflecting upon the way it actually took place?"[98] It is this injunction which renders history as the transmission of tradition "formalistic" with regard to all anticipated totalities of meaning contained within that process. That Christianity not only reflexively thematizes this process, but indeed affirms it as the comprehensive horizon of reality cannot grant it an a priori privileged status—although it may well condition its assimilative potential—in the concrete process of the interaction of religious traditions since what is at stake in this process is precisely what sort of totality of meaning is decisive and definitive and the "end" of that process is itself still indeterminate. Israel's and Christianity's valorization of history in an eschatological manner and their assertion of the same as the constitutive

---

97 Pannenberg, "Kerygma and Dogma," 1: 93.
98 Idem, "Toward a Theology of the History of Religions," 2: 91.

limits of reality and the divine is itself "at stake" in the formal process of the transmission of religious traditions. "The divinity of God himself is at stake in history."[99]

The problem is compounded further, I believe, when it is noted that Christianity not only posits reality as eschatologically valorized history, but construes that history in a specific manner. To use the language of H. White,[100] Christianity anticipatorily emplots history in a specific mode: a "comedy" sublating "tragedy" as the reconciliation of all things which becomes thematic in the symbols of resurrection from the dead and the Kingdom of God. Is it not because history eschatologically valorized is understood and hoped for in this specific manner that its corresponding *ethos* becomes "faith as trust working in love" in that both are ultimately grounded in the characterization of the divine as disclosed in the life, death and resurrection of Jesus of Nazareth; a God who is "for" men and women and who has bound itself to them as their destiny? Is it not something of an "abstraction" when Pannenberg intimates that the infinity and inexhaustability of God as the "power of the future" which is pointed to in Jesus Christ constitutes an advance in the history of religions?

> The non-Christian religions perceived the appearance of the divine mystery only in a fragmentary way because they were closed to their own transformation, to their own history. Insofar as the process of religious transformation—described by the historian of religion—takes place behind the backs of the religions, they exemplify in ever new ways the fixation of the infinite God onto the finite medium of its appearance at some time, a fixation over which the infinity of God prevails by means of this process of transformation.[101]

---

[99] "In this history of God with the world which is mediated through the Trinity, the divinity of God is at stake until it demonstrates itself in the perfection of his Kingdom. Without the coming of his Kingdom, God would not be the true God. On account of this, the future of his Kingdom is the 'place' of the reality of God as well as the truth of history as a history of his actions." Pannenberg, *"Der Gott der Geschichte,"* *Kerygma und Dogma*, 23 (March, 1977): 91. I will return in the chapter on Metz to what appears to be a consequence of Pannenberg's eschatological valorization of the essence of Christianity—one which also holds for Metz's political theology—i.e., Christianity's falsifiability.

[100] White, *Metahistory*, pp. 1-38.

[101] Pannenberg, "Toward a Theology of the History of Religions," 2: 115. See, also, "Christian Theology and Philosophical Criticism," p. 142.

The problem is that, in Christianity, not only does God appear as the "inexhaustible power of the future"; Pannenberg also designates Him as the "God of the coming Kingdom" and hence as a God whose inexhaustible power of the future is construed in a certain way. The reproach of a fixation or finitization of the appearance of the divine could just as well be directed against Christianity insofar as it "constricts" the inexhaustible power of the future with a hope of a resurrection of the dead and advent of the Kingdom of God.

In summary, there are a variety of "strategies of immunization" regarding the truth of Christian faith in the work of Pannenberg which attempt to attenuate the element of provisionality regarding the totality of meaning of Christianity: (1) the strategy of an affirmation of a common religious situation of mankind brought about by Christianity of which its eschatological historical horizon is constitutive; (2) the strategy of attempting to close the "gap" between history (A) as the process of the transmission of traditions, and history (B) as the specific constellation of Christianity's eschatological historical horizon; and (3) the strategy of an appeal to the historical verifiability of the resurrection as an event "guaranteeing" that of which this event is a prolepsis, i.e., the "end" of history as the consummation of the resurrection of the dead and the advent of the Kingdom of God. By such strategies, what is obscured is the historicality, i.e., the provisionality of the horizon or sort of totality of meaning which is projected by Christianity as (1) history eschatologically valorized, and (2) the specific mode or manner in which (1) is construed.

POSTSCRIPT: THE TASK AND STATUS OF THEOLOGICAL REFLECTION

Pannenberg's most extensive reflection on the nature of theology is *Theology and the Philosophy of Science*. Published in 1973, however, these reflections are hedged in, as it were, between two other blocks of material. On the one hand, he seeks to articulate a new self-understanding of science in general which will provide the basis for a new ordering of scientific disciplines and their methods thus providing a space for theology as "science." At least half of the text, therefore, is a critical analysis of the metamethodological positions on what constitutes science in the contemporary analytic, hermeneutical and critical-theoretical traditions. On the other hand, he attempts to describe the unity of theology in the genre of a (formal) theological encyclopedia. Bisecting these two blocks of material is the chapter "Theology as the Science of God" which could well be titled "What is Theology?" The heart of Pannenberg's constructive proposal can be seen in the following quote.

> In ordinary experience of meaning the totality of meaning is only *implicitly* anticipated, as the basis of the specificity of the particular meaning. In contrast, in religious experience there is already contained a form of *explicit* awareness of the total meaning of reality, even though it is only an indirect assumption within the awareness of the divine basis of all reality. It follows that if every experience of meaning, because it implicitly reaches out towards the totality of the process of experience which is not yet complete, proceeds hypothetically in relation to the context of meaning of all experience which is still undetermined and will emerge only from the as yet incomplete process of reality, religious awareness must have, again, a hypothetical total meaning of reality, even though it is only an indirect assumption within the awareness of the divine basis of all reality. It follows that if every experience of meaning, because it implicitly reaches out towards the totality of the process of experience which is not yet complete, proceeds hypothetically in relation to the context of meaning of all experience which is still undetermined and will emerge only from the as yet incomplete process of reality, religious awareness must have, again, a hypothetical relation to the totality of experiences of meaning available at any time because of the *implicitly* anticipated totality of meaning of reality which they contain. Therefore if theological statements...adopt a critical attitude to claims of a self-communication of divine reality in religious awareness, they must be third-order hypotheses: hypotheses about hypotheses about hypotheses. In more precise terms, theology statements are hypotheses about the truth and/or untruth of constructions of religious awareness: that is, they are about the *relation* of the implications about meaning contained in the experience of reality in its most varied forms, which are also of relevance to religion, that is, to the understanding of life as a whole. In this role theological statements are concerned both with the inadequacy of traditional and new religious assertions of meaning and with ascertaining the degree of their illuminative power. They must also decide what changes may be required in traditional assertions of meaning for the most successful integration of the present experience of meaning, and try to define their relation to other religious traditions.[102]

What is apparent is that the chapter suffers from a misnomer: theology is the science of God only indirectly, that is, as the science of religion*s*. More precisely, fundamental theology, as a moment in a Christian theology is a theology of religions.[103] The most "abstract" aspect of its task is

---

[102] Pannenberg, *Theology and the Philosophy of Science*, p. 333.
[103] Ibid., pp. 358-71.

to answer the questions (1) what is human being (human being as the open question concerning the divine in virtue of its *Weltoffenheit*)?; (2) what is the "sense" of religious discourse (religion as a "totality of meaning")?; (3) what is the reality-referent of religion (the powerful appearance of the divine in the transmission of the significant particular of positive religions)?; and (4) an exploration of the *Strittigkeit* (contestableness) of religions in the history of the transmission of traditions. Its more proximate and concrete task is the delineation of

> ... first, [the] basic forms of religious conceptions of the "sacred power" of the divine reality, second the corresponding understanding of the world and man and, thirdly, the forms of the religious relationship, i.e., of worship. To do this, philosophy of religion makes use of the work of the auxiliary disciplines of the psychology, phenomenology and sociology of religion in organizing the source material. Through their position midway between empirical investigation and conceptual systemisation these auxiliary disciplines link the two major disciplines of the science of religion, philosophy of religion and the history of religion.[104]

Yet a theology of religions is a prologomenon to the task of a Christian theology proper. The latter's task is to demonstrate reflectively the coherence of the provisional totality of meaning of Christianity with the contemporary experience and understanding of reality especially as this is found in the various sciences. Again, what Pannenberg suggests is that the (provisional) truth of Christian faith and its determinate totality of meaning is secured in its "successful integration" with the contemporary experience of meaning. The task of theology is to distill synchronically what diachronically has been termed "the history of the transmission of traditions" by mediating "for the present" the tradition in its coherence with the contemporary experience of reality. The remaining chapters of this essay are an attempt to "decenter" Pannenberg's understanding of the role and task of theological reflection in the direction indicated in the following comments.

If the reality-referent of religion is concretely given in its powerful appearance through the significant particular of positive religion, then it is rather curious that in the text under consideration Pannenberg overlooks the foundational significance of truth as disclosive and transformative event ("illuminative power") and leaves this as the mere "stuff" for reflective elucidation and subsequent correlation in "theory" with other reflective understandings of reality. The point is that the disclosive-

---

[104] Ibid., p. 368.

transformative appearance of the divine is always already a mediation of
tradition and contemporary reality which secures provisionally the truth
of that totality of meaning. The question is whether the (provisional)
truth of Christian faith is more fundamentally founded in the claims of a
theoretical correlation or in the illuminative power of the appearance of
the divine?

Second, the "history of the transmission of traditions" is itself an abstraction in which Pannenberg comes dangerously close to construing
history as the history of Ideas. Consistently, Pannenberg abstracts both
"faith" and "reason" from the specificity of the social totality which mediates both faith and reason. A theology which conceives itself in the
manner of a critical theoretical correlation (Lamb)[105] not only overlooks
its own foundation in the powerful appearance of the divine, but suc-
cumbs to the myth of pure reason surreptitiously ratifying the timelessness and spacelessness of the bourgeois as "the Subject."

Finally, in his quest for the successful correlation of the Christian totality of meaning with contemporary understandings of reality,
Pannenberg perhaps underestimates precisely what Metz highlights: the
interruptive character of Christian faith in history and society. Indeed,
the metaphor under which the task of theology is conceptualized by
Pannenberg, "integration" or "coherence," occludes the possibility that
Christianity may be a subversive religion, a subversiveness which only
can emerge after the abandonment of the "universalism" of pure reason
and a turn to viewing the true, good and beautiful as exigencies yet to be
realized in (social) praxis and after "reading" the Christian tradition
against the grain, that is, from the place of the marginalized, the silenced
and the victims of history. In short, the subversive character of
Christianity can only be preserved in the turn to praxis as discipleship
which radically questions the presuppositions of all critical theoretical
correlation by reminding it that praxis is not only the "end" of theory but
also its "foundation." Ironically, here also the idealization of history as
the history of ideas leaves Pannenberg's own construal of the task of theology uninterrupted by the surd of history in his hermeneutics of universal history—an irony that can perhaps be reduced back to the conception
of theology as embodying a critical theoretic correlation for theory cannot preserve the sensuous surd of suffering without transforming itself.

---

[105] Lamb, *Solidarity with Victims*, pp. 75-82.

AN EXCURSUS ON THE PANNENBERG-GADAMER DEBATE

Characteristic of Pannenberg is his tacit equation of "existential self-understanding" with the (merely) "ethical."

> In any case, the question of the truth of the Christian message will not permit of being narrowed down to the theme of self-understanding, but must also be carried out in the realm of the understanding of the world, too, since self-understanding and understanding of the world are always correlative. Therefore the question of the truth of the Christian message involves not only ethical but also theoretical knowledge.[106]

In part, this equation stems from Pannenberg's identification of an interpretive continuity between the liberal theology of W. Hermann and the neoorthodox theologies of Bultmann, Ebeling and Fuchs. In part, this also stems from Pannenberg's contention that the philosophical hermeneutics of Gadamer does not adequately account for the role of "assertion" in interpretation:

> . . . it is this exclusion [of "assertion" as a reconstructive-explanatory moment in interpretation] which gives rise to the equally problematic affinity of Gadamer's hermeneutic with a "theological hermeneutic of language-event" which attempts to relieve the interpretation and current appropriation of the biblical texts of the awkward problems associated with the historical facticity of the events transmitted by tradition and to reduce them to their existential relevance for present-day man.[107]

Pannenberg clearly wants to defend the necessity of "assertion" for the *reflective* interpretation of *texts*. This emphasis is important since it defines the parameters for how Pannenberg views Gadamer and from which three consequences follow. First, Pannenberg rejects Gadamer's understanding of the act of interpretation on the analogy of "the conversation as game" inasmuch as this notion is drawn from a "prereflexive" level and is inadequate to describe the methical character of reflective interpretation. Further, this concept obscures the differences between the situation of the conversation where the interpreter encounters a "subject" and that of the text where one encounters a nonhuman "object."[108] Second, Pannenberg disputes that the "fusion of horizons" in the act of reflective interpretation is grounded in an "in principle" nonobjectifiable

---

106 Pannenberg, "Faith and Reason," p. 52.
107 Idem, *Theology and the Philosophy of Science*, p. 169.
108 Idem, "Hermeneutics and Universal History," 1: 122.

linguisticality of existence as distinct from the act of understanding of the interpreter who as subject "finds a linguistic expression which combines the essential content of the text with his own contemporary horizon."[109] It is the interpreter as subject who raises to the reflective and thematic level the situation of the text, the preunderstanding of her own horizon and their fusion through "assertion." Third, insofar as the "link" of the past text in its difference from the horizon of the present is the continuity of history itself, reflective interpretation will move toward an explicit articulation of that continuity which includes the text of the past and the standpoint of the present including latter age's horizon of the future.[110] Thus, for Pannenberg, the interpretation of texts moves toward an anticipation and provisional thematization of "universal history."

> Only a conception of the actual course of history linking the past with the present situation and its horizon of the future can form the comprehensive horizon within which the interpreter's limited horizon of the present and the historical horizon of the text fuse together.[111]

My misgivings about this dispute is that Pannenberg appears to argue at cross-purposes to Gadamer. This can be drawn back to the curious title of Gadamer's text, *Wahrheit und Methöde*. As has been noted, the conjunction *"und"* has more of a disjunctive than conjunctive force. The question which arises is "How should the text be approached?"—as a description of a reflective method for the interpretation of texts or as a challenge and corrective to the Cartesian self-understanding of historicist consciousness which in an act of self-forgetfulness abstracts the subject qua historian from her effective constitution by tradition, even as a *vis a tergo*. Gadamer's argument then proceeds to lay open the play of tradition which is the condition of all human understanding and subjectivity and which is the mark of the finitude (*Geschichlichkeit*) of *Dasein*. If this is the point of *Truth and Method*, then to join the debate immediately on the issue of the reflective interpretation of texts—as Pannenberg appears to do—is to frustrate dialogue from the beginning.

With Pannenberg, I agree that at the *reflective* level the fusion of horizons of interpreter and text tends towards and finds its fullest explication in a construal of the transmission of traditions. Pannenberg's position is a corrective to a vexing lacuna of Gadamer: his suspicion and in-

109   Ibid., 1: 124.
110   Ibid., 1: 124-8.
111   Ibid., 1: 129.

difference to the "methodical" question of the interpretation of texts. With Gadamer, I agree that this reflective act of interpretation cannot raise "the effectiveness of tradition" (*Wirkungsgeschichte*) to the level of "self-transparency." In short, "we *are* more than we *know*." The issue here is that if "hermeneutical consciousness" denotes a fundamental ontology of Dasein whose mark is the identity of finitude and historicality in the play of the effectiveness of tradition, then hermeneutical consciousness does have precedence as more fundamental over the reflective and explicit delineation of the transmission of traditions. Yet the impossibility of a pure self-transparency of the subject does not invalidate a priori the project of an explicit, reflective reconstruction of *Wirkungsgeschichte* as *Überlieferungsgeschichte*. The options here are not simply those of an "either-or": either the mediation of an "in principle" nonobjectifiable linguisticality of existence or a reflective mediation of the history of the transmission of traditions as a form of "absolute knowledge." Indeed, Pannenberg's own emphasis on the proleptic character of the reconstruction of the transmission of traditions acknowledges, in distinction from Hegel, the finitude of the subject and the provisionality of all such attempts, although for Pannenberg such provisionality seems to obtain more from an awareness of the indeterminateness of the future rather than a positive acknowledgement of the "moreness" and "density" of the subject as "hermeneutical consciousness."[112] As the turn to Horkheimer and Adorno in the following chapter seeks to indicate, the concrete process to which both a prethematic as well as thematic process of mediation must refer includes a "social-political" or "materialist" mediation of tradition, lest both become ideological. Again, the acknowledgement that even this latter will not lead to the self-transparency of the subject-as-mediated-in-and-through-a-particular-social-totality does not invalidate this project either.

Perhaps most limiting for this discussion is that Pannenberg does not define his polemical use of terms such as "ethical," "self-understanding" "theoretic"—and by implication, "practical"—reason. Two separate issues must be distinguished. First, Pannenberg wants to assert that the

---

[112] Perhaps one of the most fruitful ways of comparing the positions of Gadamer and Pannenberg—and one which I have refrained from doing, but suspect would confirm my analysis—is to contrast their positions on Hegel. See Hans-Georg Gadamer, *Hegel's Dialectic*, trans. and with an introduction by P. Christopher Smith (New Haven: Yale University Press, 1976), esp. pp. 54-116; and Wolfhart Pannenberg, "The Significance of Christianity in the Philosophy of Hegel," in *The Idea of God*, pp. 144-77.

"sense" of religious discourse is never merely ethical or one of existential self-understanding but also already includes an understanding of the reality of the world. Let the former be denoted as practical[1] and the latter as theoretic[1]. A second issue concerns the history of the transmission of religious traditions. Here, a distinction may be made between those effective, but largely prereflective and informal attempts to mediate a particular religious tradition, i.e., preaching, and the reflective attempt at mediation (theoretical) which is coextensive with the task of theology which seeks in a reflective, self-conscious manner to mediate the tradition with what "counts" as reality at a given historical moment (i.e., the "sciences").[113] Let the former be denoted as practical[2] and the latter as theoretic[2]. The ambiguity of "practical" and "theoretic" arises from the fact that it can be used to denote a dichotomy in either issue.

The situation is further compounded in that some of the theologians against whom Pannenberg polemicizes appear to conjoin practical[1] with an "in principle" repudiation of the relevance and possibility of theoretic[2]."Truth" for this position rests, according to Pannenberg, in subjectivity and a decisionistic understanding of faith which actually surrenders the claim to truth of Christianity. Pannenberg is concerned to preserve the role of "explanation" in the *reflective* interpretive process; while with the former, it is not only concerning this issue that the dispute must be joined, but also the focusing on the "ethical" in the narrow sense of a dichotomy between the "senses" of religious discourse thus constricting totality of meaning to an existential self-understanding as distinct *and* separate from "worldview." More specifically, Pannenberg seems to maintain that it is the lacuna of philosophical hermeneutics regarding reflective explanation which leads to the constriction of the sense of religious discourse to the merely ethical.

The question is, "Does Pannenberg overstate his case in his polemic against Bultmann, Ebeling et. al.?" Is it the case that *prereflective* mediations of religion are by that fact alone *prerational* or *nonrational*? Is it the case that the claim to "truth" only becomes a matter for an explicit, reflective third-order discipline, theology, which seeks to provisionally demonstrate the coherence of Christianity with what is known about reality? Is it not the case that every prereflective mediation of the tradition always already includes in its disclosive and transformative power a claim to truth of the tradition in the present and is this not more foundational than the third-order reflections of theology? To the last question I

113 Idem, *Theology and the Philosophy of Science*, pp. 301-45.

would answer "Yes." To be sure, this affirmation does not entail denying the relevance and possibility of a reflective and critical theology but only claims that the latter is derivative. Only "living" religions, those which still have power to illumine reality, engage in the enterprise of theology. Further, as, for example, David Tracy and Paul Ricoeur have attempted to argue, recognition of the effectiveness of prereflective mediations of religion does not necessarily lead to decisionism which abandons the claim to truth; rather, it points to a model of the claim to truth of the work of art, truth as (provisional) disclosive and transformative appearance.

CHAPTER II

Max Horkheimer and Theodor Adorno: The Cunning of History

Gentlemen! We find ourselves in an important epoch, in a fermentation, in which Spirit has made a leap forward, has gone beyond its previous concrete form and acquired a new one. The whole mass of ideas and concepts that have been current until now, the very bonds of the world, are dissolved and collapsing into themselves like a vision in a dream. A new emergence of Spirit is at hand; philosophy must be the first to hail its appearance and recognize it, while others, resisting impotently, adhere to the past, and the majority unconsciously constitute the matter in which it makes its appearance. But philosophy, in recognizing it as what is eternal, must pay homage to it.

G.W.F. Hegel, *Lectures at Jena* 1806, Final Speech

The only sensible thing was to adapt oneself to existing conditions. . . . One must lie low, no matter how much it went against the grain, and try to understand that this great organization remained, so to speak, in a state of delicate balance, and that if someone took it upon himself, to alter the disposition of things around him, he ran the risk of losing his footing and falling to destruction, while the organization would simply right itself by some compensating reaction in another part of its machinery—since everything interlocked—and remain unchanged, unless, indeed, which was very probable, it became still more rigid, more vigilant, severer, and more ruthless.

F. Kafka, *The Trial*

INTRODUCTION

Less than a century and a half later, it appeared to a significant portion of German intellectuals—most of whom had fled their homeland to escape the nightmare of National Socialism—that the salutation of Hegel to the inexorable movement of Spirit was at best sanguine and at worst, deadly. This chapter concerns itself with two of these scholars, Theodor W. Adorno and Max Horkheimer. If Hegel greeted the movement of Spirit as a qualitative forward leap, Adorno and Horkheimer watched with horror as the spirit of Enlightenment betrayed itself through its reversion to myth. If Hegel saw the movement of Spirit in modernity as the collapse of an order of heteronomous ideas and institutions and as the realization of the Idea of Freedom in a reconciliation of the particular and the universal; Adorno and Horkheimer witnessed the collapse of bourgeois individualism and the rise of the Behemoth[1] and protested the perverted reconciliation of the particular and the universal through the extirpation of the former in submission to the demands of the latter. If, for Hegel, philosophy reached its apex in the Hegelian "system," in the self-consciousness of the necessary movement of Absolute Spirit; Adorno and Horkheimer found the aphorism, the fragment and the essay forms most appropriate,[2] because given that "the whole is the false[3]," reason could endure only by making its object the particular in negation and critique guided by "exact phantasy."[4] If Hegel's philosophy paid homage to the necessity of "what is," the coincidence of the real and the rational in history through the cunning of reason, Adorno and Horkheimer's "antisystem" protested the veiling of the *status quo* as an immutable second nature in the name of reason for "there is no remedy but steadfast diagnosis of oneself and others, the attempt, through awareness, if not to escape doom, at least to rob it of its dreadful violence, that of blindness."[5]

---

[1] Franz Neumann, *Behemoth: The Structure and Practice of National Socialism* (New York: Oxford University Press, 1942).

[2] Theodor Adorno, *"Der Essay als Form," Gesammelte Schriften*, 23 vols., ed. Rolf Tiedemann, vol. 11: *Noten zur Literatur* (Frankfurt: Suhrkamp Verlag, 1974), pp. 9-33.

[3] Idem, *Minima Moralia: Reflections from Damaged Life*, trans. E. F. N. Jephcott (London: New Left Books, 1974), p. 50.

[4] More precisely, the "concrete object" of "exact phantasy" is not the isolated (social) object as "fact," but a "constellation" or "forcefield" (*Kraftfeld*) by which the polarity or cohesiveness of discrete objects constitutes a *concrete* whole. An exposition of these two concepts in the early work of Adorno follows in n114 below.

[5] Adorno, *Minima Moralia*, p. 33.

The focus of this chapter is that cluster of themes of *Dialectic of Enlightenment* which define the substance of the first generation of critical theory.[6] The problematic of this work, published in the mid-1940's, was set by recent history itself: "the discovery of why mankind, instead of entering into a truly human condition, is sinking into a new kind of barbarism."[7] *Dialectic of Enlightenment* presents itself as both a capstone and midpoint, a distillation of the interdisciplinary work of the *Institut für Sozialforschung* as reflected in its journal, *Zeitschrift für Sozialforschung*,[8] while at the same time anticipating the final position of Adorno in *Negative Dialectics*: the collapse of all forms of domination into the prototype of "identity-thought." In order to delineate these themes, the *Dialectic of Enlightenment* will serve as a touchstone flanked by other roughly contemporaneous works of Horkheimer and Adorno as well as those of their colleagues from the *Institüt*.

The scope of this chapter is both narrow and broad. Narrow, because the work of the 1930's and 1940's has been abstracted from the intellectual developments of both men as well as the context of the work of the *Institüt* and the broader context of the development of "critical" Marxism against a "scientific" one.[9] Broad, because most of the themes which define critical theory emerged in this period: the critique of Marxist orthodoxy, of technology as instrumental reason, of the culture industry, of traditional theory; questions concerning the possibility of "autonomous

---

6 Max Horkheimer and Theodor Adorno, *Dialectic of Enlightenment*, trans. John Cumming (New York: Seabury Press, 1972).

7 Ibid., p. ix.

8 [*Institüt für Sozialforschung*], *Zeitschrift für Sozialforschung* [1932-1941], 2nd ed., 9 vols., with an introduction by Alfred Schmidt (Munich: Kosel, 1970). For an analysis of the articles contained therein, see Alfred Schmidt's *"Die 'Zeitschrift für Sozialforschung': Geschichte und gegenwartige Bedeutung,"* in the first volume of the above, pp. 5*-63*. On the significance of the *Zeitschrift* for the Institute see Jürgen Habermas, "The Inimitable *Zeitschrift für Sozialforschung*: How Horkheimer Took Advantage of a Historically Oppressive Hour," Telos 45 (Fall 1980): 114-21. Hereafter, references to the *Zeitschrift* will be cited as *ZfS*.

9 On the history of contemporary Marxism in general, and the dichotomy of "critical" and "scientific" Marxism in particular, see Maurice Merleau-Ponty, *Adventures of the Dialectic*, trans. Joseph Bien (Evanston: Northwestern University Press, 1973); George Lichtheim, *From Marx to Hegel* (New York: Seabury Press, 1971); Alvin W. Gouldner, *The Two Marxisms* (New York: Oxford University Press, 1980); Perry Anderson, *Consideration on Western Marxism* (London: New Left Books, 1970), and *In the Tracks of Historical Materialism* (London: New Left Books, 1983); and Leszak Kolakowski, *Main Currents of Marxism*, 3 vols. (New York: Oxford University Press, 1978).

art," the nature of the developments in a postmarket capitalism, the changes in the traditional (bourgeois) family structure and hence patterns of individual character formation, the psychoanalytic analysis of anti-Semitism, the material mediation of psychological and sociological constructs with one another etc. In short, Adorno's and Horkheimer's approach to their subject matter, the dialectical interpretation of the detail and the social totality through one another, follows what Adorno wrote of "properly written texts":

> The soundness of a conception can be judged by whether it causes one quotation to summon another. Where thought has opened up one cell of reality, it should, without violence by the subject, penetrate the next. It proves its relation to the object as soon as other objects crystallize around it. In the light that it casts on its chosen substance, others begin to glow.[10]

A complete exposition of these themes is beyond the scope of this chapter. To a certain degree, such an exposition is also superfluous inasmuch as a spate of introductory surveys and specialized studies have been published in the last decade.[11] Further, the republication and translation of heretofore inaccessible primary sources has helped to make critical theory a more familiar name in contemporary intellectual landscape. It is perhaps with a sense of irony to be observed that the "critical

---

[10] Adorno, *Minima Moralia*, p. 87.

[11] Martin Jay, *The Dialectical Imagination: A History of the Frankfurt School and the Institute of Social Research, 1939-1950* (Boston: Little, Brown and Co., 1973); David Held, *Introduction to Critical Theory: Horkheimer to Habermas* (Berkeley: University of California Press, 1980); Alfred Schmidt, *Zur Idee der Kritischen Theorie* (Frankfurt: Ullstein, 1974), and *Die Kritische Theorie als Geschichtsphilosophie* (Munich: Karl Hanser, 1976); Zoltan Tar, *The Frankfurt School: The Critical Theories of Max Horkheimer and Theodor W. Adorno*, foreward by Michael Landmann (New York: John Wiley & Sons, 1977); Paul Connerton, *The Tragedy of Enlightenment: An Essay on the Frankfurt School* (Cambridge: Cambridge University Press, 1980); George Friedman, *The Political Philosophy of the Frankfurt School* (Ithaca, New York: Cornell University Press, 1981); Philip Slater, *Origins and Significance of the Frankfurt School* (London: Routledge and Kegan Paul, 1977); the "introductions" in Andrew Arato and Eike Gebhardt, eds., *The Essential Frankfurt School Reader*, ed. and with introductions by Andrew Arato and Eike Gebhardt (New York: Urizen Books, 1978); Andrew Feenberg, *Lukács, Marx and the Sources of Critical Theory* (Totowa, New Jersey: Roman and Littlefield, 1981); and Helmut Dubiel, *Wissenschaftsorganisation und Politische Erfahrung: Studien zur frühen Kritischen Theorie* (Frankfurt: Suhrkamp Verlag, 1978). Also relevant are recent interviews with Herbert Marcuse and Leo Lowenthal: Herbert Marcuse, Jurgen Habermas, Heinz Lubasz and Telman Spengler, "Theory and Politics: A Discussion," Telos 38 (Winter 1978-79): 124-53; Helmut Dubiel, "The Origins of Critical Theory: An Interview with Leo Lowenthal," *Telos* 49 (Fall 1981): 141-54.

theory industry" is a relatively familiar piece of furniture in the chambers of the "knowledge industry" in general.

This chapter describes particular thematic threads of critical theory in an attempt to understand Adorno's and Horkheimer's interpretation of this piece of history, i.e., contemporary society which embodies the "dialectic of enlightenment." Dialectic of enlightenment names a movement within post-Enlightenment society, a movement from reason in the service of freedom—the leading idea of the Enlightenment *philosophes*—to a reason in the service of unfreedom. Walter Jens captured this paradox in his question "Is it really progress when cannibals eat with knives and forks?"[12] For Adorno and Horkheimer, the dialectic of enlightenment is not merely a dialectic of thought; rather, it is embedded in the contradictions of social reality. Further, in a postcapitalist and postsocialist age, the question thus arises as to whether history itself is regressing to myth.

> The interpretation of the concept of "nature" which I am trying to unravel is one dealing with a concept which, if I wanted to translate it into more common philosophical terms, could be best translated by the concept of "the mythical." Even this concept, however, is quite vague and its proper meaning cannot be shown by relying on older definitions. What "the mythical" means is "what from time immemorial simply 'is'," "what human history bears as fatefully ordained pre-given reality," "what appears to be substantial in history." What I mean by "nature" is defined in this manner. The question which arises is that concerning the relation between "nature" and what we mean by the term "history." "History" signifies every manner of human relations, every manner of relations which is characterized, above all, by the fact that in it the qualitatively "New" appears. "History" is a movement which does not play itself out in pure identity, in the reproduction of that which already is; rather, in history "the New" appears. History wins its true character through the appearance of the New in it.[13]

Dialectic of enlightenment refers to this regression-with-progress, the movement of reason as a critical force releasing humanity from tutelage towards a realization of human freedom and happiness to reason as an instrument of domination. History appears as myth today insofar as the contemporary social totality is a reification: a social, human "second nature" which approaches in its opacity and seeming immutability the

---

[12] Jens, ed., *Warum ich Christ bin*, p. 11, quoted in Lamb, *Solidarity with Victims*, p. 31.

[13] Theodor Adorno, *"Die Idee der Naturgeschichte,"* Gesammelte Schriften, vol. 1: *Philosophische Frühschriften*, pp. 345-6.

eternity and self-identity of first nature. Thus, the dialectic of the enlightenment is an "interruption," a challenge to the identification of the modern *Freiheitsgeschichte* with enlightenment and the identification of both of these with the development of postliberal society in either its capitalist or socialist form.

This chapter is divided into six parts. First, there is a description of the concept of "critical theory" largely drawn from the 1930's *Zeitschrift* articles of the Institute's director, Max Horkheimer. However, the presentation of the multitude of themes taken up by Horkheimer and Adorno does present a problem regarding the organization of the material.

Perhaps the key lies in that word which more than any other laces their writings of this period: *Herrschaft*. The "new" barbarism with which Adorno and Horkheimer were concerned was the emergence of domination in a qualitatively new, *systemic* mode. Thus, second, there is a presentation concerning the domination of first (external) nature, that is, "nature" in the commonsense understanding of the term, as the "other" of the subject—an understanding which betrays its own historicality as the product of the domination over nature. Further, an exposition of Adorno's specific "accents" in his understanding of critical theory is given in an excursus in this section. Third, there is a presentation of the domination over second (social) nature, i.e., the increasing anonymous integration of various phases of the subject's experience from above in the transformation of the social whole into the "administered world." Fourth, there is a discussion of the domination of the subject over itself, of domination internalized and directed within as "sacrifice," "renunciation" or "repression." Specifically, in these three sections, I deal with the themes of instrumental reason, the nature of postliberal capitalism, the culture industry and the possibility of autonomous art, the use of psychoanalytic categories within critical theory, changes within the pattern of family interaction and the roots of anti-Semitism. If these sections are the most "schematic," this must be risked. To attend solely to what critical theory is as a concept and avoid its material analyses would be to lose the point of critical theory itself: the attempt to think the social whole through the particular detail.[14]

---

[14] Thus Theodor Adorno: "Insight into society as a totality also implies that all the moments which are active in this totality, and in no way perfectly reducible one to another, must be incorporated in knowledge; it cannot permit itself to be terrorized by the academic division of labor" ["On the Logic of the Social Sciences," in Adorno,

The fifth section analyzes the aporia of critical theory. Here three themes are treated: the relation between theory and praxis, the tension between critical theory of society and philosophy of history and Adorno's and Horkheimer's inversion of the "end of ideology thesis." Finally, there is a specifically theological postscript which addresses the reflections of Horkheimer and Adorno on religion and suggests that, at least on this topic, their pronouncements fell behind and betrayed the very dialectical procedure which they their thought embodied.

THE CONCEPT OF A CRITICAL THEORY OF SOCIETY

One of the earliest and most programmatic statements on the nature of critical theory was published by Max Horkheimer in the *Zeitschrift für Sozialforschung* in 1937, "Traditional and Critical Theory."[15] The disjunctive nature of the two concepts of theory is crisply indicated in the opening lines of a "Postscript"[16]: "In the preceding essay I pointed out two ways of knowing: one is based on the *Discourse on Method*, the other on Marx's critique of political economy."[17] This essay, along with the essay "On the Problem of Truth"[18] are my central texts for this discussion.

The hallmark of "traditional theory" is a form of Cartesianism which is implicit in the methodological canons, the goals and the division of labor in the practice of modern science. These have been rendered reflexively thematic in the prevalent metatheory of science of the twentieth century, positivism. At the core of traditional theory is the assumption of a dichotomy between thought and being, subject and object. This dichotomy, assumed as valid, is the central problematic for a reflective metatheoretical comprehension of science as in positivism.[19] Within this framework, theory is projected as the system of principles and categories arrived at through experiential inductions, self-evident intuitions or arbitrary selection and the theorems derived therefrom which as hypotheses

---

et al., *The Positivist Dispute in German Sociology*, trans. Glyn Adey and David Frisby (London: Heinemann Educational Books, 1976), p. 120].

[15] Horkheimer, *Critical Theory: Selected Essays*, trans. Matthew J. O'Connell and others (New York: Seabury Press, 1972), pp. 188-243.

[16] Ibid., pp. 244-52.

[17] Ibid., p. 244.

[18] Idem, "On the Problem of Truth," in *The Frankfurt School Reader*, pp. 407-43.

[19] For an overview of the diverse array of positions subsumed under the label of "positivism," see Gerard Radnitzky, *Contemporary School of Metascience* (New York: Humanities Press, 1970).

are to be tested for correspondence with the "facts." The marks of a well-formed theory are not only its "verifiability," but also its "clarity," "consistency," "univocity," "lack of contradiction" and "harmony." While the notion of a unified science remains both the ideal and presupposition of traditional theory, theory becomes more and more directed towards and applied to increasingly delimited and specialized problem areas which are to be solved by theory itself and the level of technological means at hand at any given time.

The logic of such a mode of theorizing Horkheimer also terms traditional in that "it deals with the relations of unchanging concepts: how one passes from one to another judiciously and conclusively and how one develops from each what it contains. . . . This proceeds analytically, drawing out of the concept what is in it."[20] With a refinement of principles, categories and concepts and with increasing sophistication regarding the division and collection of data, there occurs within traditional theory a division of labor between "theory-making" and "empirical research": a *techne* of theory making and a *techne* of data-gathering. Yet, as a whole, traditional theory remains confined within the realm of "understanding" in Hegel's sense of the term: the subsumption of the particular (i.e., facts) under the general (i.e., theory and its hypotheses) or, more generally, the realm of classification and prediction.

Initially traditional theory was a progressive force, a force of enlightenment inasmuch as its development in disregard of the dominant political and social and religious demands constituted a liberation from theological and metaphysical—and ultimately, aristocratic-political—forms of tutelage. With the consolidation and expansion of bourgeois society, however, traditional theory has become regressive inasmuch as it is a sign of the incapacity and resignation of thought before social and cultural challenges, actual historical conflicts and struggles. "The substance underlying intellectual phenomena changes with the social totality."[21] Traditional theory constituted a liberation from hieratic sacralist authoritarianism, not to realize a unity of reason and reality, but to consolidate a new bureaucratic secularist authoritarianism which was more pernicious because it did not claim to be revelation, but the incarnation of reason itself. The utopian vision of Bacon's *The New Atlantis* has turned into the inverted utopia of Huxley's *Brave New World* even as the advent of a post-Comtean technocracy is heralded as the "end of ideology." The

---

[20] Horkheimer, "Problems of Truth," p. 436.
[21] Ibid., p. 414.

boundary of traditional theory's recognition of its relativity is limited to that theory's recognition of a pluralism of theories, i.e., the recognition of the relativity and specificity of a particular branch of science among others, not of science per se vis-à-vis a specific social whole.[22]

Horkheimer does not deny that traditional theory as modern science has yielded an almost unimaginable increase and efficiency in the means of production toward the domination of nature. Yet he does charge that traditional theory has a delusory self-understanding, even as it enables a growing domination by men and women over their natural environment, it imperceptibly shades into the domination of men and women by others of their species. This abstract self-understanding of science, Horkheimer indicates in several related observations.

First, traditional theory operative in modern science abstracts from the social preformation of conscious human activity which conditions both the subject and object of cognition. "The facts which our senses present to us are socially preformed in two ways: through the historical character of the object perceived and through the historical character of the perceiving organ."[23] Such abstraction leads to the reification of the "given" as "fact" which is put forward as the final court of appeal for all existential judgments in a forgetfulness of the mutual historical constitution of subject and object. The second and third contradictions of modern science Horkheimer tersely summarizes in his 1932 essay, "Notes on Science and the Crisis":

> First, science accepts as a principle that its every step has a critical basis, yet the most important step of all, the setting of tasks, lacks a theoretical grounding and seems to be taken arbitrarily. Second, science has to do with the knowledge of comprehensive relationships; yet it has no realistic grasp of that comprehensive relationship upon which its own existence and the direction of its work depend, namely society.[24]

In the division of labor of bourgeois society, science conceives itself as the instrument of pure reason and detached understanding thus deceiving itself by affirming its autonomy from the social totality. This self-deception, Horkheimer maintains, does not lie in the subjective opinions of certain scientists, but is embedded in the structure of traditional theory and its claim to be the sole valid instrument of knowledge, together with its dismissal of all else as subjective opinion.

---

[22] Idem, "Notes on Science and the Crisis," in *Critical Theory*, pp. 3-9.
[23] Idem, "Traditional and Critical Theory," p. 200.
[24] Idem, "Notes on Science and the Crisis," p. 8.

Insofar as science abstracts from the social totality by which it is constituted and which it helps to constitute, science's domination over nature shows itself as its own negation: the independence of traditional
theory as modern science is dependent upon the demands of the constellation of social forces dominant at any given time. In other words, the direction of research and the development of science labors abstractly for
"capital" and concretely for whomever is the bearer of that capital at a
given time. Finally, the "critical" stance of traditional theory and the abstractness of its nonpartiality—its separation of knowledge and value,
thought and action, science and politics—ideologically conceals its capitulation to the existent social totality and its own interests in preserving
and reproducing the *status quo*.

This description of "traditional theory" is itself an exercise of "critical
theory." Through a delineation of traditional theory as an affirmative
mediation of the existent societal totality in the interests of that totality's
own reproduction, critical theory seeks to inculcate vis-à-vis traditional
theory a reflexivity which would break its restriction to a purely self-
critical methodological consciousness towards one which encompasses
and comprehends the social whole in its contradictions, dynamism and
potentialities.

Yet "critical theory" cannot be reduced to a critique of traditional
theory, although in his *Zeitschrift* articles, Horkheimer did tend to define
critical theory polemically against traditional theory and positivism in
particular. By way of an initial characterization let the following quotes
stand with what follows them as a commentary.

> Critical thought has a concept of man as in conflict with himself until this
> opposition is removed.[25]

> Critical thinking is the function of neither the isolated individual nor of a
> sum-total of individuals. Its subject is rather a definite individual in his real
> relations to other individuals and groups, in his conflict with a particular
> class, and, finally, in the resultant web of relationships with the social total-
> ity and with nature.[26]

> But the critical theory of society is, in its totality, the unfolding of a single
> existential judgement. To put it in broad terms, the theory says that the basic
> form of the historically given commodity economy on which modern his-
> tory rests contains in itself the internal and external tensions of the modern
> era; it generates these tensions over and over again in an increasingly

[25] Idem, "Traditional and Critical Theory," p. 210.

heightened form; and after a period of progress, development of human powers and emancipation for the individual, after an enormous expansion of human control over nature, it finally hinders further development and drives humanity into a new barbarism.[27]

The critical theory of society . . . has for its object men as producers of their own historical way of life in its totality.[28]

The idea of a "critical theory" which could be divided into a "critical theory of science" or "of law" or "of nature" etc., is misleading. The term is an abbreviation for "critical theory *of society*," where the object of the preposition denotes both the object of critical thought as well as its subject. In this, critical theory is the heir to materialism which "challenges every claim to the autonomy of thought"[29] because it seeks to render thematic the "unconcluded" dialectic of the subject and object of thought as one mediated by the social whole at any given time. Thus even "nature" appears not as an eternal, "always the same." It is an abstract aspect of the concrete concept embodied in a specific societal totality. "There will always be something that is extrinsic to man's intellectual and material activity, namely nature as the totality of as yet unmastered elements within which society must deal."[30] Thus a theory of society forms the main content of critical theory which sublates both idealism and empirical realism. Further, insofar as critical theory has for its object the contradictory experience of contemporary society, that is, the experience of society as the product of men's and women's activity and the experience of society as a process which assimilates itself to nonhuman natural processes and confronts men and women as irrational fate and, further, insofar as this contradiction arises from the abstract form of commodity exchange and capital (the predominance of "exchange-value over use-value" for the production and growth of capital), then the content of a critical theory of society is a theory of political economy.[31]

---

26 Ibid., pp. 210-11.

27 Ibid., p. 227.

28 Idem, "Postscript," p. 244.

29 Idem, "Materialism and Metaphysics," in *Critical Theory*, p. 32.

30 Idem, "Traditional and Critical Theory," p. 210.

31 "The stability of the theory is due to the fact that amid all the changes in society the basic economic structure, the class relationship in its simplest form, and therefore the idea of the supercession of these two remain identical" [Ibid., p. 234]. Yet as Horkheimer goes on to note, even the concept of "class" is an abstract one. Its understanding is subject to the dynamism of its object in the different phases of the devel-

As distinct from the logic of traditional theory which is oriented to the analysis, selection, description and classification of "data" in accordance with appropriate categories, principles and concepts, Horkheimer specifies the logic of critical theory as "dialectical."

> A dialectical process is negatively characterized by the fact that it is not to be conceived as the result of individual unchanging factors. To put it positively, its elements continuously change in relation to each other within the process, so that they are not even to be radically distinguished from each other.[32]

The heart of dialectics is the insight that since reality is a process where subject and object are constituted by one another, there can be no absolute identity of concepts and their objects. Traditional theory is an abstraction. Its concepts abstract from the plurality of the relationships of their objects in favor of "preselected" aspects of them and they abstract from the dynamic movement of its objects in favor of their givenness or mere appearance.[33] Dialectics is the continual criticism of the knowledge of subjects and objects in their reciprocal mediations. A critical theory of society seeks to approach and mirror the concreteness of its object through an understanding of the parts both constituting and constituted by the whole and through a projection of that which "is-not" except as a tendency or potentiality of that which "is." Simultaneously, critical theory as an "unconcluded dialectic" abjures absolute knowledge and points to the necessity of praxis as the embodiment and fulfillment of that dialectic. "The theory has a historically changing object . . . it constructs a developing picture of society as a whole, an existential judgement with a historical dimension."[34] This specific procedure of critical theory Horkheimer calls "determinate negation."[35]

---

opment of capitalism. The representation of "class"—and indeed all the material concepts of critical theory—like class itself is subject to evolution.

[32] Idem, "Materialism and Metaphysics," p. 28. See, also, his essay, "The Latest Attack on Metaphysics," in *Critical Theory*, pp. 161-66.

[33] Idem, "The Latest Attack on Metaphysics," pp. 154-61.

[34] Idem, "Traditional and Critical Theory," p. 239. The theme of a "critical theory" of what "is" as witness to that which "is not" mentioned here by Horkheimer is the central theme of Herbert Marcuse's earliest interpretation of critical theory: the dialectic of appearance and essence as the dialectic of actuality and potentiality. See Marcuse's essays, "Philosophy and Critical Theory" and "The Concept of Essence," in *Negations: Essays in Critical Theory*, trans. Jeremy J. Shapiro (Boston: Beacon Press, 1968), pp. 134-58, 43-87. That this articulation of critical theory represents a rereading

Yet critical theory cannot disregard the concepts, categories and principles forged in traditional theory. Understanding must be sublated—incorporated and preserved—in dialectics, for the latter without the former is empty, while the former without the latter is abstract and hence deceptive. Exemplary in this regard, according to Horkheimer, is the work of Marx. In *Capital*, Marx laid claim to and assumed a host of categories and concepts which had been forged in the preceding history of classical British political economy: value, price, wages, labor-time, etc.. These concepts, however, were transformed from the perspective of a theory which sought to chart the tendencies of society as a whole. Through this, the basic categories were transformed into their opposites, i.e., the "just exchange" of wages for labor into an "unjust exchange" through the concept of the "surplus value" of labor.[36] Through this negation and sublation of concepts taken from traditional theory, Marxist economics becomes philosophy due to its orientation to the dynamic tendencies of the totality. It introduces "motion" into the concepts of traditional theory in an attempt to mirror an equally dynamic social reality.[37] "Concepts . . . considered individually, [they] preserve their definitions, while in combination they become aspects of new units of meaning. The movement of reality is mirrored in the fluidity of concepts."[38] It is appropriate to note at this point that both the *Institüt* and its *Zeitschrift* did not bear the name *"Soziologie"* nor *"Sozialphilosophie,"* nor did it exclusively concern itself with the "workers' movement" as it had done under the previous director, Carl Gründberg. Both bore the name, *"Sozialforschung"* which points to the comprehensiveness of critical theory understood as an interdisciplinary task. In order to achieve its task, a

---

of Marx through Hegel, see Marcuse, *Reason and Revolution: Hegel and the Rise of Social Theory* (Boston: Beacon Press, 1960).

35 Idem, "The Problem of Truth," pp. 414-22.

36 Idem, "The Social Function of Philosophy," in *Critical Theory*, pp. 253-72.

37 On the diverse meanings of the concept of "totality" in Western Marxism, see Martin Jay, *Marxism and Totality: The Adventures of a Concept from Lukács to Habermas* (Berkeley: University of California Press, 1984), esp. pp. 196-275. For a briefer presentation of the various meanings of "totality" (as longitudinal, latitudinal, expressive, decentered and normative totality), see Martin Jay, "The Concept of Totality in Lukács and Adorno," *Telos* 32 (Summer, 1977): 117-37. With the exception of the notion of "decentered" totality (which has become assimilated to "latitudinal" totality), there is a substantial identity between the frameworks presented in both the shorter and longer works. Unless noted in the text, my use of the term "totality" *simpliciter* refers to latitudinal or synchronic totality, i.e., the attempt to characterize present society as a whole.

38 Horkheimer, "The Problem of Truth," p. 437.

"theory of present society as a whole," critical theory must incorporate the spectrum of academic disciplines:

> This unifying principle by which individual investigations and their empirical strength are brought to bear on a central theoretical problem distinguishes social research (*Sozialforschung*) which the *Zeitschrift* wishes to serve from both the bare description of facts and theoretical constructions free from empirical investigation. Social research strives after a knowledge of the course of society as a whole and it presupposes that under the chaotic surface of events, a structure of effective powers is open to conceptualization. . . .In order to reach this goal—to conceptually understand the processes of social life according to the condition of knowledge possible at any given time—social research must try to bring an array of specialized disciplines to bear on its own proper problem and to make full use of them for its own purposes.[39]

At its best, critical theory represented an intense interdisciplinary endeavor around a common problem, the understanding of contemporary society. But it is the focus of critical theory in its partisanship for reason and freedom as concrete social tasks which transforms the categories and principles of traditional theory.[40] "The individual branches of knowledge only provide the material for a theoretical construction of the course of historical events. This material does not remain in the theoretical presentation what is was in the individual branches of knowledge.[41]"

[39] Idem, "*Vorwort*," *ZfS* 1 (1932), p. i. See, also, Horkheimer's address in which he assumed directorship of the Institute, "*Die gegenwartigen Lage der Sozialphilosophie und die Aufgabe eines Instituts für Sozialforschung*," in *Sozial-philosophische Studien* (Frankfurt: Fischer Tauschenbuch Verlag, 1981), pp. 31-46.

[40] In this, Horkheimer remarks, the "opposition [of critical theory] to the traditional concept of theory springs in general from a difference not so much of objects as of subjects. . . . Critical thinking is the function neither of the isolated individual nor of a sum total of individuals. Its subject is rather a definite individual in his real relation to other individuals and groups, in his conflict with a particular class, in the resultant web of relationships with the social totality and with nature" ["Traditional and Critical Theory," pp. 209, 211]. The standpoint of critical theory is partisan and, for this reason, an objective one because its standpoint is that of the victims of society, of those who live the contradictions of the present and give the lie to the identity of reason and society. See, also, for Adorno, "The experience of the contradictory character of societal reality is not an arbitrary starting point but rather the motive which first constitutes the possibility of sociology as such" ["On the Logic of the Social Sciences," p. 120].

[41] Horkheimer, "*Zum Rationalismusstreit in der gegenwartigen Philosophie*," *ZfS* 3 (1934): 22.

The question which arises, however, is that if critical theory in its materialist legacy abjures any absolute knowledge both in its critical idealist form and in the form of a materialist evolutionary determinism, then is it not driven into the position of a relativism which recoils on the claims of critical theory itself?[42] As Horkheimer argued in his 1935 essay "On the Problem of Truth," materialist dialectics as an unfinished dialectic sublates both dogmatism and skepticism within its own position. The insight that there is no absolute subject and object of cognition, but that all truth is achieved by particular historical subjects—which subjects and their objects are mutually mediated, i.e., by the social whole—does not entail relativism and skepticism. Through determinate negation whereby "every negated insight is preserved as a moment of truth in the progress of cognition, forms a determining factor in it, and is further defined and transformed with every new step" and because through this there occurs a change in both the subject and object of cognition, materialist dialectics operates within the horizon "that through nothing but this continuous delimitation and correction of partial truths, the process itself evolves its proper content as knowledge of limited insights in their limits and connections."[43] Limited and partial truth can only seem inferior from the position of an absolute knowledge. "If "the truth is the whole" and that whole is a process of materialist dialectics which cannot be a priori comprehended then truth remains immanent in the process itself and is referred to an ideal end: the identity of concept and reality.[44] The truth of theory is relative to the practical and scientific interests embodied within the particular categories and concepts of thought and is relative to the facts and circumstances to which it refers. However, if truth "nevertheless necessarily remains inconclusive and to that extent

42 Jay, "The Frankfurt Schools' Critique of Karl Mannheim and the Sociology of Knowledge," *Telos* 20 (Summer, 1974): 72-89. See, also, Theodor Adorno, "The Sociology of Knowledge and its Consciousness," in *Prisms*, trans. Samuel and Sherry Weber (Cambridge: The MIT Press, 1981), pp. 35-50. Adorno sums up the difference between critical theory and the sociology of knowledge by noting that in the latter, dialectical concepts (class, ideology, etc.) are transformed into classificatory ones abstracting from the "real laws of movement of society" [ibid., p. 43].

43 Horkheimer, "The Problem of Truth," p. 414.

44 In Horkheimer's early *Zeitschrift* articles, his anticipation of a normative totality was inseparable from his acceptance of expressive totality and its faith in the proletariat. By the end of the 1930s, given the disappearance of the latter as a critical force for change, his position on normative totality approximated that of Adorno: "the just organization of society is incorporated in the emphatic concept of truth without being filled out as an image of the future" ["On the Logic of the Social Sciences," p. 122]. Normative totality can only be articulated indirectly through negation.

'relative,' it is also absolute, since later correction does not mean that a former truth was formerly untrue."[45] Within this perspective which relativizes the claims of absolute knowledge, Horkheimer contends that there is a space whereby critical theory can avoid the relativism of a sociology of knowledge, i.e., can at least raise the claim to be "objective" and that critical theory may not be "reduced" to the theory of/for the proletariat or radicalized intellectuals, but is binding on all insofar as it truly captures the tendencies of the social whole.

The notion of the unfinished dialectic introduced by Horkheimer to characterize the stance of critical theory has a twofold significance. Negatively, it indicates the insufficiency of theory—critical or otherwise—to comprehend "once and for all" the alteration of subject and object of thought and the alteration of their interrelation. Critical theory must itself be self-critical insofar as its object is in motion. While critical theory's foundation—political economy in general and the class relationship in particular—does not change, its individual concepts and judgments cannot be abstracted from the situation which it seeks to comprehend at any given time. Thus, what "entrepreneur" might mean during the period of liberal market capitalism will differ from what it means during a period of monopoly capitalism.[46] The identity of the concepts of critical theory must be refracted through the process of historical change which in turn demands a rethinking of the constellation of concepts. "The historical development of the conflicts in which critical theory is involved leads to a reassignment of degrees of relative importance to individual elements of the theory, forces further concretizations and determines which results of specialized science are to be significant for critical theory and practice at any given time."[47]

Positively, the notion of an unconcluded dialectic recognizes the autonomy of the role of practice or praxis. The difference between theory and practice is ineradicable. "Yet as much as theory and practice are linked to history, there is no preestablished harmony between them. What is seen as theoretically correct is not therefore simultaneously realized."[48] The contradictions and the potentialities which critical theory

45 Horkheimer, "The Problem of Truth," p. 422.
46 Idem, "Traditional and Critical Theory," p. 238f.
47 Ibid., p. 234.
48 Idem, "The Problem of Truth," p. 427. See also, Russell Jacoby, "Towards a Critique of Automatic Marxism: The Politics of Philosophy from Lukács to the Frankfurt School," *Telos* 10 (Winter 1971): 119-46, and "The Politics of Crisis Theory," *Telos* 23 (Spring 1975): 221-45.

delineates are not to be resolved merely in theory, in thought alone. It demands praxis if it too is not to remain "abstract." "The verification and proof of ideas relating to man and society, however, consists not merely in laboratory experiments or the examination of documents, but in historical struggles in which conviction itself plays an essential role."[49] Although critical theory lays claim to truth, to a delineation of the objective tendencies and potentialities of bourgeois society, "the outcome cannot be predicted on a purely theoretical basis. It will be determined not by any firmly outlined unity such as the 'course of history', the principles of which could be established indivisibly for all time, but by human beings interacting with one another and with nature, who enter into new relationships and structures and thereby change themselves."[50]

Indeed, it is not an overstatement to assert that praxis is the objective mainspring of dialectics insofar as it points to the active constitution of subjects reproducing, refining and, at the limit, changing that social whole which as object is mediated back and conditions the subjectivity of the subject. In this, the goal of traditional and critical theory also differ, for unlike the former, critical theory does not seek an "increase of knowledge," but "man's emancipation from slavery." Reason is preeminently a practical (social) task. Its primacy of reason is that of the practical reason, even as theory is sublated in concrete praxis which originally summoned it forth. The telos of critical theory is the realization of reason and freedom in society—a telos which as soon as it is announced, must be unmasked as abstract. Concretely, this constant telos of critical theory can only be specified through determinate negation given the historical and changing relation of theory: "the idea of a reasonable organization of society that will meet the needs of the whole community";[51] "an association of free men in which each has the possibility of self-development";[52] "the abolition of the division of labor and the class struggle."[53]

---

[49] Ibid., p. 420.

[50] Ibid., p. 438.

[51] Idem, "Traditional and Critical Theory," p. 213.

[52] Ibid., p. 219.

[53] Ibid., p. 210. Horkheimer's ambiguity regarding the telos of critical theory and the concrete social means of realizing it is irreduccible. There are two issues here: the "what" which is critiqued and hence the telos of critical theory, and the "how" of the advent of socialism. On both issues, it has been argued that ambiguity arises within Marx's work itself. Regarding the first issue, see Albrecht Wellmer, *Critical Theory of Society*, trans. John Cumming (New York: Seabury Press, 1971); Jürgen Habermas, *Theory and Practice*, trans. John Viertel (Boston: Beacon Press, 1973); Trent Schroyer, *The Critique of Domination* (Boston: Beacon Press, 1973) pp. 75-131; and Alvin Gould-

In order to understand the relation of critical theory to praxis, one last element of Horkheimer's thought must be indicated: the relation between critical theory and the proletariat which introduces a certain ambiguity to the notion of critical theory. Indeed, a major difference between traditional and critical theory is that the latter, unlike the former, abjures the ideology of detached knowledge and seeks to enter into unity with progressive social forces and, more specifically, the proletariat, such that theory becomes a material force within society in its criticism of the social whole. However, Horkheimer's reflections on critical theory and its relation to the proletariat is far from univocal and his increasingly pessimistic position during the 1930's mirrors the internal crises of the worker's movement in Germany.

Critical theory is related to praxis not only as its *terminus ad quem*, but also as its *terminus ab quo*: "Activity is not to be regarded as an appendix, as merely what comes after thought, but enters into theory at every point and is inseparable from it.[54] In that critical theory delineates the contradictory nature of the existing societal totality as centered around the production, exchange and consumption of exchange value, the question can be raised, "How is critical theory related to experience?" If critical thought is not to remain trapped in utopian phantasy, it must have recourse to concrete historical experience and specifically to the proletariat where the contradictory tendencies of the social whole appear and the interest in overcoming these contradictions emerges. Critical theory is, then, theory sought in and with solidarity for the victims of society.

However, having stated that, Horkheimer wishes to deny to the proletariat as such or the "party" any inviolable position regarding the correct consciousness of its position, the setting of goals or the implementation of strategy. While D. Held has asserted that for Horkheimer, "Theory must conform to the 'mental (*geistigen*) and materialistic situation . . . of a particular class'—the proletariat,"[55] throughout the 1930's Horkheimer's estimation of the proletariat remained ambiguous. In one of the "fragments" from *Dammerung* written during 1926-31 entitled "The Impotence of the German Working Class," he writes

> The two revolutionary elements, the direct interest in socialism and a clear theoretical consciousness, are no longer the common property of the proletariat but are now found among different, important segments of it . . . . In

ner, *The Two Marxisms*, pp. 289-389. Regarding the second, see Stanley Moore, *Three Tactics: The Background in Marx* (New York: Monthly Review Press, 1963).

54   Idem, "The Problem of Truth," p. 420.

contemporary Germany, it expresses itself through the existence of two worker's parties.[56]

Yet neither of these two parties, in Horkheimer's estimation, is satisfactory. The Communist Party, whose unemployed members have a direct interest in socialism, has given itself over to Marxist fundamentalism. The reformer's wing of the worker's movement has abjured all theory in an attempt to reach a compromise with the capitalist status quo. Towards the end of the fragment, Horkheimer ominously asserts that "the materialist content, which means knowledge of the real world, is the possession of those who have become disloyal to Marxism."[57]

By the time of the essay "Traditional and Critical Theory," Horkheimer unequivocally asserts that "even the situation of the proletariat is, in this society, no guarantee of correct knowledge."[58] The critical theorist thus finds itself involved in not only a critique of the status quo but also in a critique of "the distracting, conformist or utopian tendencies within his own household."[59] Indeed, theory is necessary precisely because of the failure of "automatic Marxism" and the fissure between theory and the proletariat: "If such a conflict were not possible, there would be no need of theory; those who need it would come upon it without help."[60] Further, if theory contented itself with the formulations of the ideas and feelings of a particular class (i.e., the proletariat) of even an advanced sector of that class (i.e., the party) then it would not differ in kind from traditional theory where classification and prediction would be the task of thought, where "thought and the formulation of theory would be one thing and its object, the proletariat, another."[61] Yet Horkheimer did want to insist that a historically correct consciousness could be the possession of a relatively small group, i.e., critical theorists.

However, critical theory and its object should form a dynamic unity "so that his presentation of societal contradictions is not merely an expression of the concrete historical situation but also a force within it to

---

55 Held, *Introduction to Critical Theory*, p. 195.
56 Horkheimer, *Dawn and Decline: Notes 1926-1931 and 1950-1969*, trans. Michael Shaw, with an afterword by Eike Gebhardt (New York: Seabury Press, 1978), p. 62. See, also, Adorno, *Minima Moralia*, pp. 113-15.
57 Ibid., p. 64.
58 Idem, "Traditional and Critical Theory," p. 213.
59 Ibid., p. 216.
60 Ibid., p. 221.
61 Ibid., p. 215.

stimulate change."[62] Yet it is in regard to this problem—the relation of the intelligentsia to society—that Horkheimer and Adorno remain ambiguous. The critical theorist ought to "hasten developments which will lead to a society without injustice,"[63] "to reduce the tension between his own insight and oppressed humanity in whose service he thinks."[64] His thinking should be "a critical promotive factor in the development of the masses"[65] in which interaction, "an awareness comes to flower along with its liberating but also its aggressive forces which incite while also requiring discipline."[66] What is remarkable in all this is that the shibboleth of a "dynamic" unity of theorist and class masks what appears to be a spontaneity-theory regarding the relation of theory and practice, i.e., somehow the two will mesh together—and that for a man who emphasized the category of "mediation"! As we shall see, shortly afterwards, by the time of Horkheimer's essay "The Authoritarian State" (1939), the rupture between theory and practice is almost complete.

By the way of a summary, let me make three assertions. First, critical theory is *theory*. It is an interruption of the *Lebenswelt* and the quotidian attitude of men and women in acknowledgement "that all is not right with the world." As such, critical theory must guard its own autonomy from party, class and the "establishment," even while these too enter, in their historical vicissitudes, into critical theory as its object. Second, the first assertion must be qualified because the autonomy of critical theory is not absolute. Critical theory arises from and returns to praxis. Further, there is a partisanship-quality to critical theory. Most broadly, that quality is a commitment to the historical-social realization of reason and freedom for all men and women. It is precisely this quality which draws critical theory to a solidarity with the "victims," to those whose very lives give the lie that we live in a world which has achieved the coincidence of the real and the rational. Lastly, the dynamic and dialectical quality of critical theory demands its execution as a focused, yet interdisciplinary task.

[62] Horkheimer, "Traditional and Critical Theory," p. 215.
[63] Ibid., p. 221.
[64] Ibid.
[65] Ibid., p. 214.
[66] Ibid., p. 215.

THE DOMINATION OVER NATURE[67]

The phrase "the turn to the subject" usually denotes that shift in the history of ideas, associated with the figure of Descartes, when "human being" became the direct object of investigation unencumbered with the categories of a nature- or ethic-oriented objective metaphysics. In a sense, such a shift is, for Horkheimer and Adorno, a footnote to a more primordial one: the movement from magic to myth.[68] Indeed, the disjunction between magic and myth represents the primordial alternative that "men have always had to choose between their subjection to nature or the subjection of nature to the self."[69] In this disjunction and the movement from magic to myth is the true epochal shift, "the emergence of the subject."

The horizon of magic is animism and its principle is anthropomorphism—the lack of a distinction between the subject and its object. The tree, the beast, the bolt of lightening, the sickness within the body do not confront the shaman as objects, as specimens of a disenchanted nature; rather they are suffused with and embody qualities which only in retrospect, after the movement from magic, can be called "subjective." Before the "other" which holds sway and objective command, the shaman seeks in the interests of self-preservation to establish communication through

[67] The theme of the domination of nature has come to the fore today largely due to the impact of successive ecological crises and the continuing debate regarding the "limits to growth" in recent economics. So, too, various Marxists have taken up this same issue—alien to the writings of Marx himself and "novel" in those of Adorno and Horkheimer in the period under consideration. See, for example, William Leiss, *The Domination of Nature* (Boston: Beacon Press, 1974); Andre Gorz, *Ecology as Politics*, trans. Patsy Vigderman and Jonathan Cloud (Boston: South End Press, 1980); and Hans Magnus Enzenberger, "A Critique of Political Ecology," in *Critical Essays*, ed. Rheinhold Grimm and Bruce Armstrong with a Forword by John Simon, The German Library, vol. 98, (New York: Continuum Publishing Co., 1982), pp. 186-223. The perspective of these three works explicitly agrees with Horkheimer's on the priority of a specific social totality and its economic organization in understanding the domination of nature: "man's avidity to extend his power in two infinities, the microcosm and the universe, does not arise directly from his own nature, but from the structure of society" [Horkheimer, *Eclipse of Reason* (New York: Seabury Press, 1974), p. 108]. By this, their perspective is differentiated from that of Theodore Roszak, whose politics of transcendence is a nostalgic romanticism for a return to nature. Already in the theme of the domination of nature and instrumental reason, however, is to be found that ambiguity which culminates in Adorno's *Negative Dialectics*: the category of instrumental reason (as identity-thought) pivots between a discussion of a specific societal totality (late capitalism) and the philosophy of history. See Held, *An Introduction to Critical Theory*, pp. 65-70, 148-74.

[68] Horkheimer and Adorno, *Dialectic of Enlightenment*, pp. 3-42.

[69] Ibid., p. 32.

mimetic correspondence. The careful rantings and gestures of the shaman approach the fearful unknown by seeking to conform to it and hence rob it of its unfamiliarity. The shaman, like the child learns through the imitation of nature.

A qualitative shift occurs with the emergence of myth. The abode of the gods is removed to the sphere above or the sphere beneath the earth and the disenchantment of nature begins with the extirpation of the unity of deity and nature in animistic anthropomorphism. The gods merely signify the elements of nature and the ordered hierarchies of the gods in relation to one another and humans is already a rational advance beyond magic. To be sure, in myth, human beings remain in thralldom to a distantly anthropomorphized, fateful necessity, but "repetition" as the principle of myth, as the eternal in the temporal, opens up a space for rational calculability, for the emergence of the subject as such.

The excursus on the myth of Odysseus is no mere epiphenomenon to the project of the *Dialectic of Enlightenment*. The heart of Adorno's and Horkheimer's interpretation, in contradistinction to that common in the tradition of German idealism which portrayed the epic as the representation of the reconciliation of subject and object, is that "myth" is already "enlightenment,"[70] already the liberation of an instrumental reason. Odysseus is the "prototype of the bourgeois individual"[71] because myth is already enlightenment even as the enlightened bourgeois has already regressed to myth. While other aspects of their interpretation will be presented further on, only one must be noted here. Odysseus as mere mortal is dependent upon the gods who have bound themselves to human beings in a system of obeisance and sacrifice. But it is precisely this which the cunning and deceptive Odysseus manipulates for his own self-preservation.

> If barter is the secular form of sacrifice, the latter already appears as the magical pattern of rational exchange, a device of men by which the gods may be mastered: the gods are overthrown by the very system by which they are honored.[72]

By the very act of sacrifice, the gods are made to serve the interests of Odysseus as his instruments, and this doubly so, when Odysseus is able

[70] Christian Lenhardt, "The Wanderings of Enlightenment," in *On Critical Theory*, ed. John O'Neill (New York: Seabury Press, 1976), pp. 34-57; and Held, *Introduction to Critical Theory*, pp. 401-7.
[71] Horkheimer and Adorno, *Dialectic of Enlightenment*, p. 43.
[72] Ibid., p. 49.

to exploit a "loophole" in the contract between them or by fulfilling the letter of the contract, subvert its spirit. Thus the subject as such and the object as such emerge in their mutual differentiation from one another. However, on a more profound level, the situation remains largely the same and the commonality of myth and magic is revealed.

> The step from chaos to civilization, in which natural conditions exert their power no longer directly but through the medium of human consciousness, has not changed the principle of equivalence. Indeed, men paid for this very step by worshipping what they were at once in thrall to only in the same way as all other creatures. Before, the fetishes were subject to the law of equivalence. Now equivalence itself has become a fetish.[73]

The process of enlightenment which began in myth was only partial. The gods still defined an impassable boundary for men and women. Fate and necessity were still the leading themes of Greek tragedy. Even after the disappearance of the last of the pagan pantheons and the rise of Christianity which half-heartedly eschewed the identification of the deity with the world,[74] the world was still imbued with an objective *ratio* which formed a boundary for subjectivity. "Philosophy, by preserving the idea of objective truth under the name of the absolute, or in any other spiritualized form, achieved the relativization of subjectivity."[75] From a

---

[73] Ibid., p. 17. "Enlightenment" as emergence from the slime of nature as depicted by Odysseus, however, becomes socially effective in the period of the Enlightenment. Here the growing hegemony of "exchange-value" over "use-value" in a specific organization of the means of production—as increasingly that sphere stamps itself on the social whole—embodies what "instrumental reason" represents epistemologically: the hegemony of the abstract and universal over the concrete and the particular. Already, however, in this dual meaning of enlightenment is adumbrated the later dissolution of critical theory as critical theory of *society* in the reduction of the latter to what Adorno calls as "identity-thought." For an exposition of Adorno's understanding of "exchange-value," see Gillian Rose, *The Melancholy Science: An Introduction to the Thought of Theodor W. Adorno* (New York: Columbia University Press, 1979), pp. 43-8.

[74] "Half-hearted" because in the writings of Adorno and Horkheimer, the Christian doctrine of the Incarnation compromises Jewish monotheism's affirmation of the utter transcendence of God and its consequent *Verbotensbildung*. See *Dialectic of Enlightenment*, pp. 176-9.

[75] Horkheimer, *Eclipse of Reason*, p. 46. Susan Buck-Morss has claimed that "authorship of the first two chapters of *Eclipse of Reason*, for example, seems unmistakably to have been divided between them [Horkheimer and Adorno], with Horkheimer the author of pp. 3-34 and 58-72, and Adorno responsible for pp. 34-57 and 72-91" [*The Origin of Negative Dialectics: Theodor W. Adorno, Walter Benjamin, and the Frankfurt Institute* (New York: The Free Press, 1979), p. 299]. I have found no other

disclosure of the objective *ordo* of reality were derived the norms toward which individual and social life strove. Ethics and politics derived their basic terms and relations from a hegemonous metaphysics. It was only during that period of history called the "Enlightenment" and the rise of the empirical sciences that the "subjective reason" which emerged in the transition from magic to myth was brought to its culmination.

The Enlightenment which embodied Bacon's dictum that "the sovereignty of man lieth hidden in knowledge" and which held as its ideal the emancipation of men and women from all forms of tutelage—both self-imposed and that imposed by others—found its greatest ally in empirical science. While social and political forms and the Christian religion of revelation—whose normativity was already questioned by the rise of a historical science, the Reformation and the ensuing religious wars—were bluntly attacked by reason and its quest for a rational reconstruction of society and religion, the natural sciences made profound progress in the decipherment of the book of nature and the utilization of that knowledge for human ends, particularly that of preserving the self in a somewhat inhospitable world. Like myth, science sought the eradication of all animistic superstitions, symbolized by science's rejection of the explanatory value of "final causality" and the independent existence of "universals" thus concluding the disenchantment of nature by the reduction of history to facts and things to matter. Like myth, the law of science is also that of repetition and the rational calculability which takes the logical form of prediction, this time accomplished by the magic of mathematics. Indeed, by the implementation of the mathematical abstraction both movements which were embodied in myth could be brought to their conclusion: by mathematics, things could both be denuded of all ("secondary") qualities reduced to objectivity and also could be regarded as mere specimens, essentially commensurable in their abstract mathematical form and hence "substitutable" and "repeatable." The names of things could be substituted by the mathematical symbol by which all things become pure fungibles. For this reason, also, the ideal of science has always been that of the system, for in the anticipatory identification of a mathematicized world with truth is given the structure of scientific unity. "Enlightenment behaves towards things as a dictator to-

---

documentation to support that claim. It is important to note in this same work that, for Horkheimer, "the transition from objective to subjective reason was a necessary historical process" [*Eclipse of Reason*, p. 133], and hence there is no possibility of a "return" to objective reason in the form of a metaphysic [ibid., pp. 58-91]. The only recourse is a turn to a practical critical consciousness as a critical theory of society.

ward me. The man of science knows things insofar as he can make them. In this way their potentiality is turned to his own ends."[76]

For Horkheimer and Adorno, "enlightened reason" is essentially "instrumental," "subjective" reason.[77] It is concerned with the manipulation of "means" within the predicative framework of modern science. However, the banishment of the myth of an objective *ordo* of reality and the focus on the utilization of instrumental means as the task of thought has led to an irrationalism of "ends," the *terminus ad quem* of scientific investigation within the larger societal framework. The "ends" of human existence towards which science is a "means" are either authoritatively given "from above" for the reproduction of that which already is or depend upon an irrational *de facto* consensus which can appeal no further than to the fact of consensus for its normativity; either the reactionary attempt to regress to an already debunked objective *ordo* or the resignation of the designation of means to an administering technological elite. "Enlightened" reason destroys its own objective content and its progressive rationalization obliterates reason itself. In a most cruel irony, "enlightened" reason finally turns upon its own historical presuppositions as "myths" and unknowingly substitutes a new, more pernicious one.

> The objective tendency of the Enlightenment, to wipe out the power of images over man, is not matched by any subjective progress on the part of enlightened thinking towards freedom from images. While the assault on images irresistibly demolishes, after metaphysical ideas, those concepts once understood as rational and genuinely attained by thought, the thinking unleashed by the Enlightenment and immunized against thinking is now becoming a second figurativeness, though without image or spontaneity.[78]

[76] Horkheimer and Adorno, *Dialectic of Enlightenment*, p. 9.

[77] Idem, *Eclipse of Reason*, pp. 3-57. See, also, Herbert Marcuse's essay, "Some Social Implications of Modern Technology" [*ZfS* 9 (1941), pp. 414-39], where the concept of instrumental reason is connected with the emergence of modern technology, the standardization of production and consumption, the mechanization of labor, the extension of training, the bureaucratization of industry, labor and the state and the emergence of "mass" society—all themes which are to dominate *Dialectic of Enlightenment*.

[78] Adorno, *Minima Moralia*, p. 140. See, also, Horkheimer, "The End of Reason," *ZfS* 9 (1941), pp. 366-71.

This objective tendency of enlightened reason has arrived at its own self-consciousness in the "pragmatist" and "positivist" movements.[79] In the former, the instrumental and manipulative character of the knowing process per se is recognized and asserted as constitutive of all cognition. In the latter, thought itself is not spared, for scientific reason itself turns against thought and exorcises as meaningless or "conceptual poesy" that which does not submit to the criterion of verification. Thinking approaches the mathematical function and the machine and becomes subservient to the unquestioned end of the domination of humanity through the domination of nature. Thinking becomes a mirror reflecting what simply is and becomes subjected to that which it purports to dominate; like its object, thought becomes devoid of all qualities in the name of "scientific objectivity." "Impulse as such is as mythic as superstition."[80]

Perhaps the price which enlightenment extracts from thought can best be gauged by an acknowledgment of the reversal of meanings in the notions of "subjective" and "objective."

> Objective means the non-controversial aspect of things, their unquestioned impression, the facade made up of classified data, that is, the subjective; and they call subjective anything which breaches the facade, engages the specific experience of a matter, casts off all ready made judgements and substitutes relatedness to the object for the majority consensus of those who do not even look at it, let alone think about it—that is, the objective.[81]

Objectivity as the principle of repeatability and the capitulation to "the brute facts" has banished the tension, the distance between subject and object, whose play was thought. It suppresses the impulses which were constitutive of knowledge and which were preserved and transcended by thought.[82] Imagination atrophies, memory is suppressed and thought confined to the empirical givens undergoes a forgetfulness of the socially mediated nature of the "facts" themselves. Enlightenment thus regresses to myth and finds its counterpart to fate and retribution in myth in its restriction to the "facts" and its blind resignation to the reproduction of the same and in its exclusion of the qualitative and uncomprehended

---

[79] For a response to this critique by differentiating "positivism" as "scientism," "the positivist conception of science," "scientific politics" and "value-neutrality," see Russell Keat, *The Politics of Social Theory* (Chicago: The University of Chicago Press, 1981), esp. pp. 12-37.

[80] Horkheimer and Adorno, *Dialectic of Enlightenment*, p. 29.

[81] Adorno, *Minima Moralia*, p. 69.

[82] Ibid., pp. 65-74, 80-1, 122-28, 197-99.

"whole." In a cruel irony, thought which sought to dominate becomes dominated by its object and again approaches magic through its mimetic conformation to an abstracted nature.

It is the success and the progress of subjective reason that is questionable because with the rationalization of the social whole, the domination of nature for the sake of human self-preservation passes over into the domination of society and the domination of subjects for the sake of the preservation of the dominating system itself.

> With the abandonment of thought, which in its reified form of mathematics, machine and organization avenges itself on the men who have forgotten it, enlightenment has relinquished its own realization. By taking everything unique and individual under its tutelage, it left the uncomprehended whole the freedom, as domination, to strike back at human existence and consciousness by way of things.[83]

Concomitant with the dialectic of enlightenment, Adorno and Horkheimer noted a change in the role and function of "ideology" itself. During the "liberal" phase of modern society, the role of ideology can be found in the dichotomy between the transcendental and empirical ego in Kant's *Critique of Pure Reason*:

> As the transcendental, supraindividual self, reason comprises the idea of a free, human social life in which men organize themselves as the universal subject and overcome the conflict between pure and empirical reason in the conscious solidarity of the whole. This represents the idea of true universality: utopia. At the same time, however, reason constitutes the court of judgement of calculation, which adjusts the world for the ends of self-preservation and recognizes no function other than the preparation of the object from mere sensory material to make it the material of subjugation.[84]

Kant, like most of the Enlightenment philosophers, sought to replace the lost objective *ordo* of religion with one founded upon reason. Even though such a position was ideological, i.e., objectively a lie, a mask which left the objective concrete workings of society and its law of instrumental reason untouched, it at least afforded an opportunity for immanent criticism, *Ideologiekritik* and "irony."[85] As Adorno perceptively

---

[83] Horkheimer and Adorno, *Dialectic of Enlightenment*, p. 41. See, also, Horkheimer, *Eclipse of Reason*, pp. 92-127.

[84] Horkheimer and Adorno, *Dialectic of Enlightenment*, pp. 83-4.

[85] [Frankfurt Institute for Social Research], *Aspects of Sociology*, trans. John Viertel, with a preface by Max Horkheimer and Theodor W. Adorno (Boston: Beacon Press,

remarked, "it is not ideology in itself which is untrue but rather its pretension to correspond to reality."[86] Yet even these ideals of truth, the good and just society and happiness were exorcised by enlightened reason as mere superstitions, as myths. Indeed, Horkheimer and Adorno maintain that the objective morality of enlightenment as formalistic reason is not figured in the speculations of Kant, Rousseau or Voltaire, but in de Sade where "the sexual teams of *Juliette*, which employ every moment usefully, neglect no human orifice, and carry out every function . . . reveals an organization of life as a whole which is deprived of any substantial goal."[87] As Horkheimer noted, the dialectic of enlightenment has played itself out within the concept of ideology itself.

> By denying the reality of universal concepts and pointing to existing reality instead, the empiricists are right against the rationalists. On the other hand, the rationalists are right as against the empiricists in that, through what is implied in their concept of reason, they uphold the potential solidarity of men as an ideal against the actual state of affairs in which solidarity is asserted with violence and catastrophe. At the close of the liberal era, however, thinking in terms of mere existence, of sober self-preservation, has spread over the whole society. All men have become empiricists.[88]

Further on, Horkheimer adds that today, "Ideology consists more in what men are like than in what they believe. . . ."[89] What constitutes the

---

1972), pp. 182-205. See, also, Adorno's essay, "Cultural Criticism and Society," in *Prisims*, pp. 17-34, and *Minima Moralia*, pp. 209-12. For a presentation of Horkheimer's early understanding of "ideology critique," which in the 1940s increasingly approached that of Adorno, see Held, *An Introduction to Critical Theory*, pp. 183-87. By 1946 Horkheimer could write, "Formerly reality was opposed to and confronted with the ideal, which was evolved by the supposedly autonomous individual; reality was supposed to be shaped in accordance with this ideal. Today such ideologies are compromised and skipped over by progressive thought, which thus unwittingly facilitates the elevation of reality to the status of ideal. Therefore, adjustment becomes the standard for every conceivable type of subjective behavior" [*Eclipse of Reason*, p. 96]. On the history of "ideology" as a concept, see Jorge Larrain, *The Concept of Ideology* (Athens, Georgia: The University of Georgia Press, 1979), and George Lichtheim, *The Concept of Ideology and Other Essays* (New York: Random House, 1967).

[86] Adorno, "Cultural Criticism and Society," p. 32.

[87] Horkheimer and Adorno, *Dialectic of Enlightenment*, p. 88.

[88] Idem, "The End of Reason," p. 370. This essay both presents a précis of *Dialectic of Enlightenment* and documents Horkheimer's "farewell" to the "optimism" of the 1930s regarding the relation between theory and praxis and the estimate for the possibility of real change vis-à-vis the proletariat.

[89] Ibid., p. 387.

change in the role of ideology is that in postenlightenment society, ideology has dispensed with itself as "false consciousness" and its pretence towards justice, truth and the common good. Reality and ideology converge and reality becomes its own ideology. Ideology boldly presents the status quo and given atrophying thought, imagination and memory expects only one answer to the question "Where else shall we go?" Men and women today are ideology, the self-reproducing social facts where the end of self-preservation becomes the law of adaptation; the goal of emancipation becomes a grasping onto relative stability in a part of an unstable whole.[90]

Excursus: Adorno's Contributions to the Positivismusstreit
in German Sociology

The task of this excursus is twofold: to provide an introduction to Adorno's understanding of critical theory and to continue the argument against the positivism of the Enlightenment regarding the understanding of society thus forming a bridge to the next section, domination over society. Adorno's essays "Sociology and Empirical Research" and "On the Logic of the Social Sciences," which were delivered in 1961 at the German Sociological Association in Tübingen, as well as the extended "Introduction" to the volume of essays which emerged from this conference, are the primary texts for this "excursus."[91]

At the center-point of Adorno's essays stand the two categories of "totality" and "mediation," whose presence in critical theory and absence in positivism differentiates the one from the other. Totality refers not to a particular fact, nor to one central fact among a host of others, but refers to that "concept" which binds the facts or moments of a society together as a whole, i.e., the acknowledgment that there is not only a conceptuality of the knowing subject, but also a conceptuality immanent to the object. One may even go further and assert that insofar as the subject is also an object and a moment of society, that conceptuality of totality has, in the period of "late capitalism," heteronomously impressed itself upon the subject as subject. Yet such a conceptual whole, or totality, is not a thing-in-itself and independent of those moments which embody it and with which it stands in tension.

---

[90] Ibid., pp. 374-78.
[91] Adorno, et al., *The Positivist Dispute in German Sociology*, pp. 105-22, 68-86 and 1-67.

> Societal totality does not lead a life of its own over and above that which it
> unites and of which it, in its turn, is composed. It produces and reproduces
> itself through its individual moments. Many of these moments preserve a
> relative independence which primitive-total societies either do not know or
> do not tolerate. . . . System and individual entity are reciprocal and can only
> be apprehended in their reciprocity.[92]

Insofar as a conceptual totality not only appears and shapes itself in the
moments of society, but conceals itself and disguises a mediated appearance as sheer immediacy is totality simultaneously "ideology." Insofar as
such a totality takes on the appearance of a thing in itself, the appearance
of nature, myth or fate in a masking of society as subject is totality a reification. Insofar as totality heteronomously impresses itself on its constitutive moments by destroying the difference between the particular and
the general, the concrete and the abstract, by transforming all into the abstract according to its specific concept, is totality today the most real.

In the democratically governed countries of industrial society, totality is a category of mediation and not one of immediate totalitarian
domination. The description of the forms of the mediation of concept and
fact is the task of critical theory. "Theory seeks to give a name to what se-
cretly holds the machinery together,"[93] to render verbal what is hidden:
the conceptual moment of the whole which conditions the particular.
Theory seeks to force "essence" (totality) which negates itself in its appearances, to appear. This "concealed essence" as "nonessence" is affirmed by dialectical criticism, "not because of its power but instead it
criticizes its contradictions of 'what is appearing' and, ultimately, its contradiction of the real life of human beings . . . . Totality is not an affirmative but rather a critical category. Dialectical critique seeks to salvage or
help to establish what does not obey totality, what opposes it or what
first forms itself as the potential of a not-yet existent individuation."[94]
The charge of abstraction which dialectical criticism lays at the door of
positivism is that it is itself a mediation of that objective abstraction
which is the concept of the totality of industrial society, the exchange
principle.

> . . . the universal development of the exchange principle itself, which hap-
> pens independently of the qualitative attitudes of the producer and con-
> sumer, of the mode of production, even satisfy as a kind of secondary by-

---

[92] Adorno, "On the Logic of the Social Sciences," p. 107. See, also, "Introduction,"
pp. 32ff, and "Sociology and Empirical Research," pp. 81ff.
[93] Idem, "Sociology and Empirical Research," p. 68.

product. . . . The abstraction of exchange value is *a priori* allied with the domination of the general over the particular, of society over its captive membership.[95]

Like Horkheimer, Adorno emphasizes that "science is both independent and dependent: independent, insofar as it abstracts from the knowledge mediated through "real-life processes"; dependent, insofar as its autonomy, abstracted from the conditions of its genesis, can be derived from its social function. Science is not only a force of production, but also a relation of production.

Yet Adorno's major point of attack on science as positivistic is an immanent critique: science abstracts from that reality which shapes and conceals itself in its subjective and objective individual appearances. Specifically, through its taboo on the social totality which conditions the particular, that which is a mediated immediacy is converted into a pure immediacy. "Insofar as society is more than the immediate life of its members and the related subjective and objective facts, research which exhausts itself in the investigation of such immediacy misses the mark."[96] Sociology, as empirical research which relies on the average consciousness or unconsciousness of socialized subjects ignores the insight that even the most spontaneous of opinions and feelings are a mediated immediacy.[97] There is a preformation of consciousness by totality. Such an abstraction represents the *terminus ab quo* and *terminus ad quem* of what P. Lazarfeld termed "administrative research" and which today lives on in the advertising industry.[98] The theoretical development of sociological concepts, i.e., the division between "high" and "popular" culture, remains merely classifactory. It reifies the "historical" into the "natural" by disassociating the validity of concepts as research categories from the genesis of those states of affairs which are to be researched. "A social science which is both atomistic and ascends through classification

---

94   Idem, "Introduction," pp. 11-12.

95   Ibid., p. 14.

96   Idem, "On the Logic of the Social Sciences," p. 81.

97   It is important to note here that Adorno's opposition is not to empirical research as such, but to a hypostasization of "traditional theory" in its techne of "data gathering" in abstraction from an inquiry into the social whole. See Frankfurt Institute, *Aspects of Sociology*, pp. 117-28, and Friedrich Pollock, "Empirical Research into Public Opinion," in Paul Connerton, ed., *Critical Sociology*, trans. Thomas Hall, et al. (New York: Penguin Books, 1976).

98   Paul Felix Lazarsfeld, "Some Remarks on the Typological Procedures in Social Research," *ZfS* 6 (1937): 119-39, and "Remarks on Administrative and Critical Communications Research," *ZfS* 9 (1941): 2-16.

from the atoms to generalities, is the Medusan mirror to a society which is both atomized and organized according to abstract classificatory concepts, namely those of administration."[99] The objectivity of science is one of "method": an objectivity which remains content with its object as mere appearance ignoring the objectivity of the object, its mediatedness. In the negation of the objectivity of its objects, the critical force of science becomes constricted to self-criticism centered around the abstract law of noncontradiction.

> Thinking, which teaches itself that part of its own meaning is what, in turn, is not a thought explodes the logic of non-contradiction. . . . The critique of the relationships of scientific statements to that to which they refer is, however, inevitably compelled to a critique of reality. It must rationally decide whether the insufficiencies which it encounters are merely scientific, or whether reality insufficiently accords with what science, through its concept expresses about it. The separation between the structures of reality and science is not absolute. Nor may the concept of truth be attributed solely to the structures of science. It is no less meaningful to speak of the truth of a societal institution than of the truth of theorems connected with it. Legitimately, criticism does not normally imply merely self-criticism . . . but also criticism of reality.[100]

The contradiction between subject and object may not, however, be a contradiction immanent in the subject but a contradiction objective to the object which science in its true objectivity should follow. The objectivity of science can be nothing other than the objectivity, not of its methods, but of its object, as occurred in Marx's critique of political economy: "Anyone who wishes to follow the structure of his object and conceptualizes it as possessing motion in itself does not have at his disposal a method independent of the object."[101]

The puritanism of cognition which is positivistic science does, however, have its "moment" of truth in witnessing "that the facts, that which exists in this manner and not any other, have only attained that impenetrable power which is then reinforced by the scientistic cult of facts in scientific thought, in a society without freedom of which its own subjects are not masters."[102] It is against this that critical theory rebels: "despite all experience of reification, and in the very expression of this experience,

99 Adorno, "Sociology and Empirical Research," p. 74.
100 Idem, "Introduction," pp. 24-25.
101 Ibid., p. 48.
102 Ibid., p. 64.

critical theory is oriented towards the idea of society as subject, whilst sociology accepts this reification, repeats it in its methods and thereby loses the perspective in which society and its law would first reveal themselves."[103]

It may well be asked of Adorno, "What is the task of a critical sociology?" In these essays, the concept which comes to the fore is that of "interpretation." More precisely, interpretation consists in the two movements of "mediation" and "micrology" which together result in a physionomics of social appearance. "Mediation" describes the movement of understanding from above to below, in acknowledgment that the particular is always an immediacy mediated by the social totality of which it is a moment. Hence an anticipation and naming of the concept of the totality plays an integral role in interpretation. "Micrology" refers to the opposite movement, to an immersion into the detail or the particular which begins "by sharpening the sense for what is illuminated in every social phenomenon." Physiognomy refers to the concrete interpretation as a result of its reciprocal moments which is the tension between the general and the particular that critical theory as interpretation seeks to explode. Theory

> . . . must transform the concepts which it brings, as it were, from outside into those which the object has of itself, left to itself, seeks to be, and confront it with what it is. It must dissolve the rigidity of the temporally and spatially fixed object into a field of tension of the possible and the real.[104]

---

103 Ibid., p. 34.

104 Idem, "Sociology and Empirical Research," p. 69. The circle of mediational and micrological analysis, articulated in the '60s, clearly resembles Adorno's earliest articulation of the task of philosophy in the 1931 lecture, "The Actuality of Philosophy" [*Telos* 31 (Spring 1977): 120-33]. In this lecture, influenced by Walter Benjamin's notion of "constellation" in *The Origins of German Tragic Drama* [trans. John Osborne, with an introduction by George Steiner (London: New Left Books, 1977)], Adorno set out a position which was to span his career and the variegated subject matter to which he turned his attention.

In response to the question concerning the actuality of philosophy amid the liquidation and impoverishment of its contemporary forms and their claims to totality [Adorno, "The Actuality of Philosophy," pp. 120-24], Adorno asserts that philosophy must proceed not as a science of a "higher level of generality," but only as an *interpretation* of the concrete. Confronted by the "riddle-figures" of concrete existents, philosophy possesses no sure or abiding key for interpretation: "nothing more is given to it than fleeting, disappearing traces within the riddle-figures of that which exists and their astonishing entwinings" [ibid., p. 126]. Philosophy must continue to respin the threads which have been spun by previous philosophical reflection and the contemporary sciences in order to transform the ciphers of reality into a text. Yet, in doing so, philosophy must abandon the "symbolic function"—what Adorno later was to call "identity thought"—of the sciences and traditional philosophy and give its reflection over to the preponderance of the object. In this, the task of philosophy is not merely that of portraying reality as "meaningful" as the instanciation of the universal, of justifying that which is. Philosophy must realize that its text, reality, is "incomplete, contradictory and fragmentary and much in it may be delivered up to blind demons" [ibid.]. In its rejection of the equation that the reasonable is the intentional, the task of philosophy becomes criticism in "interpretation of the unintentional through a juxtaposition of analytically isolated elements and illuminations of the real by the power of such interpretation" [ibid., p. 127]. Philosophy must henceforth abandon its predilection for the "big questions" and its quest for a foundation which guarantees the particular through its suppression as a mere representation of the universal. The materialism of philosophic critique lies in its perspective of viewing its objects as historically social products, or, as expressed in the chiasm of a 1932 address which is the "companion-piece" to "The Actuality of Philosophy," "to apprehend historical being in its outermost historical determination, there where is most 'historical', as a 'natural' being; and when it reaches this, to apprehend 'nature' where it most deeply hardens into itself as a 'historical being'." [Idem, *"Die Idee der Naturgeschichte,"* pp. 354-55].

By abiding with the fragmentary and brittle concrete-particular, philosophy seeks to light up reality and, by doing so, to reveal it not as meaningful but devoid of meaning. What Adorno was later to claim as the task of art—"The task of art today is to bring chaos into order" [Idem, *Minima Moralia*, p. 222]—could equally apply to his concept of the task of philosophy. Philosophy as materialist interpretation breaks open its own closed area of knowledge because in its interpretation that reality is negated. It exists not solely in the concept or interpretation itself, but that "out of a configuration of reality the demand for its real change promptly follows" [idem, "The Actuality of Philosophy," p. 129]. Only in the abolition of philosophy's question, only in praxis, is the authenticity of philosophy's interpretation first confirmed [ibid.]. The position here is in marked contrast to that of *Negative Dialectics* at the end of Adorno's career: "Philosophy, which once seemed obsolete, lives on because the moment to realize it was missed. . . . Having broken its pledge to be as one with reality or at the point of realization, philosophy is obliged to ruthlessly criticize itself" [idem, *Negative Dialectics*, trans. E. B. Ashton (New York: Seabury Press, 1973), p. 3)]. Philosophy, thus, must not only abide with the fragmentariness of reality but, in so abiding, reveal it as fragmentary. While the direction of such interpretative criticism is specified by the materialist canon of seeing appearances as historically social, its execution can only be carried through by a construction of constellations, by exact phantasy, which follows the dynamic of its object in its relation to the whole. Such constellations, groupings and trial arrangements of conceptual material derived from the exact sciences are neither a priori nor accessible through an immediate intuition of empirical reality; rather, in the fullest sense they are provisional constructions whose legitimacy and truth lies "in the last analysis by the fact that reality crystallizes about them in striking conclusiveness" [idem, "The Actuality of Philosophy," p. 131]. Exact phantasy which immerses itself in the details of the object as presented to it by the sciences and which thus stands in opposition to any mechanical or objectivistic

"Truth" resides in motion, in the nonreconciliation of the particular and the general, in the negativity of the particular in relation to its "other"— the general—and in the negativity of the general in relation to its "other"—the particular. As long as this "difference" endures, there is a task and space for critical thought. Yet interpretation is not thereby merely arbitrary or utopian, based upon the mere negation of what is, but is irreducibly historical.

> History mediates between the phenomenon and its content which requires interpretation. The essential which appears in the phenomenon is that whereby it becomes what it is, what was silenced in it and what, in painful stultification, releases that which yet becomes. The orientation of physiognomy is directed towards what is silenced, the second level of phenomena.[105]

---

methodologism is the *ars inveniendi*, itself historic, of philosophic interpretation. It is this commitment to the concrete and the particular, the acknowledgement of the fragmentariness and brittleness of reality, as well as its complex entwinings, which demand an equally fragmentary, tentative, malleable and experimental form of communication: the essay, fragment and aphorism. Finally, it may be noted that the paratactical style of the method of constellation shatters the Marxist "doctrine" of the mechanical determination of the (socio-cultural) superstructure by the (economic) base. Such causal language is lacking in the work of Adorno and Horkheimer. What I suggest is that in the paratactical style of the method of constellation—the juxtaposition of infrastructural and superstructural appearances without reducing the latter to a causal effect of the former—as seen most clearly in Adorno's essays in *Prisms*, issues in the portrayal of a continuum of phenomena whose mode of relationship suggests coordination and conditioning—and hence a certain degree of autonomy for each—rather than the mechanical determination of causality. What results is, as Frederick Jameson observers, "that for a fleeting instant we catch a glimpse of a unified world, of a universe in which discontinuous realities are nonetheless somehow implicated with each other and intertwined, no matter how remote they may at first have seemed; in which the reign of chance briefly refocuses into a network of cross-relationships wherever the eye can reach, contingency temporarily transmuted into necessity" [Frederic Jameson, *Marxism and Form* (Princeton: Princeton University Press, 1971), p. 8]. For an excellent exposition of Benjamin's influence on Adorno in this period, as well as the notion of constellation and exact phantasy, see Buck-Morss, *The Origin of Negative Dialectics*, esp. pp. 43-110, as well as Rose, *The Melancholy Science*, pp. 11-26, for a discussion of Adorno's literary style.

105 Idem, "Introduction," p. 36. Perhaps no more clear a statement on the relation between facts, totality and history as interpretative sociology can be found than Adorno's own: "A dialectical theory of society is concerned with the structural laws which condition the facts, manifest themselves in the facts and are themselves modified by the facts. By structural laws, one means tendencies which follow more or less

The nonidentity between essence and appearance, general and particular, concept and thing is the "motor" which drives interpretation. Interpretation as physiognomy (mediation and micrology) attempts to overcome the bifurcation of theory and empirical data-gathering through a deciphering of the concrete; positivism, extolling the primacy of the individual concrete fact, denies it by ignoring its mediated objectivity thus reducing the concrete to the notion of an abstract instance of categories. Counterposed to this, the task of a critical theory would be to relativize critically through its delineation of totality the cognitive value of all appearances and to use empirical research to protect the concept of essence from being transformed into a "thing-in-itself."

DOMINATION OVER SOCIETY: THE QUESTION OF THE ECONOMY

In in its own self-understanding, critical theory decisively sides with the example of Marx's *Critique of Political Economy* rather than Descartes' *Discourse on Method*. However, it is a well-known charge and reproach that anything representing the specificity of Marx's critique of the political economy is lacking in the catalog of the Institute's work. Adorno and Horkheimer in particular, the charge continues, abandoned all concern with the economic "base" of society. Instead, they focused on the cultural "superstructure" and the way in which domination becomes internalized within and by the dominated individual. In this, they remained bourgeois critics. There is much truth to such an assertion, for one searches in vain for anything resembling extensive economic analyses in their work.

Yet it is only fair to note that the roster of members of the Institute was not devoid of "political economists."[106] Otto Kirchheimer and Friedrich Pollock, Franz Neumann and Arkadij Gurland were all members of the Institute at the time of its American emigration, and even though only Pollock could be counted as a member of the "inner circle," they all contributed towards an analysis of the changes extant in the capitalist political economy after the First World War. Such changes are

---

stringently from the historical constituents of the entire system [idem, "Is Marx Obsolete," *Diogenes* 64 (Winter 1968): 2]. See, also, *Negative Dialectics*, pp. 162-66.

[106] For an overview of the economic and political studies of the Institute, see Jay, *The Dialectical Imagination*, pp. 143-72; Held, *An Introduction to Critical Theory*, pp. 40-76; Giacomo Marramao, "Political Economy and Critical Theory," *Telos* 24 (1975): 56-80; and Andrew Arato, "Introduction," in *The Essential Frankfurt School Reader*, pp. 3-25.

signaled throughout *Dialectic of Enlightenment* by terms such as "state capitalism," "monopoly capitalism," "postcompetitive capitalism" and "postmarket society." Further, investigation of the changes in the economic "base" of society were central to the Institute's attempt to comprehend the emergence of Fascism and the Nazi state: "Whoever does not wish to speak about capitalism should also be silent about fascism."[107]

The crux of Pollock's *Zeitschrift* articles on "state capitalism" can be summarized as follows: the irrationality and periodic economic crises of liberal-market and monopoly capitalism can in principle be overcome and stabilized through central economic planning in the form of an "ideal-typical" totalitarian or democratic state capitalism such that there is not merely a quantitative, but qualitative change from earlier forms of capitalism whose contradictions and tensions are transposed from a now-stabilized economic sphere to the properly political sphere.[108] Hence the disjunction between "base" and "superstructure" is no longer mediated by the anarchy of interests of the market along the lines of class differentiation, but by an element of the superstructure itself, the state, which in its interventionist stance dominates the whole. While Pollock was almost exclusively concerned with totalitarian state capitalism, the above and following would seem to be equally applicable to its democratic forms.

The hallmark of state capitalism is its negation of the liberal market in response to the exigencies of the centralization and concentration of capital as a condition of technological advance as witnessed in monopoly capitalism, and it is also an attempt to overcome the chronic crises of both liberal and market capitalism in the form of overproduction, overcapitalization and unemployment. The inefficiency and waste of the market system where the ascertainment of what and how needs are to be satisfied is accomplished *ex post facto* must be overcome. While its existence had already been transformed by the emergence of monopolistic forces of productions in the form of capital and labor and government intervention in the credit and trade system, the market system is replaced in state capitalism by efficient and rational central administration and planning. The task of such planning is the definition "in advance" of public and private needs to be satisfied by direct allocation vs. bidding

107 Horkheimer, *"Die Juden und Europa," ZfS* 8 (1939-40): 115.
108 Friedrich Pollock, *"Die gegenwartige Lage des Kapitalismus und die Aussichten einer planwirtschaftlichen Neuordnung," ZfS* 1 (1932): 8-27; "State Capitalism," and "Is National Socialism a New Order," *ZfS* 9 (1941): 200-25, 440-55.

for the forces of production (i.e., labor, fuel, raw materials, technology) through a system of priorities and quotas concerning "the reproduction of existing resources, expansion (including defense) and the total output of consumer goods which every industry shall produce."[109] In short, given a determination of needs and resources, the task of central economic planning is the coordination and direction of production and distribution.

With the disappearance of the "natural economic laws of the market," Pollock saw no reason to question the economic stability or preservation of state capitalism. The economic *necessity* of collapse no longer obtains. Contradictions and tensions which arise in state capitalism will not enter in directly through the economic sphere, but through the political sphere. Of crucial importance here are the "ends," the recognition of what needs can be and are to be satisfied by available resources. The question of its "ends" becomes primarily a political one and herein lies the difference between totalitarian and democratic state capitalism.[110]

Horkheimer's earliest response to these developments can be seen in his 1940 article, "The Authoritarian State."[111] For him, the prelude to state capitalism, its ability to outlive the destruction of the market, can be found in the fate of the workers' organizations. In their reformist accommodations to the transformation of the economy, the workers' organizations abandoned their "unnatural" end: the destruction of capitalist exploitation. By conforming to "natural" conditions and developments, that is, to the "natural" order of capitalist development, the worker's organizations have degenerated into mass organizations. Paradoxically, in the workers' movements "men were conceived as objects, if necessary as their own"[112] which witnesses to the truth that "integration is the price individuals and groups have to pay in order to flourish under capitalism."[113]

This integration from above is consummated in the statism of state capitalism. The destruction of the liberal market through nationalization

---

[109] Idem, "State Capitalism," p. 212.

[110] Pollock's essay ends somewhat abruptly on this note. For an attempt to describe the contemporary changes in the nature and conditions of political compromise, see Otto Kirchheimer, "Change in the Structure of Political Compromise," *ZfS* 9 (1941): 264-89.

[111] Horkheimer, "The Authoritarian State," in *The Essential Frankfurt School Reader*, pp. 95-117.

[112] Ibid., p. 97. See, also, Horkheimer, *Eclipse of Reason*, p. 148ff.

[113] Ibid., p. 99. That such an objection is also applicable to the "Party" in the socialist utopia, see pp. 111f.

and socialization of industry, the absorption of the sphere of circulation into state functions, the transformation of economic questions into technical questions, the perpetuation of a state of crisis which legitimates the status quo and the "temporary" domination of the population, the atomization and leveling of all individuals to functions for the preservation and expansion of the "system" and the rationalization of all forms of public—and thereby also "private"—existence show state capitalism in its fascist, socialist and democratic form as the authoritarian state. In this, state socialism is no different from its democratic and totalitarian counterpart. The self-sufficiency and complacency of the former rests on its confusion of the notion of development with that of dialectic.

> Dialectic is not identical with development. Two contradictory moments, the transition to state control and liberation from it, are seized as one in the concept of social revolution. Revolution brings about what would happen without spontaneity in any case: the socialization of the means of production, planned management of production, and unlimited control of nature. And it also brings about what will not happen without resistance and constantly renewed efforts to strengthen freedom: the end of exploitation. Such a further outcome is not a further acceleration of progress, but a qualitative leap out of the dimension of progress.[114]

He who identifies the socialization of the means of production with the end of exploitation unwittingly capitulates to the immanent development of capitalism. The foundation of revolutionary theory lies in the difference between concept and reality, not in the concept alone whose identity with reality is universal exploitation.

What does move to the fore in this essay is the increasing negativity of critical theory. Not only does critical theory abjure all prediction given the role of praxis and the unconcluded dialectic, but also "if society in the future really functions through free agreement rather than through direct or indirect force, the result of such an agreement cannot be theoretically anticipated,"[115] but emerges from praxis itself. The stance of critical theory is solely that of "critique," of the determinate negation and not the

---

[114] Ibid., p. 107.
[115] Ibid., p. 113. The intimation here of Habermas' "ideal speech situation" of noncoercive communication is unmistakable. So, also, Adorno: "If speculation on the state of reconciliation were permitted, neither the undistinguished unity of subject and object nor their antithetical hostility would be conceivable within it; rather, the communication of what was distinguished. Not until then would the concept of communication, as an objective concept, come into its own" ["Subject and Object," p. 499].

envisionment of the socialist realm of freedom. Further, it transgresses the limits of critical theory even to specify *forms of resistance*, apart from critical theory itself, to the social totality. "Despite all the urgency with which theory attempts to illuminate the movement of the social totality even in its smallest detail, it is unable to prescribe to individuals *an effective form of resistance* to injustice. Thought itself is already a sign of resistance, the effort to keep oneself from being deceived any longer."[116] Even in this situation with the possibilities of more effective forms of domination, there still remains, however, the possibility of liberation, although this increasingly seems "abstract": the "avant-garde" who have not been purged by either the party or the state and the "sullen yearnings of the atomized masses."[117] Thus, one is left with a contradiction: concomitant to an increasing negativity of critical theory, there is an increased emphasis on the spontaneity or voluntaristic element of praxis, even as its subject becomes increasingly "abstract" and isolated.

That capitalism had witnessed profound changes in the twentieth century did not go unnoticed by Horkheimer and Adorno. However, concerning the nature and significance of these changes, there was no consensus among the political economists of the Institute itself. Pollock's view, summarized above, was opposed by Neumann for whom the term state-capitalism is a contradiction in terms. For Neumann, the latest form of capitalism in the totalitarian fascist state represented only a more advanced form of monopoly capitalism. The essential locus of social contradictions thus remain in the economic sphere.[118]

It is more difficult, however, to trace the relation of Horkheimer and Adorno to these two considerably different positions. In "The Authoritarian State," Horkheimer asserted, "State capitalism is, to be sure, an antagonistic, transient phenomenon. The law of its collapse is readily visible: it is based on the limitation of productivity due to the existence of the bureaucracies."[119] Despite his use of the term "state-capitalism," Horkheimer seems to intend by it something different from Pollock, i.e., that the collapse of state capitalism is "necessary" and that this "necessary contradiction" lies in the economic realm. In short, Horkheimer's notion of state capitalism seems closer to Neumann's "monopolistic totalitarian capitalism" than to Pollock's sense of the term.

[116] Ibid., p. 116.
[117] Ibid., p. 126. See, also, Marcuse, "Some Social Implications of Modern Technology," pp. 138-62.
[118] Neumann, *Behemoth*, pp. 221-28.
[119] Horkheimer, "The Authoritarian State," p. 109.

Scarcely a year later, however, Horkheimer wrote, referring to Pollock's article "State Capitalism," that

> Its challenging thesis is that such a society can endure for a long and terrify-
> ing period. Basing itself on the most recent economic experience, it comes to
> the conclusion that all technical economic problems that worried the busi-
> ness world can be handled through authoritarian devices. The article at-
> tempts to destroy the wishful idea that fascism must eventually disintegrate
> through the disharmonies of supply and demand, budget deficiencies or
> unemployment. The study is not confined to authoritarian society alone but
> conceives the latter as a sub-species of state capitalism, thus raising the
> question whether state capitalism might not be workable within the frame-
> work of democracy rather than terror.[120]

Interestingly enough, *Dialectic of Enlightenment* was dedicated to Friedrich Pollock.

It is difficult to locate the position of Adorno and Horkheimer in the state-capitalism/monopoly-capitalism debate within the Institute itself, and precisely this difficulty contributes to the ambiguity of critical theory as a whole. I offer the following as a tentative characterization of their position. First, both men seem to have accepted some variation of an economic "convergence thesis": in recent history, capitalism and social-ism converge in their economic essentials.[121] Further, the essence of both these forms are interpreted through the fascist state. What was a terrify-ing reality in Nazi Germany is a potentiality for socialist industrial soci-ety and democratic late capitalism. The specter of open and immediate barbarism and domination is never far from their discussion of socialism and capitalism. Second, both men seem to have accepted the thesis that both capitalism and socialism in the twentieth century have evolved to the point that the social totality and the status quo can be stabilized and reproduced through—even if never explicit—a collusion of industry, state, armed forces and communication media. Such would seem to be the import of such phrases as "integration from above," "the adminis-tered world" and "the anonymity of a hegemonic totality." Here the lan-guage of the "technological veil" and hence the illusion of an "end of ideology" tends to replace that of the commodity fetish and, further, permit the transference of ideas and concepts (i.e., mass culture, the role of prejudice, etc.) originally worked out in the context of an attempt to understand fascism to democratic late capitalism and the authoritarian

120   Idem, "Preface," *ZfS* (1941): 198.
121   Adorno, "Is Marx Obsolete," pp. 1-16.

socialist state.[122] Third, however, unlike Pollock, they hesitated to transfer the antinomies of the societal whole from the economic sphere to the
political; rather, they tended to derive the latter from the former as its
hidden grammar. Rejecting Pollock's notion of a state capitalism in the
context of democratic reform, when it came to an articulation of the liberative possibilities of the present world, they continued to employ
"traditional" Marxist language concerning the contradictions of the relations and forces of production—even while simultaneously asserting the
disappearance of the proletariat as such! In short, to a great extent,
Horkheimer and Adorno remained "orthodox" Marxists. The tacit acceptance of the stabilization thesis of Pollock, yet their persistence in delin-
eating the structure of revolutionary social possibilities in the contradictions of the economic sphere conditioned the peculiar constellation of
critical theory in its later development: its pessimism about the possibility of change and a lack of specificity concerning that sphere in which
social antinomies are generated, the economy. Fourth, it must be asserted
that the virtual absence of any sustained reflection on the concrete eco-
nomic-political developments of either the authoritarian socialist state or
democratic late capitalism remain a major lacuna of Horkheimer's and
Adorno's critical theory.

THE DIALECTICS OF CULTURE AND KITSCH: THE CULTURE INDUSTRY AND AUTONOMOUS ART[123]

In a sense, the path Adorno and Horkheimer were to travel was ini-
tially explored by one who never had a formal relationship with the
Institute, Georg Lukács. In 1923 Lukács published his seminal work,
History and Class Consciousness—a work which he was later to repudiate

---

[122] For example, see Horkheimer and Adorno, *Dialectic of Enlightenment*, pp. 120-
208, where the analysis of the development of capitalist society and the extirpation of
"difference" and the demise of the "individual" is refracted through a discussion of
the "culture-industry" and "anti-Semitism," and Horkheimer, *Eclipse of Reason*, pp.
139-61, where the decline of the individual is related to the "technological veil" of the
concentration of capital in service of increased productivity and efficiency.
[123] For a general presentation on "art and mass culture" (or the "culture industry"),
see Jay, *The Dialectical Imagination*, pp. 173-218, and Held, *An Introduction to Critical
Theory*, pp. 77-109. For a general exposition of Adorno's aesthetics, see Jay, *Adorno*
(Cambridge: Harvard University Press, 1984), pp. 111-60, and Rose, *The Melancholy
Science*, pp. 109-37.

under pressure from the Soviet Communist Party.[124] In the essay "Reification and the Consciousness of the Proletariat," he asks, "How may the structure and nature of capitalist society in its totality be portrayed?" The key, for Lukács, does not lie in the notion of labor as a source of surplus-value, nor even in the distinction between "exchange" and "use" value in its economically precise sense, but in the commodity structure whose essence is "fetishistic" and "reified," i.e., that social relations between men and women are masked and take on a "phantom objectivity" assuming the character of a relation between people and things or between things and things. Through this rearticulation of the nature of capitalism, Lukács could assimilate Marx's notion of the production of exchange value to Weber's notion of the "rationalization" of the *Lebenswelt* through bureaucracy—if not also to Simmel's notion of culture as "objectification."

> . . . the problem of commodities must not be considered in isolation or even regarded as the central problem in economics, but as the central, structural problem of capitalist society in all its aspects. Only in this case can the structure of the commodity be made to yield a model of all the objective forms of bourgeois society together with all the subjective forms, corresponding to them.[125]

If this is the case, it means that "'ideological' and 'economic' problems lose their mutual exclusiveness and merge into one another."[126] If the cultural superstructure could neither be dismissed as the reflection of specific class interests ("vulgar" Marxist criticism") nor be accepted as a wholly autonomous sphere for the higher life of *Geist* ("conservative cultural critics"), but if it embodies the same structural form as the capitalist base and hence *in nuce* embodies the antinomies of capitalist society, that is, if the superstructure could be interpreted as a "code language for pro-

---

124 For an exposition of the work of the early Lukács and *History and Class Consciousness* in particular, see Andrew Arato and Paul Breines, *The Young Lukács and the Origins of Western Marxism* (New York: Seabury Press, 1979).

125 Georg Lukács, "Reification and the Consciousness of the Proletariat," in *History and Class Consciousness*, trans. Rodney Livingstone (Cambridge: The MIT Press, 1971), p. 83. See, also, his essay in the same volume, "What Is Orthodox Marxism," pp. 12-15.

126 Idem, "The Marxism of Rosa Luxemburg," in *History and Class Consciousness*, p. 34.

cesses taking place in society,"[127] then an area unexplored and ignored by traditional Marxists opens up. It is not without exaggeration that I suggest that the discussion concerning "Marxism and aesthetics" of the middle of this century is perhaps the most abiding legacy of western or critical Marxism.[128] In what follows in this section, the word "culture" will refer preeminently to the work of art in contemporary society—an metonymy which nevertheless is true to the use of the term "culture" by Adorno and Horkheimer. Further, if in what follows the work of Adorno is almost exclusively focused on, it is because of the extent of his work in this area as well as the breadth of the various facets of the question which he considered. Lastly, I would suggest that in the seeming disjunction, yet convertability of the terms "sociology of art" or "aesthetics" is contained the crux of Adorno's thought on the relation of art (culture) and society.[129]

A great part of the difficulty in outlining Adorno's reflections on art and society is its intransigence to facile classification. His protean thought remains equidistant from populist, elitist, administrative and radical approaches to culture. Against the populist who advocates the enlightening and liberative function of the "media explosion" and the eclipse of aesthetic aura in the mechanical work of art, Adorno points to the stultifying and regressive effects of the culture industry. Against the elitist who points to culture as the realm of eternal values, as a bulwark against the catastrophe which is modernity, Adorno argues that this itself is a *proton pseudos* and false consciousness and that "the reification of life

---

[127] Horkheimer, "Ten Years on Morningside Heights: A Report on the Institute's History, 1934-1944" (unpublished, 1944; Lowenthal collection), cited in Jay, *The Dialectical Imagination*, p. 177.

[128] For an attempt to sketch and situate the position of the Frankfurt School within the wider context of German Idealism, see Sherry M. Weber, "Aesthetic Experience and Self-Reflection as Emancipatory Processes," in O'Neill, ed., *On Critical Theory*, pp. 78-103. For an excellent exposition of the various forms the Marxist theory of art has taken, see Aronowitz, *The Crisis of Historical Materialism* (New York: McGraw Hill Book Co., 1973), pp. 225-80. Two of the best detailed studies on the "debate" concerning art in contemporary Marxism are Jameson, *Marxism and Form*, and Eugene Lunn, *Marxism and Modernism: A Historical Study of Lukács, Brecht, Benjamin and Adorno* (Berkeley: University of California Press, 1982). Finally, many of the most important primary texts, previously unpublished in English, of Bloch, Brecht, Benjamin, Lukács and Adorno have been published in Ronald Taylor, ed., *Aesthetics and Politics*, trans. Harry Zohn, et al., with an Afterword by Frederic Jameson (London: New Left Books, 1977).

[129] Adorno, "Theses on the Sociology of Art," *Working Papers in Cultural Studies*, 2 (Spring 1972): 121-28.

results not from too much enlightenment but from too little."[130] Against
the administrative approach which mechanically used *Ideologiekritik* of
the work of art in a subsumptive and classificatory manner, Adorno argues that such a use of *Ideologiekritik* is a reification, given that today
"ideology is not simply reducible to a partial interest. It is as it were
equally near the center in all its pieces."[131] Against the radical who in
recognition of the ideological foundation of culture counsels its whole-
sale dismissal, Adorno argues that the "dialectical critic of culture must
both participate in culture and not participate"[132] and that what often
disguises itself under the banner of radicalism is a prelude to open barbarism.

The fundamental antinomy of culture lies, for Adorno, in the potential of freedom which it signifies and claims as existing and the reality of
domination.[133] Ultimately, this antinomy is to be drawn back to the division of labor which is the condition of the possibility of culture. In the
separation of mental and physical labor, "all culture shares the guilt of
society. It ekes out its existence only by virtue of injustice already per-
petuated in the sphere of production."[134] This tension in the objective
origin of culture is deceptively negated through its claim to autonomy
and the positing of itself as an *an sich*. By claiming distance from that
from which it derives, culture takes on the appearance of a mythic obdu-
racy and its consolation "to offer universal security in the middle of a
universal dynamic"[135] is only achieved through its isolation from the life
processes of society and its renunciation of interference in them. Culture,
in order to preserve itself, must thus negate what it seeks to offer—the
potential of reason and freedom—except within its own hermetic con-
fines.

Even in its separation and isolation, in its positing of itself as an "in
itself," culture remains unable to manage the separation between the so-

---

130   Idem, "Culture Criticism and Society," p. 24.

131   Ibid., p. 31.

132   Ibid., p. 33.

133   See, also, Horkheimer, "Art and Mass Culture," in *Critical Theory*, pp. 273-90,
and Herbert Marcuse, "The Affirmative Character of Culture," in *Negations*, pp. 88-
133.

134   Adorno, "Culture Criticism and Society," p. 26. Perhaps the most quotable expression of this point was Benjamin's: "The products of art and science owe their existence not merely to the effort of the great geniuses that created them, but also to the
unnamed drudgery of their contemporaries" [Walter Benjamin, "Edward Fuchs:
Collector and Historian," in *The Essential Frankfurt School Reader*, p. 233].

135   Ibid., p. 22.

cietal whole and itself because this very separation between the reality of
oppression and suffering and the appearance of freedom and reason is
potentially subverted through the "beautiful appearance" of the work of
art. The disjunction in culture of the appearance of directly helping freedom while indirectly mediating domination through its claim to autonomy is managed by culture through kitsch.[136] As "pure entertainment,"
kitsch is the crisis management of culture which proclaims "nothing
must change" in the invariance and simplicity of its formal elements. The
artistic grammar of kitsch is infantile; its invariant reservoir of clichés
(perhaps best seen in sitcoms and soap operas) represent the dregs of
artistic history. It is the prototype of the culture industry minus the latter's integration and concentration. The triumph of kitsch is in its internalization, in the cries for more and for entertainment, amusement and
diversion which relieves one from labor solely to return one to it. What
culture could not do, kitsch accomplishes, because the disjunction between freedom and suffering is overcome in that "people cling to what
mocks them in confirming the mutilation of their essence by the smooth-
ness of its own appearance."[137] Yet the epochal change in culture and its
claim to freedom and enlightenment lies in the transformation of its relation to its "other," kitsch. If kitsch is as old as culture itself, culture had
previously proscribed its own bad conscience, half-aware that its message of "nothing must change" was only the dark side of its own claims
to freedom and reason. Yet in our own times, "culture no longer impotently drags its despised opponent behind it, but is taking it under its direction."[138] Indeed, the difference between the two is eroding and culture
in "administering the whole of mankind, administers also the breach between man and culture"[139] and thus negates itself. Today culture has
been devoured by kitsch and organized as industry.[140]

   Yet if the negation, fulfillment and surmounting of culture is only to
be envisioned in the abolition of the division of labor from which it arises
or that the "end of art" is possible only in a society which had achieved

---

[136] For a response to the position of Adorno and Horkheimer, see Herbert Gans,
Popular Culture and High Culture (New York: Basic Books, 1974).
[137] Adorno, *Minima Moralia*, p. 147.
[138] Ibid.
[139] Ibid.
[140] Idem, "Culture Industry Reconsidered," *New German Critique* 6 (Fall 1975): 12-
19.

satisfaction,[141] it does not follow that culture is to be ignored as an epiphenomenon or denounced as mere ideology. While the former stance allows kitsch by omission to run wild and thus collaborates in its reproduction, the latter "replaces insight into a bad reality with insight into the badness of ideas."[142] True criticism of a barbaric culture cannot be content with a barbaric denunciation of culture. It must recognize overt uncultured barbarism as the *telos* of that culture and reject it, but it cannot crudely proclaim the supremacy of barbarism over culture simply because barbarism has ceased to lie.[143] A dialectical theory of culture can only maintain itself by both not participating (a critique of the culture industry) and participating (raising the question of "autonomous art" today) in culture and in retaining its mobility with regard to culture through a clear recognition of criticism's position within the societal whole.

There is, however, a difference in the mode of criticism dependent on the nature of the object treated: culture industry or autonomous art. While a cursory reading of "Culture Criticism and Society" conveys the impression that the critic of culture must choose between immanent criticism or transcendent criticism, it seems to me that recourse is made to a form of transcendent criticism in regard to the culture industry. To be sure, this form of transcendent criticism is not the sort of transcendent criticism rejected by Adorno, i.e., that mode which takes up a standpoint outside the sway of existing society in its presupposition of a longitudinal and expressive notion of totality, of a *Gesamtsubjekt* mediating the *Gesamttotalität* of history, which would then ground a mechanical and reified use of *Ideologiekritik*.

For Adorno, immanent critique is inherently dialectical, even if it too must presuppose a normative totality in a negative manner. In his description of immanent criticism, the moment of micrological analysis is dominant, for by seeking

> . . . to grasp through an analysis of their [the work of art's] form and meaning, the contradiction between their objective idea and that pretension [to correspond to reality] . . . names what the consistency or inconsistency of the work itself expresses of the structure of the existent.[144]

141   Idem, *Philosophy of Modern Music*, trans. Anne Mitchell and Wes Blomster (New York: Seabury Press, 1980), p. 15.
142   Idem, "Spengler after the Decline," in *Prisms*, p. 66.
143   Idem, "Veblen's Attack on Culture," in *Prisms*, p. 91.
144   Idem, "Culture Criticism and Society," p. 32.

Through the micrological analysis of the level of technique which is constitutive of the work of art and through which the work's subject matter is sublated into an aesthetic whole, immanent criticism is dialectical, focusing and shedding light on the puzzle-character (*Rätselcharakter*) of the work of art and the social whole which appears in it through the mediation of aesthetic form and technique.[145] Yet, here, immanent criticism must acknowledge its own limits, for it threatens to revert to sheer idealism: "even the most radical reflection of the mind on its own failure is limited by the fact that it remains only reflection, without altering the existence to which its failure bears witness."[146]

This is not all that threatens immanent criticism because under the force of the integration of the subjective and objective moments of the societal totality "even the immanent method is eventually overtaken by this. It is dragged into the abyss by its object. The materialistic transparency of culture has not made it more honest, only more vulgar."[147] Attendant upon the change in the nature of the work of art as kitsch (which parallels that of ideology) from affirmative culture to a bare advertisement for the already existent is raised the question of the possibility of immanent criticism which is simultaneously the question about the possibility of autonomous art today: the recalcitrance of the work of art towards its co-optation into a commodity through the culture industry.

Indeed, Adorno notes that with the debasement of culture into kitsch something rather distinct from a mechanical and reified transcendent criticism is required.

> Hence, the task of criticism must not be so much to search for the particular interest groups, to which cultural phenomena are to be assigned, but rather to decipher the general social tendencies which are expressed in these phenomena and through which the most powerful interests realize themselves. Cultural criticism must become social physiognomy.[148]

---

[145] Idem, "Theses on the Sociology of Art," pp. 127-28, and "Commitment," in *Aesthetics and Politics*, pp. 177-95.

[146] Idem, "Culture Criticism and Society," pp. 32-33.

[147] Ibid., p. 34. A corollary to this is the threat posed to even the autonomous work of art: "Today every phenomenon of culture, even if a model of integrity, is liable to be suffocated in the cultivation of kitsch" [idem, "Commitment," p. 194]. For an example of this, see Adorno's essay, "Bach Defended against His Devotees," in *Prisms*, pp. 133-46.

[148] Ibid., p. 30.

Yet such a task is also different from that of immanent criticism. With regard to culture as kitsch, a form of transcendent criticism emerges in the work of Adorno, not with regard to a longitudinal and expressive notion of totality which presupposes a reconciliation of the subject and object of history, but with regard to a synchronic notion of totality which calls by its true name the hegemony of the social whole and unmasks its products as "insignias of the absolute rule of that which is."[149] In the theory of the culture industry, of the integration of the production, distribution and consumption of culture as a commodity, emerges that moment of thought towards totality in recognition that the synchronic whole is the false, the rigidification of society and history into a "second nature." Thus there emerges in Adorno's work a two-pronged mode of procedure: a form of transcendent criticism in the theory of the culture industry by which its "one-dimensional" products are analyzed through reference to the force of the false synchronic totality, and a form of immanent criticism of autonomous art in which the analysis of the form and technique of the work of art articulates the antinomies of the synchronic totality thus bearing a mute and broken witness to a normative whole, the reconciliation of subject and object.

"Culture industry" refers to the systematic character of kitsch today which as industry is the interlocking of production, distribution and consumption which forms a self-reproducing whole.[150] If formerly the nature of the work of art was its never altogether contradictory claim to a purposefulness-without-purpose, then that of the products of the culture industry today is a purposelessness-with-purpose, i.e., a liberation from thought which acts in the interests of the anonymous whole to insure that things will remain as they are.

> If one were to compress within one sentence what the ideology of mass culture actually adds up to, one would have to represent this as a parody of the injunction: "Become that which thou art": as the exaggerated duplication and justification of already existing conditions and the deprivation of all transcendence and critique.[151]

The genius of the culture industry is that by passing off its commodities as mere "diversion," as that which has no power over people's existence, it entraps them in that existence all the more tightly, even as it simulta-

---

149   Ibid., p. 34.
150   Horkheimer and Adorno, *Dialectic of Enlightenment*, pp. 120-67, and Adorno, "Culture Industry Reconsidered," passim.
151   [Frankfurt Institute], *Aspects of Sociology*, p. 202.

neously cheats them of the *promesse du bonheur* of traditional affirmative culture. Culture industry accomplishes what in fascism was only accomplished through the slogan of "crisis": the negation of the distinction between the private and public sphere with the former organized as an appendage to the latter. Mass culture as produced and marketed by the culture industry is the 20th century opiate of the people which, unlike its 19th century counterpart, suppresses the sighs of the oppressed into boredom and triviality.

> Amusement under late capitalism is the prolongation of work. It is sought after as an escape from the mechanized work process, and to recruit strength in order to be able to cope with it again. But at the same time mechanization has such a power over a man's leisure and happiness, and so profoundly determines the manufacture of amusement goods, that his experiences are inevitably after images of the work process itself.[152]

The products of the culture industry are stamped with the mark of their origin. The message of that industry—the sheer representation of *das Immergleiche*—migrates into the inner consistency of the work itself. In the sphere of music this one-dimensionality reveals itself in the dialectic of standardization and pseudoindividuality of contemporary popular music whose contrast is the integral mediation of the detail as containing and leading to the whole and the whole summoning forth the specific detail in the traditional work of art.[153] This dynamic interrelation of part and whole becomes a static one between a predigested framework and the fungible detail. The identity-nonidentity between part and whole mediated by compositional technique is reduced to an identity of framework and specious detail whose synthesis is the elusive "commercial hit." In comparison to the level of technique of "good art," "popular music constitutes the dregs of musical history" which, precisely because of its fixation on a compositional "lowest denominator" which is regarded as a second nature, demands that "the standardization of that music should be interpreted not so much intramusically as sociologi-

[152] Horkheimer and Adorno, *Dialectic of Enlightenment*, p. 137.
[153] The bulk of the following analysis is drawn from Adorno's essays: "On Popular Music," *ZfS* 9 (1941): 17-48; "A Social Critique of Radio Music," *Kenyon Review* 8 (Spring 1945): 208-17; and "The Radio Symphony: An Experiment in Theory," in *Radio Research 1941* (New York: Harper and Bros., 1941). That such an analysis is not simply confined to the sphere of music, see Adorno, "Television and the Patterns of Mass Culture," in Bernard Rosenberg and David Manning White, eds., *Mass Culture: The Popular Arts in America* (New York: The Free Press, 1957), pp. 474-88.

cally."[154] It should be interpreted as the direct immanence of the societal whole in the sphere of music. Further, "structural standardization aims at standardized reactions";[155] it accomplishes a preformation of listening such that "the composition itself hears for the listener."[156] It functions to impart to the listener that he or she is always "on safe ground." The sense of familiarity and security in the face of the trivial and its attendant deconcentration of listening which is relieved not by "structural listening"[157] but the glimmer of recognition leads subjectively to the regression of listening even as it leads objectively from music into *Muzak*. This structurally infantile grammar, a pastiche of clichés whose hallmark is stereotypical aesthetic residues fostering a specious personalization and identification, is common to all the products of the culture industry.

It is perhaps in the sphere of distribution that the transformations in the work of art become manifest. Formerly, the "use-value" of the work of art was its "uselessness." Its autonomy was defined by its resistance to the system of exchange-value, from which it offered a moment of respite. In "mass culture," however, there is a change in the nature of the work itself: the very uselessness of the work becomes something quite useful for the service of capital, and this signifies the transformation of the work into "exchange-value," a commodity from which a profit is to be made. Under the conditions of late capitalism, the life of art is kitsch and, more specifically, kitsch as commodity.[158]

Within the sphere of distribution, the commodity character of the culture industry's products can be seen in the concepts of "administrative research" and "advertising." While the former represents an internal control mechanism for the rationalization of production and distribution through research of market preferences (which themselves are socially mediated), the latter through various strategies ("plugging," the fetishization of "stars," etc.) seeks to break down the resistance "to the ever-equal or identical by, as it were, closing the avenues of escape from the ever-equal. It leads the listener to become enraptured

154   Adorno, *Introduction to the Sociology of Music*, trans. E. B. Ashton (New York: Seabury Press, 1976), p. 29.
155   Idem, "On Popular Music," p. 29.
156   Ibid., p. 22.
157   For Adorno's "phenomenology" of "listening" to music as "expert," "good listener," "culture consumer," "emotional listener," "resentment listener," and the listener to "music as entertainment," see *Introduction to the Sociology of Music*, pp. 1-20.
158   Adorno, "Culture and Administration," *Telos* 37 (1978): 98-99, and *Minima Moralia*, pp. 225-27.

with the inescapable."[159] Advertising and culture industry merge, because both have the same task: the pseudoindividualization of the standardized.

> Advertising and the culture industry merge technically as well as economically. In both cases the same thing can be seen in innumerable places, and the mechanical repetition of the same culture product has come to be the same as that of the propaganda slogan. In both cases the insistent demand for effectiveness makes technology into psychotechnology, into a procedure for manipulating men. In both cases the standards are the striking yet familiar, the easy yet catchy, the skillful yet simple; the object is to overpower the customer, who is conceived as absent-minded or resistant.[160]

The counterpart to kitsch as exchange-value is that its abstractness migrates into the subject through its consumption. As distinct from "empirical sociology," critical theory maintains that "the fetish character of the commodity is not a fact of consciousness; rather, it is dialectical, in the sense that it produces consciousness" and that the force of the culture industry is "less a matter of single experiences than of cumulative effect."[161] In encountering its own social product abstractly, as a "second nature," subjectivity—or, in the case of music, the listening ear—regresses in a mimesis of the commodity:

> The counterpart to the fetishism of music is a regression of listening. . . . Regressive listening is tied to production by the machinery of distribution, and particularly by advertising. . . . The fetish character of music produces its own camouflage through the identification of the listener with the fetish.[162]

The subject becomes the consumer who has "empathy with exchange-value" (Benjamin), that is, with something other than the work.

The regression of listening to a distracted, deconcentrated and atomistic posture where "understanding" becomes the subjective satisfaction of recognition imparting a sense of novelty to the trivial along with a sense of ownership over that which is recognized is an adequate response to the one-dimensionality of the culture industry.[163] However,

---

159 Idem, "On the Fetish Character in Music and the Regression of Listening," in *The Essential Frankfurt School Reader*, p. 280.
160 Horkheimer and Adorno, *Dialectic of Enlightenment*, p. 163.
161 Idem, "Theses on the Sociology of Art," p. 123.
162 Idem, "Fetish Character of Music," pp. 286-88.
163 Idem, "On Popular Music," pp. 32-37.

the force of the culture industry under the regression of listening is that the distinction between popular and high culture is abolished even as it is posited by that industry's market strategies, because the latter also takes on a fetish character in its reproduction and distribution and is abstractly consumed. The ear does not hear the work but screens out the complex into a purified melody and abstracts from the dynamism of the concrete whole by focusing on the detail. Listening becomes pervasive inattention punctuated by attentive excitement at the "high" points of a work. Distracted listening deconstructs serious music into "Muzak of the sublime."[164] Distracted listening, as second nature, is the reification of the subject and witnesses not only to a regression of capability for aesthetic experience, but since art, at its best, has always had a cognitive dimension; it witnesses to a regression of thought itself, a resignation to a return of the same which degrades the subject into an object: "the liquidation of the individual is the real signature of the new musical situation."[165]

The life of traditional serious art today is a mere semblance of life—it survives as something "other than art"—as kitsch and a trigger for emotions otherwise socially repressed and thus as a rationalized sphere for the irrational. There is more than just a tinge of sadomasochism in "mass culture": rage and boredom lie near the surface and erupt in the phenomenon of "fadism" and the merciless and sadistic "parodying" of its commodities by the culture industry itself particularly in film and television.[166] In late industrial society, kitsch not only endures but becomes through the culture industry inescapable, and the response of the subject "corresponds to the behavior of the prisoner who loves his cell because he has been left nothing else to love."[167] Indeed, the culture industry is

---

[164] Georg Steiner, *In Bluebeard's Castle* (New Haven: Yale University Press, 1971), p. 119.

[165] Adorno, "The Fetish Character of Music," p. 276.

[166] Idem, "On Popular Music," pp. 42-48 on the ambivalence and "latent sadism" of popular music. To a great extent, Adorno's objection to both jazz and the music of Stravinsky was that in its primitivistic objectivism, such music signified the sadistic triumph of the collective over the individual, the unconscious over the ego. On jazz, see Hektor Rottweiler [Adorno], "*Über Jazz*," *ZfS* 5 (1936): 235-57; Adorno, review of *American Jazz Music*, by Wilder Hobson, and *Jazz Hot and Hybrid*, by Winthrop Sargeant, *ZfS* 9 (1941): 167-78; and "Perennial Fashion—Jazz," in *Prisms*, pp. 121-32. On Stravinsky, see *Philosophy of Modern Music*, pp. 135-217, esp. pp. 139-48, 157-72, 175-81.

[167] Idem, "The Fetish Character of Music," p. 280.

that "prism" through which industrial society is interpreted by Adorno and Horkheimer.

The core of Adorno's reflections on art and society is that its object is given in *both* the historical and socially mediated relations to historical and socially mediated forms, where the latter refers not only to specific aesthetic genres but also to the level of technique and *Durchbildung* in the work of art.[168] Axiomatic for Adorno is his defense of the centrality of "technique" to the work of art as *art* and hence his defense of the avant-garde and the position that the mediation of society into the work is precisely through this formal element. "Society determines in the work of art what is expressed in its content by means of its formal structures."[169] In the compositional techniques of the work of art are the traces of the social totality. Thus sociology of art and aesthetics converge.

This, too, affects the question of "autonomous art" today which is historically and socially mediated and not a "once and for all" achievement. "The hermetic work of art belongs to the bourgeois, the mechanical work belongs to fascism, and the fragmentary work, in its complete state of negativity, belongs to utopia."[170] More specifically, for the last as autonomous art:

---

[168] More precisely, "aesthetics" *is* the "sociology of art" where the latter is not mere empirical research but a dialectical consideration of the vicissitudes of the work of art in its production, distribution, circulation and consumption. Insofar as "production" does not refer to the psychology of the artist but the level of compositional technique which makes the work of art an aesthetic whole, the sociology of art preserves within itself the classical concerns of aesthetics.

[169] Adorno, *Aesthetische Theorie*, ed., Gretel Adorno and Rolf Tiedemann (Frankfurt: Suhrkamp Taschenbuch, 1970), p. 342. Here it may also be noted that at the crux of Adorno's dispute with Georg Lukács was the former's insistence on the centrality of compositional technique for the work of art—as in the works of the avant-garde—as distinct from any "realism" of its "subject-matter." See Adorno, "Reconciliation under Duress," in *Aesthetics and Politics*, pp. 151-76. Helpful as a "guide" to Adorno's *Aesthetische Theorie* is Martin Zenck, *Kunst als Begriffslose Erkenntnis* (Munich: Fink, 1977); Karol Auerland, *Einfuhrung in die Aesthetik Adornos* (Berlin: Fink, 1979); and Richard Wolin, *Walter Benjamin: An Aesthetic of Redemption* (New York: Columbia University Press, 1982).

[170] Idem, *Philosophy of Modern Music*, p. 126. What Adorno here terms the "hermetic" work of art is what is also often termed the "affirmative" work of art—affirmative in that it positively and concretely exhibits the *promèsse du bonheur* of reconciliation. The "fragmentary" work as an art of *Grausamkeit* witnesses as a determinate negation of "what is" to utopia which it refuses to depict and which, for Adorno, is the form of autonomous art today. Indeed, one of the major differences between Adorno's and Marcuse's aesthetic theories is that the latter still continued to look at

> A successful work . . . is not one which resolves objective [societal] contradictions in a spurious harmony, but one which expresses the idea of harmony negatively by embodying the contradictions, pure and uncompromised, in its innermost structure.[171]

There are three contexts which circumscribe Adorno's position on autonomous art and his defense of aesthetic modernism which received its quintessential expression in the posthumously published *Aesthetische Theorie*. Each moment inheres in and specifies the others and each begets its own antinomy. Taken together as a "constellation," they define what autonomous art is today as well as its fragility. Needless to say, what follows is not a full exposition of Adorno's aesthetics and defense of modern art, let alone its relation to the aesthetics of Brecht, Benjamin and Lukács to which it is intimately, if negatively, related.

Autonomous art exists today, first, as the art of the avant-garde, as art of "advanced technique."[172] In this context, appeal is most often made to the sphere of music which functions as a privileged aesthetic sphere for Adorno insofar as it is that sphere which most completely sublates its subject matter into compositional technique.[173] The ideal of the aesthetic *Durchbildung* and *Durchformung* of the work of art—the preeminent example is Adorno's defense of Schönberg in *Philosophy of Modern Music*—is a systematic deconstruction of the second nature of traditional aesthetic forms which, in the case of music, leads to a radical revolution in the tonal system: a rejection of the elements of triadic construction, of the difference between major and minor keys and of the difference between consonance and dissonance which seeks to reconstitute the whole solely from the exigencies of technical composition.[174] "Progress" in art refers to this progressive technicization and sublation of subject matter into form, and as the "technological work of art," autonomous art today protests the reification of artistic technique to the "traditional" or "classical."[175] To be sure, if to understand tradition is to understand it differently (Gadamer), there is a continuity within the rupture: modern

the *promèsse du bonheur* as the hallmark of the work of art, while for Adorno that "promise" could only be present in its absence.
[171] Idem, "Culture Criticism and Society," p. 32.
[172] Idem, "Reconciliation under Duress," pp. 153, 159-68.
[173] Idem, *Minima Moralia*, p. 223.
[174] Idem, *Philosophy of Modern Music*, pp. 48-71, and "Arnold Schoenberg, 1874-1951," in *Prisms*, pp. 149-72.
[175] Idem, "Music and Technique," *Telos* 32 (1977): 79-86, and "Music and the New Music," *Telos* 32 (1977): 124-28, 132-33.

music in its commitment to compositional autonomy and the integration of all musical parameters (melody, harmony, counterpoint and rhythm) continues that ideal which also permeated traditional music but which only was manifest in that music's inconsistencies and fissures.

The antinomy of such an approach is the tension between technique and aesthetic "aura," where the latter refers to the "power," "spell," and "uniqueness" of the work of art—its claim to represent something absolute, its gesture of authenticity, of being-just-so-and-not-otherwise. As technically advanced, autonomous art today represents a deauraticization (*Entzauberung*) of art.

> Throughout the course of history the artist becomes more and more consciously and freely the master of his material and his forms and thus works against the magic spell of his own product. But it is only his incessant endeavor towards achieving this conscious control and constructive power, only the attack of artistic autonomy on the magic element from which this selfsame element draws the strength to survive and to make itself felt in new and more adequate forms . . . the only possible way to save the "spell" of art is the denial of this spell by art itself.[176]

The complete eradication of "aura," however, would be the self-liquidation of art. The deauraticization of art through technique is left with the task of dialectically sublating magic in technique: "Aura itself, liberated from its claim to be real, is an aspect of enlightenment. Its illusory appearance deauraticizes the deauraticized world. This is the dialectical ether in which art lives today."[177] Indeed, it is this dialectic which underlies Adorno's reticence concerning Schönberg's consistent "row technique." This reduces the work of art to a technological whole in which the abolition of the subject by the compositional technique through which the work attains objectivity is at the same time the dominance of the abstract subject over the work.[178] Certainly, this is not to return music back to pure subjective intention, but "objectivity itself calls this subject home to the composition."[179]

Second, autonomous art today is that art which resists the trivialization of the culture industry. It was noted that the culture industry's power lies in its ability to abolish the distinction between "high" and

[176] Idem, "Theses upon Art and Religion Today," *Kenyon Review* 7 (Fall 1945): 680-81.
[177] Idem, *Aesthetische Theorie*, p. 93.
[178] Idem, "Music and Technique," pp. 90-94.
[179] Ibid., p. 191.

"popular" culture. Through its fidelity to "advanced technique" autonomous art is art which unmasks the reification of the subject by renouncing effortless consumption. Its asceticism, its taboo on ornamentation serving diversion and its renunciation of an affirmative communicative meaning is its response to subjective regression under the sway of the culture industry.

> The terror which Schönberg and Weber spread, today as in the past, comes not from their incomprehensibility but from the fact that they are all too correctly understood. Their music gives form to that anxiety, that terror, that insight into the catastrophic situation which others merely evade by regressing.[180]

Yet this, too, brings its own antinomy. Autonomous art as the "societal antithesis to society" risks becoming impotent and elitist in its recalcitrance to the hegemony of the culture industry. Its reception either becomes obstructed or "planned" for groups of experts.[181] Further, it is made dependent upon those institutions against which it rebels.[182] Ironically, private commission and patronage reemerge as the objective, social condition of the work and art's autonomy is tainted with a complicity which threatens the loss of its own inner tensions.

> The word "New Music" confirms the relegation of this music—in terms of institutional or yellow-page categories—to studios, special organizations and presentations, thus involuntarily limiting its own claim to truth and consequent general validity, while without such organized help this music would atrophy hopelessly.[183]

At best, marginalization is its fate; at worst, trivialization.

Finally, autonomous art exists today only as an *Entkunstung*, a deaestheticized art which is an art of *Grausamkeit*. It is art which gives a voice to those silent victims whose lives—and deaths—give the lie to the affirmation that all is right in the world. Its social substance is "shock," "dissonance" and "suffering" which tears the mask from the illusion of false happiness.[184] It witnesses to the subject by representing her as

---

[180] Idem, "The Fetish Character of Music," p. 298. See, also, "Music and New Music," pp. 128-33, 135.
[181] Idem, "Music and New Music," pp. 134-35.
[182] Idem, "Culture and Administration," pp. 101-2.
[183] Idem, "Music and New Music," p. 125.
[184] Idem, *Philosophy of Modern Music*, pp. 29-46, 112-33, and "Music and New Music," passim.

maimed and dominated by society—and therein resides the "truth" of Schönberg's "twelve tone technique." Its meaning is the absence of meaning, and in its renunciation of expression and communication this art becomes cognition, cognition of the horror which is. Through its renunciation of a representation of the *promesse du bonheur*, of the "beautiful appearance" which is the hallmark of the traditional work of art, it witnesses to this promise, albeit indirectly and negatively. Autonomous art exists today only as critique, as a negative dialectics which inscribes itself in the very form of the work itself.

> The unresolved antagonisms of society return in the work of art as the immanent problems of its form....Art apprehends the essence of social reality and forces this essence to appear against the appearances of society. Art becomes knowledge of society because it seizes and takes up the essential and not because it discusses, depicts or imitates society directly.[185]

Refracted in the technical composition of autonomous art is the untruth of the whole. The rupture with the affirmative art of bourgeois culture occurs here. In an age when the reconciliation of subject and object has taken on the guise of the subjugation of subjects as objects to an anonymous social totality, the affirmative and reconciliatory moment of the traditional work of art is a form of false consciousness: a masking of the objective situation, even while through the substitute gratification of its pleasure, it functions to affirm the status quo thus betraying the very reconciliation of subject and object and promise of happiness which it affirms. The force and meaning of the first two moments receive their full articulation only in this third.

Crucial in this respect is the role which Auschwitz, the Holocaust, came to play in the thought of Adorno. It is the "caesura" "which defies human imagination as it distills a real hell from human evil" and which inscribes the lie of all culture in general, affirmative culture in particular and mass culture *par excellence*.

> To write poetry after Auschwitz is barbaric . . . .[186]

> All post-Auschwitz culture, including its urgent critique, is garbage. . . .[187]

> Perennial suffering has as much right to expression as a tortured man has to scream; hence it may have been wrong to say that after Auschwitz you

185   Idem, *Aesthetische Theorie*, pp. 16, 384.
186   Idem, "Culture Criticism and Society," p. 34.

could no longer write poems. But it is not wrong to raise the less cultural question whether after Auschwitz you can go on living. . . .[188]

After Auschwitz, affirmative art is not merely false consciousness but blasphemous. Autonomous art today can exist only as a witness in solidarity with the victim. In the mediation of constructive-technical and mimetic-expressive moments in the work of art, suffering finds a voice which does not immediately betray it by transmuting it into meaning.

> The abundance of real suffering tolerates no forgetting . . . it also demands the continued existence of art while it prohibits it; it is now virtually in art alone that suffering can find its own voice, consolation, without immediately being betrayed by it.[189]

If the existence of suffering today demands the continued existence of art, this too is not unproblematic because the primordial wound of art generates its own antinomy: that its representation is already reconciliation.

> The so-called artistic representation of the sheer physical pain of people beaten to the ground by rifle-butts contains, however remotely, the power to

---

[187] Idem, *Negative Dialectics*, p. 367.

[188] Ibid., p. 362.

[189] Idem, "Commitment," p. 188. It is also worth noting at this point that this same exigency to remember suffering also establishes critical theory's relationship with "tradition." "It is inhuman to forget because accumulated pain will be forgotten. The historical trace in things and words, colors and sounds is always the trace of past suffering. On account of this, tradition today stands before an insoluble contradiction. No tradition is available to take one's oath on—each person extinguishes it and thus begins the march into barbarism." [Idem, *"Thesen uber Tradition,"* in *Ohne Leitbild: Parva Aesthetica* (Frankfurt: Suhrkamp, 1967), p. 35]. Here I would also further suggest that the reflections of Adorno on the task and status of the work of art today parallels those of Metz on revelation as circumscribed by the *memoria passionis et resurrectionis Jesu Christi*. Both are conjoined in the exigency to preserve—without noetic reconciliation—the sensuousness of suffering as having a final claim on the attention of men and women and as a protest against the social whole because "it is part of the mechanism of domination to forbid recognition of the suffering it produces. . . ." [Adorno, *Minima Moralia*, p. 63]. Finally, I suggest that if the theological understanding of "revelation" has its formal parallel in the philosophical understanding of "the work of art," then Metz' implicit understanding of revelation has more of an elective affinity with Adorno's understanding of the autonomous work of art today—within the context of aesthetics as a sociology of art—than with Gadamer's understanding of the "classic."

elicit enjoyment out of it. The moral of this art, not to forget for a single moment, slithers into the abyss of its opposite.[190]

Autonomous art exists today only tenuously, fragilely. Its contradictions are those of a society become barbaric even while "enlightened." "It has become self-evident that nothing which concerns art is self-evident any longer: neither art taken on its own terms nor in its relation to society as a whole or even its very right to exist."[191]

DOMINATION OVER SELF[192]

Let me begin this section by describing two different topics which appear extraneous to each other: the first concerns the interpretation of Odysseus and "sacrifice" within the *Dialectic of Enlightenment*; the second concerns the proletariat in the early work of Lukács. A transformation of the notion of sacrifice is symbolized in Odysseus. Sacrifice which once witnessed the antagonism of the collective and the individual, and the objective claims of the self-preservation of the former over the latter, becomes internalized within the heroic subject. Sacrifice lives on as self-renunciation and self-denial for the sake of self-preservation.[193] The crucial transformation is that the self-to-be-preserved is the rational subject as "ego": as the center of organization and control, manipulation and domination.

---

[190] Ibid., p. 189.

[191] Idem, *Aesthetische Theorie*, p. 9.

[192] For an overview regarding Marxism and psychoanalysis, see Reuben Osborn, *Marxism and Psychoanalysis*, with an introduction by James Strachey (New York: Octagon Books, 1965); Paul A. Robinson, *The Freudian Left: Wilhelm Reich, Geza Roheim, Herbert Marcuse* (New York: Harper and Row, 1969); Bruce Brown, *Marx, Freud, and the Critique of Everyday Life* (New York: Monthly Review Press, 1973). For an overview of the "Frankfurt School's" appropriation of Freud, see Jay, *The Dialectical Imagination*, pp. 86-112; Held, *An Introduction to Critical Theory*, pp. 111-47; and, especially, Russell Jacoby, *Social Amnesia: A Critique of Contemporary Psychology from Adler to Laing* (Boston: Beacon Press, 1975). For perhaps the best attempt to retrieve the original but now suppressed political dimension of psychoanalysis, see Jacoby, *The Repression of Psychoanalysis: Otto Fenichel and the Political Freudians* (New York: Basic Books, 1983). An indispensable collection of primary source material regarding the uneasy alliance between Marxism and psychoanalysis can be found in Hans Jorg Sankuhler, ed., *Psychoanalyse und Marxismus: Dokumentation einer Kontroverse* (Frankfurt: Suhrkamp Verlag, 1970).

[193] Horkheimer and Adorno, *Dialectic of Enlightenment*, pp. 43-58.

The adventures of Odysseus, the noble landowner who barters and haggles with the gods, are so many attempts to detour him from his course, to swallow up the ego which has emerged. The idyll of the Lotus-eaters, the barbaric age proper of hunters and herdsmen who lack any organization of social labor (Cyclops Polyphemus) and the magic stage, symbolized by Circe and her enticement of resignation to "animal" instinct, are all impermissible for one who has embarked upon the course of rational self-preservation. Yet the plight of men and women, in thralldom to nature yet able to outwit it by cunning, is best depicted in Odysseus' adventure with the Sirens. Odysseus will not resist the temptation of their chthonic song, but also will not forgo the rational self control which has been attained. Nature is mastered, but the price it exacts, sacrifice and renunciation, betrays it as the true master. Yet in this process is not more given away than vindicated?

> In class history, the enmity of the self to sacrifice implied a sacrifice of the self, inasmuch as it was paid for by a denial of nature in man for the sake of domination over non-human nature, and over other men. This very denial, the nucleus of all civilizing rationality, is the germ cell of a proliferating mythic irrationality: with the denial of nature in man not merely the telos of outward control but the telos of man's own life is distorted and befogged. As soon as man discards his awareness that he himself is in nature, all the aims for which he keeps himself alive—social progress, the intensification of all his material and spiritual powers, even consciousness itself—are nullified and the enthronement of the means as an end, which under late capitalism is tantamount to open insanity, is already perceptible in the pre-history of subjectivity. Man's domination over himself, which ground his selfhood, is almost always the destruction of the subject in whose service it is undertaken; for the substance which is dominated, suppressed, and dissolved by virtue of self-preservation is none other than that very life as functions of which the achievements of self-preservation find their sole definition and determination: it is, in fact, what is to be preserved. . . . The history of civilization is the history of the introversion of sacrifice. In other words: the history of renunciation. Everyone who practices renunciation gives away more of his life than is given back to him: and more than the life that he vindicates.[194]

---

[194] Ibid., p. 54. See, also, *Eclipse of Reason*, pp. 105-12, where "ego" is explicitly identified with the functions of domination, command and organization, such that "the history of Western civilization could be written in terms of the growth of the ego as the underling sublimates, that is internalizes, the commands of his master who has preceded him in self-discipline" [ibid., p. 106].

Lukács' theoretical position is contextualized by two rather contradictory positions. On the one hand, he accepts Rosa Luxemburg's mechanical theory of the crisis of capitalism which guarantees the integrity of a *Gesamttotalität* of history and society. On the other hand, there is his acceptance of Lenin's voluntarist understanding of the revolutionary organization of praxis. The intersection of these is Lukács theory of the reification of the class consciousness of the proletariat by which the *Gesamttotalität* of history is mediated and necessarily realized by the proletariat.

For Lukács, the proletariat is the subject-object of history. It assumes this privileged role insofar as it is, along with the bourgeois, the only "pure" class in capitalist society.[195] The self-consciousness of the proletariat is inextricably bound with a knowledge of the objective conditions of society. In understanding itself, the proletariat must understand society as a totality, that is, society as it is and its immanent potential. In understanding society as a totality, the proletariat understands itself. The crux of this self-knowledge is to see through the reification of bourgeois society in all its manifestations where "reification" is understood as a uneasy unification of Marx's fetish of the commodity as exchange-value, Weber's rationalization through bureaucratization of the social world and Simmel's understanding of the objectification of the cultural world as objective *Geist* as "alienation." This defines bourgeois society where for its participants "their own social movement possesses for they themselves the form of a movement of things under whose control they stand, instead of controlling it."[196]

The problem which arises is that the proletariat is subject to the reifying form of consciousness which is the historical product constituting capitalist society. The proletariat itself undergoes a process of "embourgeoisement." Thus a distinction between the "empirical" and "imputed" class consciousness of the proletariat is necessary. While empirically the proletariat is unable to achieve true self-consciousness and grasp society as a whole in relation to its and hence society's final goal, the realm of freedom, the imputed class consciousness is attained by inferring

---

[195] Lukács, "Reification and the Consciousness of the Proletariat," pp. 149-208, and "Class Consciousness," in *History and Class Consciousness*, pp. 46-78.
[196] Karl Marx, *Capital*, 3 vols., trans. Ben Fowkes and David Fernback, with an introduction by Ernest Mandel (New York: Vintage Books, 1977-82), 1: 173.

. . . the thoughts and feelings which men would have in a particular situation if they were able to assess both it and the interests arising from it in their impact on immediate action and on the whole structure of society.[197]

Given this gap between empirical and imputed class consciousness, there is a need for a mediator, the "party," to assume control, organization and direction of the proletariat and to practically mediate what it theoretically knows inevitably to be the case given the economic contradictions of capitalism.[198] For Adorno and Horkheimer, Lukács' recourse to the "party" was as questionable as the notion of an expressive totality which underlies his work as a whole. If the latter reduced the indeterminateness of history to mere appearance through what was ultimately an economic scientism, the former merely justified a situation of domination for the sake of the proletariat which subsequent history has all too concretely shown to be barbaric.

In the ensuing void given the impotence of the proletariat in those contexts in which their consciousness was theoretically anticipated to be most advanced, the task arises to discover "why men passively adjust to a condition of unchanged destructive irrationality or why they enroll in movements whose contradiction to their own interests is in no way difficult to perceive."[199] At this juncture and as distinct from the example of Lukács, Gramsci and Korsch whose appeals to subjectivity were considered "abstract," Horkheimer and Adorno turn to appropriate Freudian psychoanalysis whose categories yielded, they believed, a more concrete depiction of the vicissitudes of the subject.

Analytic psychology is appropriated in order to delineate the subjective mediation of objective society where the irrationality of the societal whole migrates into the inner consistency of the subject who conforms to and reproduces that whole. The use of the categories and theoretical framework of Freud takes the form of a "negative psychoanalysis:"[200] a

---

[197] Lukács, "Class Consciousness," p. 51.

[198] Idem, "Towards a Methodology of the Problem of Organization," in *History and Class Consciousness*, pp. 295-342.

[199] Adorno, *Stichworte*, pp. 182-83, cited in Jacoby, *Social Amnesia*, p. 78. It is this rupture between the identity of the *Gesamtsubjekt* and *Gesamttotalität* of history which specifies and marks the earliest appropriation of Freud by the Frankfurt School. As that identity crumbles in history, recourse to the framework of psychoanalysis is made to "explain" the continuing acquiescence to domination which is not in the "rational" interests of those dominated. See Horkheimer, "*Geschichte und Psychologie*," *ZfS* 1 (1932): 135.

[200] Jacoby, *Social Amnesia*, pp. 73-100.

theory of the ruptures and fissures of the subject, not as an isolated "in it-self" but as the dialectical counterpart to the objective whole. Psychoanalysis "discovers the historical dynamics of society in the microcosm of the monad, as it were, in the mental conflicts of the individual."[201] As a nonsubjective theory of the subject, the use of such categories by the two men is to describe the price which the subject as the concrete nexus between nature and society pays on behalf of the societal whole.

> As long as economic rationality remains partial and the rationality of the whole problematic, irrational forces will be harnessed to perpetuate it. The irrationality of the rational system emerges in the psychology of its trapped subjects.[202]

It is this perspective which forms the context of the Institute's studies on authority and the family and anti-Semitism.

Concomitant with an appropriation of Freud's thought, Adorno and, to a lesser degree, Horkheimer maintained a strident polemic against Freudian revisionists. The crux of the issue was that they substituted for the conflict-model of character formation and its key notions of the Oedipal situation and the "biological" parameters of the psyche in the theory of instincts either a model of socialization based upon a diffuse notion of "role-modeling" or a reification of subjectivity where the crises of a subject were managed through the "common sense" of adjustment or self-actualization. What appeared questionable to Adorno and Horkheimer was that under the guise of an "advance" beyond Freud through the introduction of a cultural dimension to counteract his alleged "biologism" and "mechanistic scientism," there occurred the harmonization of actual conflict under the assumption of a homogeneity of the subject and society.[203] By this, revisionism showed itself to be the ally of the emergent institutionalized "helping professions" (industrial psychology, social work, family therapy, marriage/sex counseling, juvenile jurisprudence) and the victim of its own reformist, progressivist ideol-

---

[201] Horkheimer, in *Tensions that Cause War*, ed. Hadley Cantril (Urbana: University of Illinois Press, 1950), p. 38, cited in Jacoby, *Social Amnesia*, p. 34.

[202] Adorno, "Sociology and Psychology," *New Left Review* 46/47 (December 1967/January 1968): 72.

[203] Idem, *Minima Moralia*, pp. 58-66, and "*Die rividierte Psychoanalyse*," in *Gesammelte Schriften*, vol. 8: *Soziologische Schriften I* (Frankfurt: Suhrkamp, 1972), pp. 20-41.

ogy.[204] Further, the transition in emphasis from theory to therapy fetishized the subject precisely to the degree to which it was already occluded. The humanism of Freud lay in the witness of his theory to the conflictual character of the subject.

> The greatness of Freud, like that of the other radical bourgeois thinkers, consists in that he allowed such contradictions to stand unresolved. He scorned the pretense that there was a systematic harmony where the thing itself is in inner strife.[205]

To be sure, Freud himself is censured for his tendency to transmute the intrapsychic into the doubtfully factual and thus hypostasize the particular conjuncture of psyche, nature and society as an eternal "in itself."[206] Yet the eclipse of the contradictions between society and humans as a part of nature, and the taboo on a theory of depth psychology in favor of a one-dimensional therapy of optimistic conformism witnesses to the false consciousness of the revisionists: "it perpetuates conceptually the split between the living subject and the objectivity that governs the subjects yet derives from them."[207] The conclusion is, to paraphrase a thought which Adorno articulated in another context, psychology and sociology are both torn halves which do not add up to an integral whole. Like sociology as critical theory, the truth of psychology endures in critique. "The only totality the student of society can presume to know is the antagonistic whole. . . . Every 'image of man' is ideology except the negative one."[208]

In the first part of this section, the quote from *Dialectic of Enlightenment* states that the affirmation of the self as "ego" is only at the expense of that which is repressed, the self as a piece of nature, as "id" and that this opposition of ego and id is the conflictual basis of all civilization and society. However, in the same work, a different aspect of the subject matter comes to the foreground.

> The individual . . . arose as a dynamic cell of economic activity. Emancipated from tutelage at earlier stages of economic development, he was interested only in himself: as a proletarian, by hiring his services through the labor market, and through continual adaptation to new techni-

[204] See, for example, Christopher Lasch, *Haven in a Heartless World: The Family Besieged* (New York: Basic Books, 1977).
[205] Adorno, "Die revidierte Psychoanalyse," p. 40.
[206] Idem, "Sociology and Psychology," p. 86.
[207] Ibid., p. 69.
[208] Ibid., p. 94.

cal conditions; and, as an entrepreneur, through tireless attempts to approx-
imate to the ideal type *homo economicus*. Psychoanalysis represented the internal "small business" which grew up in this way as a complex dynamic
system of the conscious and the unconscious, the id, ego and superego. In
the conflict with the superego, the social check mechanism of the individual,
the ego holds the psychological drives within the limits of self-preservation.
The friction surfaces are large, and neuroses—the *faux frais* of this instinctive
economy—are inescapable. However, the complex mental apparatus made
possible to some extent that free interplay of subjects on which the market
economy was based. But in the era of great business enterprises and world
wars the mediation of the social processes through innumerable monads
proves retrograde. The subjects of the economy are psychologically expropriated, and the economy is more rationally operated by society itself. The
individual no longer has to decide what he himself is to do in a painful inner dialectic of conscience, self-preservation and drives. Decisions for men
as active workers are taken by the hierarchy ranging from trade associations
to the national administration, and in the private sphere by the system of
mass culture which takes over the last inward impulses of individuals, who
are forced to consume what is offered to them. The committees and stars
serve as the ego and superego, and the masses, who have lost the last semblance of personality, shape themselves more easily according to the models
presented to them than the instincts ever could by the mechanism of inner
censorship. In the system of liberalism, individuation of a sector of the population belonged to the process of adaptation of society as a whole to technological development, but today the operation of the economic apparatus
demands that the masses be directed without any intervention from individuation.[209]

The focus here is not on the opposition of ego and id but the abolition of
that opposition. The id appears as the object of direct manipulation
through the "psychoanalysis in reverse" of the culture industry and socially sanctioned and mediated "ritual sacrifices" such as anti-Semitism.
The ego which is inherently dialectical, representing both the "psychic
and extrapsychic, a quantum of libido and the representative of outside
reality"[210] itself regresses. The reality principle of the ego for the sake of
self-preservation becomes the principle of conformism which must re-
nounce rationality within an irrational whole for the purpose of self-
preservation. In order to function at all, ego "has to join forces with the
unconscious."[211] "The ego hardly has any other choice than either to

---

[209] Horkheimer, *Dialectic of Enlightenment*, pp. 203-4.
[210] Adorno, "Sociology and Psychology," p. 96.
[211] Ibid., p. 79.

change reality or to withdraw back to the id."[212] Further, in contemporary society there is a weakening of conscience, the superego, together with a desublimation of archaic id impulses. For both Horkheimer and Adorno, the weakening of the superego and the resulting crisis of internalization points to a transformation of the bourgeois family and the expropriation of superego functions by the collective as in fascism. They postulate a gradual merger of superego as collective ego-ideal and the id where the former permits the desublimation of the latter even while simultaneously serving as a source of narcissistic gratification. Given this context what follows below is a brief description of Horkheimer's work on the family and Adorno's on anti-Semitism.

One further observation should be added here. The first quotation from *Dialectic of Enlightenment* implicitly affirms the opposition of ego and id as the universal foundation of civilization and as a necessary condition for the emergence of the "self." The second suggests a specific historical context for the emergence of "psychoanalytic man" as conditioned by the emergence of capitalism as well as his abolition by the very dynamic of that objective structure. As Adorno wrote in another context, "The prebourgeois order does not yet know psychology, the oversocialized society knows it no longer."[213] This double perspective is irreducible throughout *Dialectic of Enlightenment* points to the limits of Adorno's and Horkheimer's appropriation of Freud.[214]

The most proximate influence on Horkheimer's and Adorno's understanding of the "family" was Erich Fromm who was a member of the *Institüt* in the 1930's and, in particular, his essays "The Method and Function of an Analytic Social Psychology" and "Psychoanalytic Characterology and its Relevance for Social Psychology."[215] Fromm's

---

[212] Ibid., p. 86f.

[213] Ibid., p. 95.

[214] This impasse was most strikingly stated by Adorno: "The cultivation of the superego arbitrarily breaks off the process of psychoanalytic enlightenment. But to make a public profession of consciousness is to sanction atrocity. So heavily weighs the conflict of social and psychological insight" [ibid., p. 85]. See, also, Jessica Benjamin, "The End of Internalization: Adorno's Social Psychology," *Telos* 32 (1977): 42-64.

[215] Erich Fromm, "The Method and Function of an Analytic Social Psychology," and "Psychoanalytic Characterology and Its Relevance for Social Psychology," in *The Crisis of Psychoanalysis* (New York: Holt, Rinehart and Winston, 1970), pp. 138-87 and *The Working Class in Weimar Germany*, trans. Barbara Weinberger, ed. with an introduction by Wolfgang Bonss (Cambridge: Harvard University Press, 1984). In addition to Lasch's *Haven in a Heartless World*, a discussion of various critical approaches to the

thesis was that the family constitutes the mediating link between society, nature (libido) and the individual and, further, that the specific "libidinal structure" of the bourgeois family is productive of an "anal-retentive" or patricentric character which is the subjective condition for the objective reproduction of capitalist society.

> The phenomena of social psychology are to be understood as processes involving the active and the passive adaptation of the instinctual apparatus to the socioeconomic situation. In certain fundamental respects, the instinctual apparatus itself is a biological given; but it is highly modifiable. The role of the primary formative factors goes to the economic conditions. The family is the essential medium through which the economic situation exerts its formative influence on the individual psyche. The task of social psychology is to explain the shared, socially relevant, psychic attitudes and ideologies—and their unconscious roots in particular—in terms of the influence of economic conditions of libidinal strivings.[216]

In his contribution to the *Institüt* project, *Studien über Autorität und Familie*, Horkheimer continued the line of reflection outlined above. Like Fromm, Horkheimer emphasizes the historical particularity of the bourgeois family: it mediates the exigencies of economic reproduction where the second nature of paternal authority reflects the second nature of capitalist society in general.

> The family, as one of the most important formative agencies, sees to it that the kind of human character emerges which social life requires, and gives this human being in great measure the indispensable adaptability for a specific authority-oriented conduct on which the existence of the bourgeois order largely depends.[217]

More particularly, the child within the bourgeois family is presented with an either/or: either purely sensuous pleasure in its own body or recognition through parental love. The latter has as its condition submission to the authority of the father. The ambivalence thus created is negotiated through an identification with the "father."[218] With the internalization of duty there also arises a compulsive sense of guilt which di-

family, including the Frankfurt School, may be found in Mark Poster, *Critical Theory of the Family* (New York: Seabury Press, 1978).

[216] Fromm, "Analytic Social Psychology," p. 149.
[217] Horkheimer, "Authority and the Family," in *Critical Theory*, p. 98. See, also, Fromm, "Analytic Social Psychology," p. 144ff, and "Psychoanalytic Characterology," p. 177f.
[218] Ibid., pp. 107-12, 122-26.

minishes the subjective capacity to criticize the objective whole even as this subject's "virtues" are an objective condition for the reproduction and expansion of bourgeois society: "The self control of the individual, the disposition for

> work and discipline, the ability to hold firmly to certain ideas, consistency in practical life, application of reason, perseverance and pleasure in constructive activity.[219]

As Fromm notes, however, both the familial structure and character type specific to the bourgeois were also to be found in the proletariat. This was simultaneous with a crisis and mutation of the bourgeois family as Horkheimer emphasizes.[220] Indeed, these two developments are related—the embourgeoisement of the proletariat family was but a brief moment in a far more general movement which overtook and negated them both.

> In the bourgeois golden age there was a fruitful interaction between family and society, because the authority of the father was based on his role in society, while society was renewed by the education for authority which went on in the patriarchal family. Now, however, the admittedly indispensable

---

[219] Ibid., p. 101.

[220] Thus, in one of his earliest essays, "*Geschichte und Psychologie*," Horkheimer presumed that the structure of the instincts and the unconscious would assume a different form according to class. The same question is asked by Fromm regarding the endurance of forms of bourgeois character among the proletariat ["Psychoanalytic Characterology," pp. 185-86] and answered by a somewhat enigmatic reference to the structure of the family and "other traditional cultural factors" which change more slowly than the forms of economic organization. By 1940, however, as witnessed in the essay "The End of Reason" (Fromm was already marginalized from the Institute because of his Freudian revisionism), given the collapse of the working class, the emergence of the authoritarian state and state capitalism, Horkheimer had completely abandoned the position of "*Geschichte und Psychologie*" in acknowledgement that the demise of the individual knew no class lines ["The End of Reason," pp. 376-87]. Whereas previously, in the era of bourgeois liberalism the "father" enjoyed the undisputed role of authority in the family due to his objective role as economic provider, in late capitalism, with the undermining of his objective social and economic power, that role had become ideological. The "metaphysical aura" which once was attached to the father was now attached to social institutions and movements which now seemed immune from criticism. The extirpation of the "subject" (psychoanalytic human) and the emergence of the administered world and integration from above are thus simply different sides of the same irrational whole.

family is becoming a simple problem of technological manipulation by government.[221]

In general terms, this change was an erosion of the family's economic, educational, recreational and protective functions by the social whole which left the family with the abstract function of providing emotional and affective "depth." Its task was, in Christopher Lasch's words, to provide a "haven in a heartless world." With the abolition of the private sphere—the targeting of the family as the fundamental unit of consumption by producers of consumer goods via the advertising complex—this function too was eroded: consumption becomes the substitution for love and happiness, or better, its language and medium. The inverse side psychologically to this development sociologically was the destruction of paternal authority and its replacement by the authority of the collective. In a society "without the father," the authoritarian bourgeois character was not negated but only intensified—minus the "virtues" of the classic bourgeois character type.

> What is affected is not so much belief in authority *per se*, which in a way is stronger today than it used to be during the last century, but the formation of an integrated, continuously functioning superego. The consistent ego and superego, the essential traits of the traditional middle class idea of the individual, are necessarily undermined in modern society.[222]

Today, "the child, not the father, stands for reality as the direct representative and advertisement for the collective."[223] It is here—and one is tempted to amend the quote above to read "consistent ego *through* superego"—that the ambiguity of Horkheimer's position becomes clear. Under the impact of the recognition that society without the father was not utopia, but only more barbaric, there is an affirmation of the necessity of the internalization of authority implicitly identified with the negotiation of the Oedipal situation before the possibility of liberation from that authority could arise. Indeed, this leads to a curious turn in Horkheimer's language: what in his contribution to the *Studien* was known as the punishing superego with its "compulsive sense of guilt," later becomes the benevolent superego which is the bulwark against the extirpation of the subject by the social whole. Thus there arises an in-

---

[221] Horkheimer, "Authority and the Family," p. 128. See, also, his essay, "The Lessons of Fascism," pp. 227-29.
[222] Idem, "The Lessons of Fascism," p. 217.
[223] Idem, "The End of Reason," p. 381.

creasing "nostalgia" for the patriarchal family simultaneous with an acknowledgement of its historical-social particularity and fragility.

One of the first major statements by Horkheimer and Adorno concerning anti-Semitism was a joint one: "Elements of Anti-Semitism" in *Dialectic of Enlightenment*.[224] Here they sought to delineate that conjuncture of historical factors which resulted in fascist anti-Semitism. The hallmark of all their writings about this topic, however, is their approach to the structure of anti-Semitism as an instance of "something else," i.e., prejudice, demand for identity, etc. What follows is a brief exposition of the four major motifs of "Elements of Anti-Semitism" where the general context and content of their approach may be seen and Adorno's article "Freudian Theory and the Pattern of Fascist Propaganda" where the psychoanalytic exposition of the dynamics of mass prejudice is most acute.

First, in the pogrom, the ghetto and the concentration camp, the dialectic of enlightenment becomes concrete: the "polishing off" of that which refuses to capitulate to the status quo.[225] On a broad level, modern secular anti-Semitism is a rage against nonidentity. The extermination of the Jews is society's revenge for the absence of a second circumcision at the time of the Emancipation: the voluntary negation of the Jew as Jew and assimilation into enlightened European society as non-Jew. The promise and threat of liberalism comes to light in fascism: the price of emancipation is identity as the negation of difference and the demand for equality is the elimination of the "other" as "other."[226] "Today race has become the self-assertion of the bourgeois individual integrated within a barbaric collective."[227]

Second, "bourgeois anti-Semitism has a specific economic reason: the concealment of domination in production."[228] Through the stereotypical generalization of the "Jew" as carnal, money-hungry and a Shylock, the Jew as such is made a scapegoat in that the economic injustice suffered

---

[224] Horkheimer and Adorno, *Dialectic of Enlightenment*, pp. 168-208. According to the "Introduction," the first three fragments were written in conjunction with Leo Lowenthal [ibid., xvii].

[225] Adorno, *Negative Dialectics*, p. 362.

[226] Horkheimer and Adorno, *Dialectic of Enlightenment*, pp. 168-72, 179-82.

[227] Ibid., p. 169.

[228] Ibid., p. 173. See, also, Horkheimer's statement, "Research Project on Anti-Semitism," *ZfS* 9 (1941): 124-43, which outlines various theories of anti-Semitism, a capsule overview of anti-Semitism and mass movements in Western society from the time of the crusades, a summary of anti-Semitism in the Enlightenment philosophies, a typology of configurations of the form of anti-Semitism, and the Jew's role in economic society and under National Socialism in particular.

by an entire class is attributed to them. Since the economic activity of the Jews has historically been restricted from immediate ownership of the forces of production, the economic niche which they have occupied is that of the sphere of circulation and finance, if they themselves were not reduced to mere penury. As the financier of middlemen, it is the Jew who calls credit due or presents the bill to the seller. He appears as the immediate cause of the impoverishment of the *petit bourgeois* and in this role he functions to conceal domination in production. "The lower strata become aware of their

> miserable conditions not so much through intercourse with those who are really mighty (the leaders of industry and politics) but through contact with the middleman, the merchant and the banker.[229]

With the emergence of a monopoly or state capitalism, the once indispensable economic function of the "Jew" in a liberal capitalist economy has been eliminated while their "image" endures. The "Jew" is thus depicted as being a parasite on society and the hatred and rage felt by the dominated may thus be directed at a socially marginal group which has ceased to supply a necessary function and this hate can attain some gratification without endangering the system itself.[230]

Horkheimer and Adorno note, third, that Christian anti-Semitism is the essential prehistory of modern racial anti-Semitism and that the former is not anti-Semitic by accident but by the logic of its identification of the absolute with the finite in the Christ. The denunciation of the Jew is the left hand of the affirmation of the Christ. Those who "persuaded themselves with a heavy conscience that Christianity was their own sure possession, had to affirm their eternal salvation as against the worldly damnation of all those who did not make the dull sacrifice of reason."[231] What lives on in the husk of objectified religion as a private commodity form is sublated into fascism: unconscious longing is channelled into nationalistic rebellion.

The final motif concerns the role of mimesis and projection (paranoia) in anti-Semitism.[232] In anti-Semitism there is a censuring of uncontrolled mimesis which is stereotypically projected on the "Jew":

[229] Horkheimer, "Research Project on Anti-Semitism," p. 137.
[230] Ibid., pp. 137f, 140f. See, also, Horkheimer and Adorno, *Dialectic of Enlightenment*, pp. 173-76.
[231] Horkheimer and Adorno, *Dialectic of Enlightenment*, p. 179.
[232] Ibid., pp. 179-200.

the "Jew" becomes a stereotypical pastiche of mimetic ciphers denoted as "race traits." Precisely what is held up to arouse disgust is that which civilization and modern society in particular has sought to suppress: uncontrolled mimesis.

> Civilization has replaced the organic adaptation to others and mimetic behavior proper, by organized control of mimesis, in the magical phase; and, finally by rational practice, by work, in the historical phase. Uncontrolled mimesis is outlawed.[233]

What is repressed in oneself as the price of adaptation to the social whole cannot be tolerated in the "other." Yet the anti-Semite cunningly partakes in what he despises. The mocking imitation and jeering of the Jew, the laughter at her and the scorn heaped upon her allows the anti-Semite the opportunity of a "mimesis of mimesis" under the pretext of exorcising the same. "Fascism is also totalitarian in that it seeks to make rebellion of suppressed nature against domination directly useful to domination."[234] Anti-Semitism becomes the celebration, permitted and encouraged by authority, of what is otherwise forbidden.

The psychological mechanism which Horkheimer and Adorno identify with such behavior is the "false projection" of the paranoiac that inverts mimesis: the projection onto the intended victim of what is forbidden to oneself.[235] While conscious projection is intrinsic to all knowledge, it consummates itself in the awareness of the external world as something other than itself. False projection, whose noetic moment is stereotypical thought, is impervious to experience and produces a false immediacy which remains unbroken by thought:

> Objectifying (like sick) thought contains the despotism of the subjective purpose which is hostile to the thing and forgets the thing itself, thus committing the mental act of violence which is later put into practice.[236]

---

[233] Ibid., p. 180. See, also, by the same author, *Eclipse of Reason*, pp. 114-19.

[234] Ibid., p. 185.

[235] Ibid., p. 187.

[236] Ibid., p. 193. The social counterpart to "false projection" is the "stereotype": "In the world of mass series production, stereotypes replace individual categories. Judgements are no longer based on a genuine synthesis but on blind subsumption" [ibid., p. 201]. For an expanded treatment of "stereotype" and "stereotypical thinking"—itself one might suspect to be a prime example of what Adorno later calls "identity-thought"—see Adorno, et al., *The Authoritarian Personality* (New York: The Norton Library, 1969), pp. 606-8.

With fascism, anti-Semitism becomes the socialization of paranoia as the politics of the "in-group/out-group." Above all, this *is* the dialectic of enlightenment. "Auschwitz confirmed the philosopheme of pure identity as death."[237]

From the time of *Dialectic of Enlightenment* until roughly 1951, Horkheimer, but especially Adorno, were preoccupied with the question of fascism, mass prejudice, propaganda, the authoritarian personality and anti-Semitism.[238] Notable in this context are Adorno's contributions on the role of political, economic and religious ideologies in prejudice in *The Authoritarian Personality* and his study of the rhetorical devices of fascist propaganda in "The Psychological Technique of Martin Luther Thomas' Radio Addresses." They fall, however, outside the limited scope of this section.

In the essay "Freudian Theory and the Pattern of Fascist Propaganda," there is a qualitative shift in approach from previous considerations of the topic. Now the focal question is "what makes the masses into masses."[239] The theoretical context for an "answer" is no longer false projection as paranoia or the distinction between in-group and out-group, or an analysis of fascist propaganda as "wish-fulfillment"; rather the theoretical context is narcissism and the dynamics of idealization and identification with a powerful authority figure, the leader.

In "Sociology and Psychology," Adorno defines narcissism as that splitting and regression of the ego which is provoked by an increasingly contradictory reality. "In narcissism the self-preserving function of the ego is, on the surface at least, retained, but, at the same time, split off from that of consciousness and thus lost to rationality."[240] The reality

237 Adorno, *Negative Dialectics*, p. 362.
238 The major articles in this regard, in addition to the ones already cited, are Horkheimer, "Sociological Background of the Psychoanalytic Approach," and Adorno, "Anti-Semitism and Fascist Propaganda," in *Anti-Semitism: A Social Disease,* ed. Ernst Simmel (New York: International Universities Press, 1946), pp. 1-10, 125-37; Adorno, "Freudian Theory and the Pattern of Fascist Propaganda," in *The Essential Frankfurt School Reader*, pp. 118-37; and Adorno, "The Psychological Technique of Martin Luther Thomas' Radio Addresses," in *Gesammelte Schriften*, vol. 8.1: *Soziologische Schriften* (Frankfurt: Suhrkamp Verlag, 1975), pp. 12-141, and "The Stars Down to Earth: *The Los Angeles Times* Astrology Column," *Gesammelte Schriften*, vol. 9.2: *Soziologische Schriften* (Frankfurt: Suhrkamp Verlag, 1976), pp. 11-120.
239 Adorno, "Freudian Theory and Pattern," p. 121.
240 Idem, "Sociology and Psychology," p. 88. See, also, "Freudian Theory and Pattern," p. 134f.

testing of the ego in the service of self-preservation must be occluded in order to effect the renunciations paradoxically imposed by the affluent society. Thus a part of the ego itself is consigned to the sphere of the unconscious. This regression and feedback of ego into the id affects not only ego, but also the id.

> The ego that withdraws back into the unconscious does not simply cancel itself out but retains several of the features it had acquired as a societal agent. But it subordinates them to the dictates of the unconscious. . . . With the transposition of the ego into the unconscious the quality of the drives is modified in turn; they are diverted towards characteristic ego-goals which contradict those of the primary libido.[241]

This occlusion of the ego is an objective condition for fascist propaganda whose "organized flight of ideas" and language negates the logic of argument in place of the calculation of its effects on the unconscious.[242] If the therapeutic motto of psychoanalysis is "where id once stood, let ego come forth," then that of fascist propaganda as "psychoanalysis in reverse" is its inverse: "where ego once stood, let id come forth!"[243]

In the dynamic of idealization and identification, narcissism becomes social in the libidinal bond formed between the follower and leader. Adorno intimates that the objective condition for such subjective formations is the crisis of internalization and subsequent externalization of the superego. The fascist personality

> . . . fails to develop an independent autonomous conscience and substitutes for it an identification with collective authority which is as irrational as Freud described it, heteronomous, rigidly oppressive, largely alien to the individual's own thinking, and, therefore, easily exchangeable in spite of its structural rigidity.[244]

As the ego regresses, so too does the independent superego. In fact the superego proper ceases to exist for the term "identification" refers to a pre-Oedipal mode of libidinal bonding tied to the oral phase of the organization of the libido where identification as an act of "devouring," "of making the beloved object part of oneself" takes the form of the projection of the subject.[245] "Idealization" refers to that process whereby nar-

241   Ibid.
242   Adorno, "Anti-Semitism and Fascist Propaganda," p. 125f.
243   Idem, "The Stars Down to Earth," p. 65.
244   Idem, "Freudian Theory and Pattern," p. 178, n. 11.
245   Ibid., p. 125.

cissistic libido is partially transferred to an object other than the self. It is
this pattern of identification through idealization, "by making the leader
his ideal he loves himself,"[246] that the psychological squaring of the circle
can be accomplished for the follower: "the twofold wish to submit to authority and to be the authority himself."[247] In the image of the leader, the
primal omnipotent father appears with which the follower can identify,
not as the heteronomous "other," but as the self. Virtually all the standard rhetorical strategies of fascist propaganda ("great little man,"
"unity-trick," "lone-wolf," etc.),[248] exhibit this pattern of fostering identification through idealization while allowing expression of transformed
id-impulses in the form of social aggression.[249]

Previously in this section, I provisionally noted two criticisms of
Horkheimer's and Adorno's appropriation of Freud: their seeming
"bifocal" vision and the assertion of internalization as the condition of
individuation. A third may be added here. Unlike their former colleague,
Herbert Marcuse, the two men's appropriation of Freud remains

[246] Ibid., p. 126.

[247] Ibid., p. 127.

[248] See Adorno, "Martin Luther Thomas' Radio Addresses," and Adorno, et al., *The
Authoritarian Personality*, pp. 605-783. For an additional study of the rhetoric of fascist
agitation and the psychological mechanisms which such rhetoric "triggers" and
which proceeds in the same vein as the "Martin Luther Thomas" study and explicitly
credits Adorno, see Leo Lowenthal and Norbert Guterman, *Prophets of Deceit: A Study
in the Techniques of the American Agitator* (New York: Harper and Brothers, 1949).
Again, the social phenomenon of the "masses" bound together by a "herd instinct" is
not merely a datum, but a result of a prior process. The bond by which the "masses"
are formed into the "masses" is itself of a libidinal nature and the outcome of a psychic mechanism. The "awakening of archaic inheritance" is brought about by the re-
animation of the idea of the primal father who receives his personalization and embodiment in the fascist leader. This identification translates libido into the bond between leader and follower. Yet this process of identification is accompanied by or accomplished through the further mechanisms of idealization. The dilemma of a
"strongly developed rational, self-preserving ego agency and the continuous failure
to satisfy their own ego demands" leads to narcissistic impulses which are satisfied
"only through idealization as the partial transfer of the narcissistic libido to the object" [idem, "Freudian Theory and Pattern," p. 125]. The rhetoric of fascist propaganda is the true coincidence of opposites which seeks to evoke and sustain such
identification through idealization through its depiction of the fascist leader himself,
who must appear as a superman giving open vent to that rage which the follower se-
cretly harbors but dare not say, yet also and simultaneously appears as "average";
that he must present his position as immediately threatened, yet also a *fait accompli*.

[249] Idem, "Freudian Theory and Pattern, p. 133f. On the "ritual" dimension of fascist propaganda, see Adorno, "Anti-Semitism and Fascist Propaganda." p. 136f.

"fragmentary," that is, confined to essays written over a long period of time which leads to an extreme fluidity of concepts crucial to their object of a negative psychoanalysis and the delineation of the eclipse of "psychoanalytic being." What "ego," "id," "superego," "ego ideal," "internalization," "individuation," "oedipal complex," etc. mean is often vague, even if it might be conceded that precisely this vagueness is a reflection of the crisis of the subject today.[250]

SUMMARY

Perhaps the vision held by Adorno and Horkheimer in *Dialectic of Enlightenment* is best evoked by Walter Benjamin whose death witnesses to the terror of modernity as its victim. Written shortly before his suicide in a French border town, Benjamin names the lie which most are wont to call "progress."

> A Klee painting named "Angelus Novus" shows an angel looking as though he is about to move away from something he is fixedly contemplating. His eyes are staring, his mouth is open, his wings are spread. This is how one pictures the angel of history. His face is turned toward the past. Where we perceive a chain of events, he sees one single catastrophe which keeps piling wreckage upon wreckage and hurls it in front of his feet. The angel would like to stay, awaken the dead, and make whole what has been smashed. But a storm is blowing in from Paradise; it has got caught in his wings with such violence that the angel can no longer close them. The storm irresistibly propels him into the future to which his back is turned, while the pile of debris before him continues to grow. This storm is what we call progress.[251]

Not without a certain congruence, Benjamin's "Theses on the Philosophy of History" were planned for a never-published special memorial issue of the Institute's journal in the same year as Horkheimer and Adorno began their collaboration on the *Dialectic of Enlightenment.*

---

250   Thus Adorno could assert, "Psychoanalysis in its most authentic and by now already obsolete form comes into its own as a report on the forces of destruction rampant in the individual amidst a destructive society. What remains untrue about psychoanalysis is its claim to totality" ["Sociology and Psychology," pp. 95-61].

251   Walter Benjamin, "Theses on the Philosophy of History," in *Illuminations*, trans. Harry Zohn, with an introduction by Hannah Arendt (New York: Schocken Books, 1969), pp. 257-58.

CRITICAL REFLECTIONS

Theory, Praxis and Determinate Negation

In the eleventh thesis on Feuerbach, Marx wrote, "The philosophers have only *interpreted* the world in various ways; the point is to *change* it."[252] Perhaps as much has been written about this single sentence as about any other in the history of philosophy. Interpretations abound, and while I neither intend nor can give an exposition of them, minimally, four assertions are expressed here. First, there is the conviction that something is askew, the world is not as it ought or can be. Something is wrong in that complex of nature-history which defines our world, but there are also latent possibilities, humanly realizable, for the ameliorization of the same. Second, the task of philosophy (theory) is the delineation of these possibilities in the world that would realize human liberation and autonomy. Philosophic reason is, above all, a practical, that is, historical and hence social task. Third, the "change" referred to in these is not a merely contemplated change. There is an infinite qualitative difference between "contemplating social change" and "actually changing society." Lastly, it is an exigency for responsible philosophy (theory) to establish a connection with concrete praxis. Indeed, the hallmark of Marxism and those projects which bear a family resemblance to it is the so-called theory-praxis nexus, i.e., that theory emerges due to the exigencies of praxis and is sublated back into that whence it emerged.

As various critics, however, have pointed out, it is precisely this theory-praxis nexus which became and remained problematic for Horkheimer and Adorno. Apart from his *Zeitschrift* articles during the 1930's when Horkheimer still wrote as if the proletariat could yet realize the project of a transformation of society, there is little further mention made in the works of the two men which can be interpreted as an attempt to establish a connection between critical theory and praxis. When one recollects that Horkheimer became director of the *Institüt für Sozialforschung* in 1931 and that the first issue of the *Zeitschrift für Sozialforschung* appeared in 1932 and that the forced emigration of the Institute began in 1933, there is little wonder that the remarks of both men concerning praxis were "abstract!" What is remarkable is that even

---

[252] Karl Marx, "Concerning Feuerbach," in *Early Writings*, trans. Rodney Livingstone and Gregor Benton, with an introduction by Lucio Colletti (New York: Vintage Books, 1975), p. 423.

in 1937 ("Traditional and Critical Theory") mention was still made of the proletariat!

> The whole thrust of Frankfurt School activity, though centralizing the problem of "praxis", was ultimately academic: "praxis" was a theoretical category, not a constituent of a concrete revolutionary struggle. . . . While stressing the revolutionary role of the critical intellectual, "critical theory of society" could not formulate itself as a practical theory of ideological struggle.[253]

While I shall return to the first part of Philip Slater's statement, the injustice of the second part should be noted. Given his own avowal that none of the major political options existent during the Weimar Republic was without serious weaknesses, it appears to me to be unjust to fault forced emigrés for not formulating their critical theory as a practical theory of ideological struggle. In the debacle which was the collapse of the Weimar and the emergence of what is still today the most unspeakable evil of history masquerading as a "state," the elaboration of such a theory was unthinkable. Having said this, it must also be noted that even during the ferment of the 1960's, Adorno, unlike Marcuse, could not condone the revolutionary practical tactics of his students: when in May 1969 students occupied the *Institüt* in Frankfurt, Adorno did nothing to stop the police from evicting them.

This rupture of the theory-praxis nexus by Adorno and Horkheimer was not an unreflective act but a deliberate one based upon the demands of the historical moment itself. In 1944, Adorno wrote

> . . . (s)ince Utopia was set aside and the unity of theory and practice demanded, we have become all too practical. Fear of the impotence of theory supplies a pretext for bowing to the almighty production process, and so fully admitting the impotence of theory . . . in the face of the lie of the commodity world, even the lie that denounces it becomes a corrective.[254]

Twenty-five years later, in an article entitled "Resignation" addressed to the student revolutionaries, Adorno's position had not changed:

> The often evoked unity of theory and praxis has a tendency to give way to the predominance of praxis. . . . One clings to action because of the impossi-

---

[253] Slater, *Origin and Significance*, p. 55.
[254] Adorno, *Minima Moralia*, p. 44.

bility of action. . . . Repressive intolerance toward a thought not immediately accompanied by instructions for action is founded in fear.[255]

The historical problem with the demand for the establishment of a theory-praxis nexus was that under the current system of domination such attempts at praxis could easily be co-opted by the system itself[256] and serve the interests of domination and, further, calls for a theory-praxis nexus gradually pass over into what Adorno and Horkheimer saw to be the very problem itself, i.e., another form of instrumental reason.

The position by which Adorno and Horkheimer responded to this dilemma was not so much a fixed position as it was a constellation of motifs. First, in the face of a growing eradication and extirpation of the subject, the only locus left for critical theory is the remnant of individuality.

> In face of the totalitarian unison with which the eradication of difference is proclaimed as purpose in itself, even part of the social force of liberation may have temporarily withdrawn to the individual sphere. If critical theory lingers there, it is not only with a bad conscience.[257]

One need only add from the position of a historical retrospective view that the "temporary withdrawal" has become a permanent exile. Second, in the face of an ever increasing and integratory system of domination, the stance of the critic could only be one of "isolation" and "homelessness."

> The best mode of conduct, in face of all this, still seems an uncommitted, suspended one: to lead a private life, as far as the social order and one's own needs will tolerate nothing else, but not to attach weight to it as something socially substantial and individually appropriate . . . it is part of morality not to be at home in one's own home.[258]

Third, Slater is correct. For the Frankfurt School "praxis" became a category of theory. More precisely, in a situation where freedom has become contracted to pure negativity, "theory" has become praxis. "The self-crit-

---

255 Idem, "Resignation," *Telos* 35 (Spring 1978): 166.
256 Praxis, even of the most revolutionary type, is thus threatened by cooptation, just as the most nonconformist and "new" works of art are potentially assimilable by the culture industry. See, also, Herbert Marcuse, "Repressive Tolerance," in *A Critique of Pure Tolerance* (Boston: Beacon Press, 1965), pp. 81-123.
257 Adorno, *Minima Moralia*, p. 18.
258 Ibid., p. 39. See, also, pp. 26-33.

icism of reason has become the truest morality."[259] Isolated before the seemingly inviolable system of domination, the only recourse is to negative thought: "If there is any chance of changing the situation, it is only through undiminished insight."[260] Finally, there is an awareness, particularly on Adorno's part, that even this stance is unsatisfactory, that "whatever the intellectual does is wrong." If he chooses to overlook the social, political and economic base which supports and tolerates his work, "he shoots into thin air." If he immerses himself in it, he risks "sinking to the level of what he is dealing with."[261] Most of all, even if after informing oneself of this base he foreswears any alliance with it, then he "is seduced into the vain and unrelated substitution of the reflection for the thing."[262] It was this last alternative which Adorno and Horkheimer seemingly judged to be the best among bad alternatives and which supplies the reproach laid at their door: that determinate negation elevated into a program of negative dialectics was the dervish dance of elitist intellectuals who nevertheless remained fixed to one spot.

Having made this first, somewhat lengthy observation, the remaining two can be made with more dispatch, inasmuch as they have already been alluded to. The second observation is that for Adorno and Horkheimer, the potential subject of history had disappeared. With a general amelioration of their material state in life, the proletariat lost their revolutionary character and became supporters of the status quo under increasingly intense and pervasive pressure from a culture industry which reified the status quo and leveled the differences between the proletariat and their historical antagonists. What Benjamin tersely observed about the failure of the German Workers Movement and the Social Democrats can be generalized.

> Nothing has corrupted the German working class so much as the notion that it was moving with the current. It regarded technological developments as the fall of the stream with which it thought it was moving. From there it was but a step to the illusion that the factory work that was supposed to tend toward technological progress constituted a political achievement.[263]

[259] Ibid., p. 126.
[260] Idem, "Resignation," p. 167. See, also, "*Marginalien zu Theorie und Praxis,*" in *Gesammelte Schiften*, vol. 10.2: *Kulturkritik Gesellschaft* (Frankfurt: Suhrkamp, 1978), pp. 759-83, esp. pp. 780-83.
[261] Idem, *Minima Moralia*, pp. 132-33.
[262] Ibid., p. 132.
[263] Benjamin, "Theses on the Philosophy of History," p. 258.

"Automatic Marxism" was refuted by the fact that the revolution just did not come where it was expected, that it was betrayed where it did come and that whatever latent possibilities there were for it, the system of domination seemed to successfully suppress. Further, unlike Marcuse, Horkheimer and Adorno remained orthodox Marxists, nostalgically abiding with the broken hopes of a co-opted proletariat, while Marcuse found fragmentary agents of liberation in the blacks, students, the "Third World" and, finally, the feminist movement.[264]

The third observation concerns the nature of that "reason" which constitutes the method of critical theory. Certainly "subjective reason" which forges an identity of the real and the rational through the subjugation of the former to the interests of domination is not what is referred to. It is the problem. Equally decisive is their rejection of any naive return to "objective reason." Aside from their assertion that the transition from objective to subjective reason was necessary—which is not to say progress—and that any contemporary return to some *ordo* of objective reason would simply be manipulated by the demands of subjective reason itself, objective reason also forges an identity of the real and the rational by subjecting the latter to the heteronomy of the former. Subjective and objective reason are simply different sides of the same coin: "affirmative reason," because both seek to forge an identity of the real and the rational.[265] To this, Adorno and Horkheimer opposed "negative

---

[264] See Adorno, "Is Marx Obsolete," *Diogenes* 64 (Winter 1968): 1-16; Horkheimer, "Marx Today—An Address," in *Post-War German Culture: An Anthology*, ed. C. McClelland and S. Scher (New York: E. P. Dutton and Co., 1974), pp. 128-38; and Marcuse, "The Obsolescence of Marxism," in *Marx and the Western World*, ed. Nikolaus Lobkowicz (Notre Dame: University of Notre Dame, 1967), pp. 409-17. While for both Adorno and Horkheimer the contemporary conflict in society was still to be analyzed in terms of the clash between the forces and relations of production, for Adorno this clash had itself become an object of administration and hence taken on the appearance of a frozen second nature, while for Horkheimer all he could suggest was the addition—or integration?—of a study of the Marxist interpretation of history and society in the school curriculum. For Marcuse's position after the obsolescence of Marxism and the loss of its subject, see *An Essay on Liberation* (Boston: Beacon Press, 1969) and *Counter-Revolution and Revolt* (Boston: Beacon Press, 1972).

[265] Horkheimer, *Eclipse of Reason*, pp. 162-87. "The task of philosophy is not stubbornly to play the one against the other, but to foster a mutual critique and thus, if possible, to prepare in the intellectual realm the reconciliation of the two in reality. . . . Since isolated subjective reason in our time is triumphing everywhere, with fatal results, the critique must necessarily be carried on with an emphasis on objective reason rather than on the remnants of subjectivistic philosophy. . . . Applied to concrete reality, this means that only a definition of the objective goals of society that includes

reason": reason as the determinate negation. It is the tension, the distance, the nonidentity of the real and the rational that is the true wellspring of reason whose task is "to brush history against the grain."[266] In the false seduction of the negation of the negation, reason loses itself, its orientation to truth and becomes its "other," untruth.

> But as soon as thought repudiates its inviolable distance and tries with a thousand subtle arguments to prove its literal correctness, it founders. If it leaves behind the medium of virtuality, of anticipation that cannot be wholly filled by any single piece of actuality, in short, if instead of interpretation it seeks to become mere statement, everything it states, becomes, in fact, untrue.[267]

Like the Jewish prohibition against graven images of the Holy One, critical theory refused to delineate in an affirmative manner the nature of the "utopia," the "good" and the "truth" towards which it is oriented.[268] It remains with the determinate negation, the reading of the falsity of the thing in the thing itself. Hence reason can only endure as a self-critique, as the negation directed against its own affirmative reasonableness.

> Reason can realize its reasonableness only through reflecting on the disease of the world as produced and reproduced by man; in such self-critique, reason will at the same time remain faithful to itself, by preserving and applying for no ulterior motive the principle of truth that we owe to reason alone.[269]

It is here that the more fundamental and profound reason lies for the rupture of the theory-praxis nexus in the work of Adorno and Horkheimer and which intensifies the two other observations. The problem is negative reason itself. It is impossible to establish, let alone sustain, a connection with concrete praxis on the basis of reason as determi-

---

the purpose of the self-preservation of the subject, the respect for individual life, deserves to be called objective" [ibid., pp. 174-75].

[266] Walter Benjamin, *Über den Begriff der Geschichte: Gesammelte Schriften* 6 vols., ed. Rolf Tiedemann and Hermann Schweppenhauser, vol. 1.2: *Abhandlungen* (Frankfurt: Suhrkamp Verlag, 1974), p. 697, cited in Buck-Morss, *Origin of Negative Dialectics*, p. 48.

[267] Adorno, *Minima Moralia*, p. 127.

[268] Horkheimer and Adorno, *Dialectic of Enlightenment*, p. 23, and *Dawn and Decline*, p. 236f. For an analysis of the relation between Judaism and Idealism, see Jürgen Habermas, "The German Idealism of the Jewish Philosophers," in *Philosophical-Political Profiles*, trans. Fred Lawrence (Cambridge: The MIT Press, 1983), pp. 21-43.

[269] Idem, *Eclipse of Reason*, p. 177.

nate negation alone. Critique does not suffice for praxis because the latter inherently demands *positive* directions and concrete strategies if it is to exist, particularly in socially manifest forms. Yet it was precisely this which both men rejected with their *Verbotensbildung* and reliance on negative reason alone.

> The concept of the negative—be it that of the relative or of evil—contains the positive as its opposite. Practically speaking, the denunciation of an act as evil at least suggests the direction a better one would take. . . . The critical analysis of society points to the prevailing injustice. The attempt to over-come it has repeatedly led to greater injustice. . . . If one wishes to define the good as the attempt to abolish evil, it can be determined.[270]

The ambivalence of theory to praxis is concisely summed up in this aphorism by Horkheimer. The positive can only be defined as the oppo-site of the negative, as a "not-this." In this, however, the positive loses precisely what is necessary for social praxis: specificity. To put it crudely, determinate negation as praxis could never be determinate enough or negative enough as the determinate negation of thought. The definition of the good as the attempt to abolish evil is too diffuse a notion in its negative formulation to ground a social praxis. It is as if the fear of founding a greater injustice or compromise with the object of critique prevented the establishment of a connection with concrete social praxis.

Critical Theory of Society or Philosophy of History

In *The Tragedy of Enlightenment*, Paul Connerton makes a trenchant criticism concerning the project of the Frankfurt School (for him, Adorno, Horkheimer, Marcuse and Habermas). On the one hand, for Marx, men's and women's appropriation of nature is a "constant," an ahistorical given.

> Labor, then as the creator of use-values, is a condition of human existence which is independent of all forms of society; it is an eternal natural necessity which mediates the metabolism between man and nature, and therefore human life itself.[271]

On the other hand, Connerton detects a tendency in the work of the Frankfurt School—and *Dialectic of Enlightenment* in particular—to hy-

---

270   Idem, *Dawn and Decline*, p. 236.
271   Marx, *Capital*, 1: 133.

postasize humanity's appropriation of nature as "domination" as such and then to confuse this with the capitalist process of social organization which conditions humanity's appropriation of nature. In Connerton's estimate, what renders the human/nature nexus problematic or an instance of domination is the specific mode of social organization in which this appropriation of nature is embedded. "Domination" over nature is, thus, derivative from and a function of the social organization of the forces of production.[272] This confusion makes the task of a "critical theory of society" impossible. Such a task has, in Connerton's opinion, as its object the description of the "laws" of the rise, development and demise of a given social totality. However, given a generalized and ahistorical notion of domination, this proves impossible.

> . . . an attempt is being made here to relate together two quite distinct historical transformations. There is the transition from myth to enlightenment, where the pre-Socratic cosmologies may be said to mark the point of transition because they are rationalizations of the mythic mode of apprehension. And there is the transition from pre-capitalist communities to capitalist social formations, which is established by the institution of wage-labor. But what is seen as the decisive break in history, the transition from myth to enlightenment, is never brought into clearly articulated connection to the specific break between pre-capitalist formations and capitalist formations. Because of this the critique of domination becomes dispersed.[273]

This tension in the writings of the Frankfurt School leads to the question, "What constitutes the 'primary process of domination'?" Is the process of domination primarily due to instrumental reason, affirmative reason or identity-thought which culminates in capitalism? Or is capitalism the particular societal configuration in which these forms of reason becomes a means of the domination of nature? It is only on the basis of the latter that the construction of a critical theory of society becomes possible because on the basis of the former, domination is not seen as conditioned by any specific social situation.[274]

---

272 Connerton, *The Tragedy of Enlightenment*, pp. 71-9. For an presentation of "nature" in Marx's thought, see Alfred Schmidt, *The Concept of Nature in Marx*, trans. Ben Fowkes (London: New Left Books, 1971).

273 Ibid., p. 78.

274 Thus, Horkheimer could assert, "It is not technology or the motive of self-preservation that in itself accounts for the decline of the individual; it is not production per se, but the forms in which it takes place—the interrelationships of human beings within the specific framework of industrialism" [*Eclipse of Reason*, p. 153]; while Adorno could write, "It is not technology that is fatal, but the fact that it gets matted

Connerton continues and suggests that this confusion arises from two major influences.[275] First, the concept of "critique" is compromised by the retention of the "enlightenment myth" of universal history. Granted, both Horkheimer and Adorno held equivocal positions regarding the concept of universal history. They reject this concept insofar as it entails an affirmation of the necessary self-realization of an autonomous subject of history in theological form (history as the realization of God for us) or idealist form (history as the realization of Absolute Spirit through the cunning of reason) or its Marxist form (history as the realization of the proletariat as the subject-object of history). What is rejected in all three forms is the affirmation of the existence of a "subject" of history *and* the affirmation of the necessary self-realization of that subject in history. Over and against this, Horkheimer and Adorno suggest in *Dialectic of Enlightenment*—and this becomes an explicit theme for Adorno in *Negative Dialectics*—a construal of "world history" as the history of domination: domination over self (renunciation) which is the condition of the emergence of the subject-ego; domination over society which is the condition of the emergence of culture or civilization; and domination over nature which is the condition of the emergence of science. In contemporary times such modes of domination have become interconnected, systemic, and self-reproducing. To what extent the transition from "prehistory" to history necessarily must take the form of domination remains obscure as does the extent to which capitalism represents a qualitatively "new" development of history and hence the extent to which it may be considered in abstraction from prior history which conditions its emergence. The notion of universal history is thus inverted, but formally retained; and "critique" as criticism of concrete historical, social structures and configurations becomes dissipated.

Second, Connerton notes that there is a "tragic pessimism," an all-encompassing vision of heteronomy which is pervasive in classical and contemporary German sociology (Weber, Simmel, Tönnies, Gehlen). The problem is that in the reactions of these sociologists to Marx, features specific to an analysis of capitalism (i.e., exchange value) were conflated with a concept of instrumental reason with the result that the former lost

---

together with the social relations that surround it" ["Is Marx Obsolete," p. 9]. Throughout this chapter, I have cited material to indicate that in their explicit statements Horkheimer and Adorno held the latter position. However, their implicit procedure and construction drew them in the direction of the former position, and it is this unresolved conflict which defines the "tragedy" of critical theory.

[275] Connerton, *The Tragedy of Enlightenment*, pp. 109-31.

its historical specificity and the latter became "over-inflated." The material results of such a trend in sociology and the retention of the notion of a universal history, was that it was inevitable that *Dialectic of Enlightenment* appear as the marriage of the two.

I find myself in substantial agreement with Connerton's analysis. There is an essential duality of perspective in *Dialectic of Enlightenment*—simultaneously a philosophy of history and a critical theory of society. Recourse to the epic of Odysseus in this work, for example, is not merely a sophisticated literary device—it is at one and the same time a document from the childhood of Western civilization and a cipher of contemporary society and its use in the *Dialectic of Enlightenment* is the attempt par excellence to mediate philosophy of history and critical theory of society. Throughout this work, "domination over nature" is depicted as the primordial form of domination leading to power over the "other" and the renunciation of the self which founds history culminating in contemporary society.

> The pressure of circumstances around them has forced men to overcome their own problems and produce material and intellectual works. The thinkers from Democritus to Freud who have stressed this fact are not wrong. The resistance of external nature to which the pressure can ultimately be reduced continues through the classes in society, and acts on every individual from childhood on as the obduracy of his fellows . . . terror and civilization are inseparable.[276]

> A philosophical interpretation of world history would have to show the rational domination of nature comes increasingly to win the day, in spite of all deviations and resistance, and integrates all human characteristics. Forms of economy, rule and culture would also be derived from this position.[277]

In part, the "pessimism" of critical theory lies in this convergence of philosophy of history and critical theory of society.

Here I would like to suggest a further line of reflection which incorporates Connerton's two criticisms. My thesis is that at the transition point of a critical theory of society to a philosophy of history through the concept of the domination of nature, there is a shift of analytical tropes which govern the use of the term "domination," one which moves from "reification" to "objectification." While it has become fashionable to define the two terms through a reference to the differences between Marx

[276] Horkheimer and Adorno, *Dialectic of Enlightenment*, p. 217.
[277] Ibid., p. 223.

and Hegel—an assertion which says everything and yet nothing—I wish to define the two terms by referring to the specific difference between the two: reification takes as its context of reference a specific interpretation of a concrete societal totality, while objectification does not. This is more than the assertion of a logical tautology (i.e., philosophy of history = objectification and critical theory of society = reification). Horkheimer and Adorno sought to hold on to both moments. What threatens their work is that in the movement from a critical theory of society to a philosophy of history, there is the tendency to collapse reification into an "instance" of objectification viewed as a universal anthropological constant. Thus the difference between the two analytical tropes is, I suggest, twofold: first there is the difference of its "bearer" (i.e., a particular social totality versus the subject or thought as such) and, second, given the ascendancy of the latter over the former, there is the reduction of the former to an "instance" of the latter.

First, to the best of my knowledge, the term reification (*Verdinglichung*) nowhere occurs within the work of Marx. In the early manuscripts the focal concept is the "alienation of wage labor," while in his mature writings, the focal concept is "exchange-value." Assuming an interpretive continuity on this issue between Marx's early and later works and that the latter concept can sublate the former, "exchange-value" refers to the structuring of the forces of production for the production of commodities through an appropriation of the surplus value of labor by the socially and historically structured relations of production. To be sure, there is the *locus classicus* discussion of "commodity fetishism" in the first volume of *Capital*, yet as the remainder of that volume makes clear, it is the analysis of "exchange-value" which sets the interpretive context for "commodity fetishism" and not the reverse.

Second, the term "reification" is first given systematic use in the Marxist tradition in the work of Georg Lukács, preeminently in his *History and Class Consciousness*, where the focal concept is "commodity fetish." Here it appears that the "proportions" are reversed: from the structure of commodity fetishism within the context of the production of exchange-values to the production of exchange-value within the context of the structure of commodity fetishism. The latter encompasses the former as its instanciation and specification and thus allows Lukács to incorporate within his analysis of reification qua commodity fetishism the rationalization of the social world through its bureaucratization as described by Weber as well as to postulate an identity of form, commodity fetish, in the base and the superstructure. In this movement, the seeds are already sown for the generalization of commodity fetishism qua "instrumental reason," although, and this remains decisive, for Lukács this generalization remains inextricably intertwined with a specific social totality—capitalism and the primacy of the sphere of the economy.

Third, although little work is done on the topic of political economy, in the early essays of Horkheimer critical theory is described as a theory of society whose focus is the sphere of the economy, a position which is most explicit in Marcuse's essay, "On the Concept of Essence." Yet by the end of the 1930's the accent and emphasis changes. By "The End of Reason" (1941), the concept of "technological fetish" has eclipsed and replaces "commodity fetish" and the former is explicated in the major writings of the 1940's—the *Dialectic of Enlightenment* and *Eclipse of Reason*—as the domination of nature through instrumental or subjective reason. Further, in a late essay, "Culture and Administration," Adorno identifies scientific rationality with administration, but what is most notable, explicates both not in terms of a specific social totality, but in terms of what in *Negative Dialectics* is called "identity-thought."

> For that which is administered, administration is an external affair by which it is subsumed rather than comprehended. This is precisely the essence of administrated rationality itself, which does nothing but order and cover over. . . . Aporia prevails between the absolute purpose of the cultural and the absolute rationality of administration, which is nothing but the rationality of scientific rationality.[278]

In *the Melancholy Science*, Gillian Rose successfully argues that Adorno, the retrieval of Marx's notion of "exchange value" culminates in his concept of "identity-thought."[279] In *Negative Dialectics*, Adorno not only renewed his reflections on the dialectic of enlightenment but transposed his reflections on a "new" plane: the perspective of thought and reason itself where the dialectic of enlightenment appears as a dialectic between identity thought qua subjective reason and negative dialectics. A brief description of the two types of reason has been given above. Here I only need to add that while reason as negative dialectics, as self-critique and hence as critique of reality fulfills the role of reason through its constitutive orientation to truth through the negation of untruth, reason as "identity-thought" as the subsumption and forced coercion of the particular by the universal remains the inevitable and inescapable tempta-

[278] Adorno, "Culture and Administration," p. 97.
[279] Rose, *The Melancholy Science*, pp. 43-51. See, also, Held, *Introduction to Critical Theory*, pp. 210-22.

tion—if not presupposition—for reason as negation. In the concept of identity-thought, exchange-value as interpreted by Adorno is transposed to an anthropological "constant." What once named the logic of capital now becomes the immanent drive and goal, albeit fissured, of mind as such.

> When thinking follows its law of motion unconsciously it turns against its own sense, against what has been thought, against that which calls a halt to the flight of subjective consciousness. . . . Regression of consciousness is a product of its own lack of self-reflection. We can see through the identifying principle, but we cannot think without identifying. Any definition is identification.[280]

The will to identity is seen in each act of synthesis of the copula. The corresponding critical task of negative reason is not only the criticism of objective mind, but of consciousness itself—a task which is fulfilled not in a critical theory of society, but in a deconstructive mimesis of the particular under the sway of the universal through a philosophical program of negative dialectics and contemporary autonomous art which negatively witnesses to the hope of a rational identity.[281] As soon as reason resigns itself to its own immanent drive towards identity, it becomes its opposite—"unreason"—even as the aporia of critical reason is that as negation it presupposes the subjective affirmative from which derives and historically it must presuppose that domination of nature, which creates the space simultaneously founding history, the subject and civilization. It is not by mere chance that in *Negative Dialectics* critical theory of society and reference to a specific societal totality is edged out by the section "World Spirit and Natural History." What was the dark underside of the *Dialectic of Enlightenment* becomes thematic.

> Universal history must be construed and denied. After the catastrophes that have happened, and in view of the catastrophes to come, it would be cynical to say that a plan for a better world is manifested in history and unites it. Not to be denied for that reason, however, is the unity that cements the discontinuous, chaotically splintered moments and phases of history—the unity of the control of nature, progressing to rule over men, and finally to that over men's inner nature. No universal history leads from savagery to humanitarianism, but there is one leading from the slingshot to the megaton

---

[280] Adorno, *Negative Dialectics*, p. 149.
[281] Thus what Adorno wrote concerning a social utopia—"An emancipated society, on the other hand, would not be a unitary state, but the realization of universality in

bomb. It ends in the total menace which organized mankind poses to organized men, in the epitome of discontinuity. It is the horror that verifies
Hegel and stands him on his head. . . . The world spirit, a worthy object of
definition, would have to be defined as permanent catastrophe. Under the
all-subjugating identity principle, whatever does not enter into identity,
whatever eludes rational planning in the realm of means, turns into fright-
ening retribution for the calamity which identity brought on the non-identi-
cal. There is hardly another way to interpret history philosophically without
enchanting it into an idea.[282]

These comments on *Negative Dialectics* are not meant as even a partial
summary of that work. They simply indicate the intensification yet continuity of the later work of Adorno with the project of *Dialectic of
Enlightenment*. That continuity can be seen in that domination which is
seen as the content and subject matter of world history is "traced back"
to the ambiguity of reason itself and its constant temptation to lose itself
in "identity-thought." At the close of this second critical constellation
what I wish to suggest is that precisely at this point there occurs explicitly what was already implicit: the fragmentation of a critical theory
of society into a philosophy of (universal) history.

Critical Theory and the "End of Ideology"

In May 1962, President John Kennedy pronounced that

. . . most of us are conditioned for many years to have a political view-
point—Republican or Democratic, liberal, conservative or moderate. The
fact of the matter is that most of the problems . . . that we now face are technical problems, are administrative problems. They are very sophisticated
judgements, which do not lend themselves to the great sorts of passionate
movements which have stirred this country so often in the past. [They] deal
with questions which are now beyond the comprehension of most men. .
. .[283]

---

the reconciliation of differences" [*Minima Moralia*, p. 103]—itself derives from his image of the reconciliation of subject and object, see p. 164f..
[282] Adorno, *Negative Dialectics*, p. 320.
[283] John F. Kennedy, Press Conference, May 12, 1962, cited by Christopher Lasch,
The Culture of Narcissism (New York: Warner Books, 1979), p. 145. The following
month, in his 1962 commencement address at Yale University, the President again re-
turned to the question of government "management": "What is at stake is not some
grand warfare of rival ideologies . . . but the practical management of a modern
economy. What we need is not labels and clichés but more basic discussion of the so-

Through the 1960's the advent of "scientific politics" and the ideal of a rational management of society as a whole was celebrated as the "end of ideology."[284] What is notable in the writings of both Horkheimer and Adorno is that there also arises a variant qua inversion of the thesis of the "end of ideology"—not as the object of celebration and expectant greeting but with a recoiling terror before the specter of a "brave new world with a human face." From *Dialectic of Enlightenment* forward, this is increasingly conveyed in phrases such as "the administered world," "integration from above," "the extirpation of the subject," "the reification of consciousness" and the change in the function of ideology itself. It witnesses to the regression of this (enlightenment-capitalist) piece of history to myth; *die versteinte Gesellschaft* condemned to the eternal repetition of the same; the automatic reproduction of the societal whole through the convergence of its subjective and objective moments.

> For while the mind extricated itself from a theological-feudal tutelage, it has fallen increasingly under the sway of the status quo. This regimentation, the result of the progressive socialization of all human relations, did not simply confront the mind from without; it immigrated into its immanent consistency. It imposes itself as relentlessly on the autonomous mind as heteronomous orders were formerly imposed on the mind which was bound. Not only does the mind mould itself for the sake of marketability, and thus reproduce the socially relevant categories. Rather, it grows to resemble the *status quo* even where it subjectively refrains from making a commodity of itself. The network of the whole is drawn ever tighter, modelled after the act of exchange. It leaves the individual consciousness less and less room for evasion, preforms it more and more thoroughly, cuts it off *a priori* as it were from the possibility of differencing itself as all difference degenerates to a nuance in the monotony of supply. At the same time, the semblance of freedom makes reflection upon one's own unfreedom more difficult than formerly when such reflection stood in contradiction to manifest unfreedom, thus strengthening dependence.[285]

Such sentiments were not limited to Adorno. In Horkheimer's 1968 preface to the collection and publication of his *Zeitschrift* essays—signifi-

---

phisticated and technical questions involved in keeping a great economic machinery moving ahead. . . . [T]echnical answers, not political answers must be provided" [*Speeches of John F. Kennedy*, commencement address at Yale University, June 11, 1962 (Washington, D. C.: U. S. Government Printing Office, 1964), cited in Robert B. Reich, *The Next American Frontier* (New York: Times Books, 1983), p. 80].
284 Daniel Bell, *The End of Ideology* (New York: The Free Press, 1960).
285 Adorno, "Culture Criticism and Society," pp. 20-21.

cantly subtitled *Eine Dokumentation*—he asserts that greater social organization and integration as the bill of technological advance is the price of material amelioration. The preservation of the remnants of the private sphere of the individual, once decried as abstract and false, becomes the task today:

> To protect, preserve and, where possible, extend the limited and ephemeral freedom of the individual in the face of the growing threat to it is far more urgent a task than to issue abstract denunciations of it or to endanger it by actions that have no hope of success.[286]

For Adorno, the last refuge of reason against the end of ideology and the impotency of praxis is the renewal of philosophy as a self-critique, as negative dialectics.

> Philosophy, which once seemed obsolete, lives on because the moment to realize it was missed. The summary judgement that it merely had interpreted the world, that resignation in the face of reality had crippled it in itself, becomes a defeatism of reason after the attempt to change the world miscarried . . . . Theory cannot prolong the moment its critique depended on. . . . Having broken its pledge to be as one with reality or at the point of realization, philosophy is obliged ruthlessly to criticize itself.[287]

The thesis of the "end of ideology" is, at best and worst, a tendential one—a premature thought which may yet be vindicated by this society's endurance and growth. It denotes the *tendency* of the societal whole. Here lies both its untruth and its truth. Its untruth is the absence of the complete reification of consciousness and the potential crises of the crisis management of societal subsystems. Its truth lies in the co-optive power of society. The truth of the "end of ideology" is that even overt revolt and disruptive potentials can be "managed": detoothed and exhibited as a witness to tolerance; subtly transmuted through a specious coming to grips with the issues they raise; capitalized upon and commoditized into industry; merely endured, hoping that exhaustion and fatigue will lead to resignation and dispersion; or, at the limit, squelched through indirect political and economic coercion or the direct coercion of the bullet. Nevertheless, widespread resignation, boredom and cynicism today can erupt into revolutionary praxis, or, into a new barbaric atrocity. Posed between one unspeakable horror some generation earlier and an unimag-

---

[286] Horkheimer, "Preface," in *Critical Theory*, p. viii.
[287] Adorno, *Negative Dialectics*, p. 3.

inable one perhaps yet to come, the conditions which led to them both endure.

Thus I may be forgiven if I do not underplay the force of this thesis for Adorno and Horkheimer. It may be "premature," not yet a *fait accompli*, but that does not equal the negation of the negation—neither in the form of the "right" who have understood but not comprehended the antinomies of liberal democracy and hence are content with reformism; nor in the form of the "left" who parrot Marx and close their eyes to the betrayal of socialism in the authoritarian socialist state (or if more liberal, become "tourists of the revolution"); nor in the form of the academician and scholar who usually fall neither into the right nor the left, but who almost always espouse a "trickle down" theory of revolutionary change. The counterthesis (not antithesis) to the "end of ideology" endures only as an abstraction, a hope against hope or else it becomes an objective delusion itself supporting the status quo. Perhaps this too may be accused of resignation and pessimism. If so, however, it is a realism borne from fear and has the truth of a corrective.

A THEOLOGICAL POSTSCRIPT: FOUR ALLUSIONS

I

What credible justification can be given for being a partisan of reason today, for a commitment to reason and freedom as historical and hence social tasks? Unless one is willing to explain it through a facile reference to gene structures, environmental conditions (both physical and sociological), a personal distaste for the alternative as a conservativism which clings to the "outmoded" standards of Western culture; unless one is willing to explain it by these or through an explanation of a similar nature, then something more is needed. Even the appeal to self-preservation seems insufficient because as Horkheimer and Adorno observed, it is an ironic truism in our present society that the path of least resistance is the surest avenue of self-preservation both socially and psychologically. To appeal to self-preservation within the wider framework of the preservation of the species-being merely begs the question at a further juncture. Why concern ourselves with a species-being—itself a bloodless abstraction—which seemingly has had little concern for us?[288] In a soci-

---

[288] Robert L. Heilbroner, "What Has Posterity Ever Done for Me?," in *An Inquiry into the Human Prospect*, rev. ed. (New York: W. W. Norton and Co., 1980), pp. 179-86.

ety characterized by narcissism, is the "cash-value" of such an appeal a sentimental attachment to one's parents or progeny? There is nothing particularly wrong with that, but there seems to be something of a "disproportion" in ascribing one's partisanship in reason to such provisional ties. After all, parents die and artificial contraception has made progeny predictable to the point where the quest for sexual pleasure may be met with little concern for the potential toddling tyke. If one does escape such facile sentimentality regarding the preservation of the "species-being" to a solidarity with the oppressed past in a spiritual "care for the dead" and an anticipation of a transformed world for those whom we will never know, a not so absurd question which the taboo of silence has not rendered any less urgent necessarily arises, "Why?". Perhaps at this point, theology as a question may enter in. "Even a critical social theory cannot avoid an 'ultimate' in which its criticisms is rooted because reason itself is rooted therein. Otherwise criticism itself becomes positivistic and contingent."[289]

II

In an iconoclastic essay, "Anamnestic Solidarity: The Proletariat and Its *Manes*," Christian Lenhardt probes the concept of "solidarity" in the Marxist tradition. At the core of this attempt to probe Marx's ideal of the "total recovery of many," stands a thought experiment:

> ... let us introduce a simple generational typology where G_1 stands for the generation of enslaved predecessors (*Vorwelt*), G_2 for the generation of enslaved contemporaries who, according to Marx, will emancipate themselves (*Mitwelt*), and G_3 for the generation of emancipated successors (*Nachwelt*). It is quite conceivable, albeit not likely, that Marx saw the solidarity of a liberated mankind simply in terms of an interpersonal principle of harmony amongst the members of G_3. This would reduce the exploited predecessors (G_1) and those who struggle for the revolutionary cause (G_2) to the status of nonentities or deadwood in the evolution of mankind, primitive stages which had to be overcome, and whose existence had better be forgotten. . . . According to this view, the human species can only actualize itself when it overcomes the debilitating ballast of remembrance, i.e., when it *forgets* its historical genesis.[290]

[289] Paul Tillich, review of *Reason and Revolution*, by Herbert Marcuse, in *ZfS* 9 (1941): 478.
[290] Christian Lenhardt, "Anamnestic Solidarity: The Proletariat and Its Manes," *Telos* 25 (Fall 1975): 135-36.

If such is the case, Lenhardt asks "Is Marxism really the theory and practice of emancipation from remembrance? Is it a synonym for a pervasive
world-historical amnesia? Is it so entranced by the prospects of the future
that it believes an emancipated mankind could accept the sacrificial self-
abnegation of 'pre-historic' man without sadness and without scru-
ples?"[291]

Assuming as truthful Benjamin's dictum that the core of revolutionary practice is more "nourished by the image of enslaved ancestors
rather than that of liberated grandchildren,"[292] Lenhardt seeks to expose
the aporia of "anamnestic solidarity" in the thought experiment introduced above.

> According to him [Benjamin], there is little virtue in the contemporaries
> sacrificing themselves for posterity. Rather their proper outlook and moti-
> vation is an empathetic regard for the exploitation of the dead predecessors.
> And if G_2 feels that he has a debt towards G_1 because the ancestors pro-
> vided, however blindly and unknowingly, the historical opportunity for a
> great cataclysmic overthrow of the aggregate conditions of unfreedom, how
> much greater must be the debt owed by G_3 to the memory of G_1 and G_2, and
> yet G_3 cannot pay it off in the same self-sacrificial manner in which G_2 pays
> off its debt to G_1. The members of the humanized socialist society enjoy their
> social praxis, their labor becoming creative, and so on. But how can this
> daily redemption of debts which G_2 effected by making a revolution of
> vengeance? If a redemptive attitude is part and parcel of the idea of an
> emancipated mankind, is it not rather an unenviable destiny to belong to the
> successor generation (G_3), for what can it do, practically and existentially, to
> equalize the burden of injustice borne by its predecessors (G_1 and G_2)?[293]

The suppression of the question directly raised here indirectly affirms,
Lenhardt claims, an amnesic pride which operates "with the premise that
only visible suffering creates a barrier to happiness, and once this visible
suffering is gone, a boundlessly affirmative appropriation and understanding of the world becomes possible" while ignoring the fact that
while "the evils of pre-history may have been overcome, they will linger
on in the collective *anamnesis* of liberated mankind."[294]

It is this aporia of anamnestic solidarity which conditions, Lenhardt
suggests, the "pessimism" of the Frankfurt School or, more exactly, the
thought of Benjamin and Horkheimer in the latter's assertion that "past

---

[291] Ibid., p. 136.
[292] Benjamin, "Theses on the Philosophy of History," p. 260.
[293] Lenhardt, "Anamnestic Solidarity," p. 137.
[294] Ibid., p. 138.

injustice will never be made up; the suffering of past generations receives no compensation."[295] The *Naturwuchsigkeit*,[296] the slime of history as the embeddedness of the human being in nature, fractures the very demand for a universal solidarity which is the real, subjective condition of revolutionary praxis and critical theory for not only "nature"—as Marx is maintains in the third volume of *Capital*—but also "history" as the unredeemable suffering of the past constitutes a sphere of "necessity" which interrupts the myth of a pure self-transparent collective appropriation of the social world. In the face of this aporia Lenhardt posits the necessity of a form of "ancestor worship" which acknowledges the claim of the "dead past" even in the state of utopia:

> The felicity of the lucky successors will have an admixture of displeasure owing to the exclusion of the ancestors from the feast of their grand-children. Dead and gone, the predecessors have a rightful claim to being remembered. Perhaps that will make their lower world habitable—if it exists and if they exist. If not, then the anamnestic homage of the living at least serves the purpose of assuaging their own guilt. Posterity will have to maintain that hypothesis (that it owes its existence to the manes) in the face of all evidence to the contrary.[297]

The most ambitious attempt to respond theologically to this aporia of anamnestic solidarity is Helmut Peukert's *Wissenschaftstheorie-Handlungstheorie-Fundamentale Theologie*.[298] In this work he attempts to elaborate a fundamental theology as a theory of society and history which clusters around the exigencies of "communicative action." Most tersely stated, Peukert's argument is that the concrete practice of communicative action and its demand of a universal solidarity implies the assertion of a reality that saves the innocent one from "death" which is implicitly correlated with the religious traditions of Judaism and Christianity which provide a concrete locus for the experience of freedom in universal solidarity.

My own misgivings concerning Peukert's constructive proposal involve his transcendental orientation: the transition from his construal of the conditions of the possibility of communicative action (qua universal

---

[295] Horkheimer, "Materialism and Metaphysics," in *Critical Theory*, p. 26.

[296] See, also, Jeremy J. Schapiro, "The Slime of History: Embeddedness in Nature and Critical Theory," in *On Critical Theory*, pp. 145-63.

[297] Lenhardt, "Anamnestic Solidarity," p. 144.

[298] Helmut Peukert, *Wissenschaftstheorie-Handlungstheorie-Fundamentale Theologie* (Frankfurt: Suhrkamp, 1976).

solidarity) to an assertion that if, in fact, such communicative action is the case, then the reality which saves the innocent one from death exists. Such a procedure is, I believe, yet another strategy to secure the truth claims of the Christian tradition without risking them in history. In fact, Peukert appears to overlook how the truth claims, mediated by the Christian tradition, *already* condition his construal of communicative action itself—a fact which becomes clear when Peukert's position is juxtaposed to Lenhardt's.

Perhaps the most that can be said is that at the juncture of the aporia of anamnestic solidarity, Christian faith and theology can only stand as an overdetermined question—overdetermined by the weight of its own traditions and a question as to whether the worship of the *Manes* does not a priori inscribe in advance pessimism as constitutive of critical theory. Here, the question must be tolerated as a *question*—only that and nothing more. In short, the conjuncture between critical theory (a theory of communicative action) and Christian faith is far more fragile than Peukert himself appears to assume—a fragility which derives from the experience of the Christian "significant particular" as interpreted in a particular and determinate manner.

III

Both Adorno and Horkheimer, but especially the former, had precious little to say about the phenomenon of positive religion.[299] Much of what they did say was stated obliquely or as ancillary to other concerns. Indirectly or directly stated, almost all their comments are negative. It is curious that these men who saw as clearly as any the dialectic of enlightenment at this point seem to capitulate to a one-dimensional reception of the enlightenment critique of religion: knowledge (*Wissen*) of God would occlude the consciousness of the *Verlassenheit* of men and women thus relieving humanity of the exigency for self-creative praxis inasmuch as God would act as the guarantor of meaning and value; religion masks and transmutes the negativity of evil and the seriousness of suffering; religion, much like *prima philosophia*, is the popular positing of a *proton*

---

[299] For an exposition of the explicit statements of Horkheimer and Adorno on religion, see Rudolph Siebert: "Horkheimer's Sociology of Religion," *Telos* 30 (Winter 1976-77): 127-44; "Adorno's Theory of Religion," *Telos* 58 (Winter 1983-84): 108-14; and *Horkheimer's Critical Sociology of Religion: The Relative and the Transcendent* (Washington, D. C.: University Press of America, 1979).

pseudos.300 The subsequent and increasing instrumentalization of religion in contemporary society was, for Adorno and Horkheimer, a sign of the hollowness of its claim to truth even as it served another untruth.301 If Marx wrote, "the criticism of religion is the premise of all criticism,"302 then it seems that for both men such criticism was not so much a task as finished business. The incompatibility of religion and materialism was not so much an issue as an assumption.

However disparaging or noncommittal their remarks concerning positive religion (i.e., Judaism and Christianity), there is a "religious dimension" to critical theory which is certainly not thematic, almost always subliminal, and only occasionally erupts into view culminating in Horkheimer's 1969 interview with Helmut Gumnior, *Die Sehnsucht nach dem ganz Anderen*—an interview as much remarkable for its content as for the tacit silence which succeeded it on the part of the "left."

In a 1935 letter to Benjamin, Adorno wrote,

> . . . a restoration of theology, or better yet, a radicalization of the dialectic into the glowing center of theology, would at the same time have to mean the utmost intensification of the social-dialectical, indeed economic, motifs.303

---

300 In this regard, Horkheimer's assertion is typical: "Consciousness of our aloneness, our finitude, is no proof that 'God exists'....If we had absolute certainty that 'God exists," then our knowledge of the aloneness of humanity would be a deceit for we could not then actually have that knowledge." Horkheimer, *Die Sehnsucht nach dem ganz Anderen: Ein Interview mit Kommentar von Hellmut Gumnior* (Hamburg: Furche, 1970), pp. 56-57.

301 See, for example, Horkheimer, *Eclipse of Reason*, pp. 63-70, and *Die Sehnsucht nach dem ganz Anderen*, pp. 66-71. Horkheimer's tacit position here is that the "liberalization" and "secularization"—and these terms are nowhere explicated by him—of religion as a farewell to what Ricoeur calls "first naïveté" inevitably destroys the certainty which is constitutive of religious belief and hence leads to its social pragmaticization.

302 Marx, "A Contribution to the Critique of Hegel's Philosophy of Right," in *Early Writings*, p. 243.

303 Adorno, "Adorno-Benjamin Correspondence," in *Aesthetics and Politics*, p. 114. So, also, Benjamin could write, "Remembrance can make of the unfinished (i.e., happiness) something that is finished and, conversely, it can make the finished (i.e., past suffering) into something that is unfinished. This is theology. Yet in remembering we gain the knowledge that we must not try to understand history in fundamentally atheological terms, just as we would not want to write history in straight-forwardly theological terms" [Benjamin, unpublished manuscript entitled, "*Passagen*," cited in Lenhardt, "Anamnestic Solidarity," pp. 141-42].

To be sure, the use of the term "theology" here is highly idiosyncratic. Some interpretation of this term, however, may be gleaned from the last fragment of *Minima Moralia*, entitled "Finale."

> The only philosophy which can be responsibly practiced in the face of despair is the attempt to contemplate all things as they would present themselves from the standpoint of redemption. Knowledge has no light but that shed on the world by redemption. Perspectives must be fashioned that displace and estrange the world, reveal it to be, with its rifts and crevices, as indigent and distorted as it will appear one day in the messianic light.[304]

Lest the theologian prematurely rejoice and claim Adorno as an unwitting ally, the last line of the fragment must be added: "But beside the demand thus placed on thought, the question of the reality and unreality of redemption itself hardly matters."[305] Hope and the future become the very medium of transcendence and the appearance of truth.

> In the end hope, wrested from reality by negating it, is the only form in which truth appears. Without hope, the idea of truth would be scarcely even thinkable, and it is the cardinal untruth, having recognized existence to be bad, to present it as truth simply because it has been recognized.[306]

As an extreme form of "negative theology," a religious dimension exists within the core of critical theory in its allegiance to a "Wholly Other" or a "transcendence without a Transcendent" which reveals the world as mere appearance.[307] Thus also Horkheimer could assert the ultimate and intimate conjunction of "theology" and "politics" which grounds the negation of the positivistic bad facticity of "what simply is."

> Politics which does not preserve theology in itself but adapts itself remains, in the final analysis, mere business....Everything which concerns moral matters goes back in the last analysis to theology. All moral matters, at least in the West, are grounded in theology.[308]

---

[304] Idem, *Minima Moralia*, p. 247.
[305] Ibid.
[306] Ibid., p. 98.
[307] Horkheimer, *Die Sehnsucht nach dem ganz Anderen*, pp. 57-60, 77.
[308] Ibid., pp. 60-61. This last consideration of religion by Horkheimer stands in notable contrast to some of his earliest thoughts (i.e., "Materialism and Metaphysics," pp. 10-46, and "Thoughts on Religion," in *Critical Theory*, pp. 129-31). The following selection of quotes may help illustrate this: "Consciousness of our aloneness, of our finitude, is no proof that 'God exists'; rather this can only summon forth the hope

Three brief comments may be added at this juncture. First, the theologian must beware not to posthumously baptize agnostic Jews. Horkheimer's and Adorno's refusal to acknowledge the validity and truth claims of any particular positive religion or even to give serious intellectual consideration to any positive religious tradition must be granted its autonomy, even if not accepted as authoritative. Yet it appears valid to suggest that a critical theory which decisively, either implicitly by omission or explicitly by assertion, cuts its roots from a religious dimension, that is, from a dimension which transcends the merely existent, withers.

Second, I suggest that for all its "emptiness," there is a specific grammar of the religious dimension as articulated by both men: history as mediated by society is set as the parameters of that dimension. In this critical theory partakes of the remnants and residue of a specific religious tradition(s)—most proximately Judaism and, more distantly, Christianity—where history is valorized as a totality of meaning which sets the context for the sort of transcendence to be sought.

Lastly, the question can be raised whether a religious dimension—already implicitly determined as of a specific sort—can exist without a positive, social embodiment, religion? As "immediate," a religious dimension which does not recognize its own specific dependence as mediated by a particular religious grammar is not only inadequate to its own concept as a false immediacy abstracted from a mediated immediacy, but

---

that there exists a positive Absolute....'Theology' here signifies the consciousness that the world is appearance, that it is not the absolute truth, the last thing. Theology is....the hope that this consciousness together with the injustice which characterizes the world does not abide, that injustice may not be the last word....Theology is an expression of a yearning, a yearning that the murderer may not triumph over his innocent victim....Religion can make humanity aware of its finitude, that each must suffer and die. Even under suffering and death, the yearning remains that this earthly being may not be absolute, may not be the last thing....The yearning for a complete and perfect justice....This, however, can never be actualized in the secular world. Even if a better society redeems the present social dis-order, the misery of the past will not be made good and the lack in an unyielding nature will not be overcome" pp. 56, 61, 62, 67, 69]. Horkheimer's position in this last interview seems clear: the divine is a "limit," in Kant's sense of the phrase, which is subjectively held not in the modality of "certainty," but a "hopeful yearning." Of the object of this hopeful yearning, nothing can be said, even as it plays a constitutive function in disclosing the world as "appearance." Finally, this hopeful yearning itself is constitutive of the interest in reason of praxis and critical theory itself. As I suggest immediately below, Horkheimer's very articulation of the divine as "limit" is always already an overdetermined one, and hence not simply a "limit" per se.

precisely in being inadequate threatens its own existence by discarding that by which it is mediated. The severing of the two moments, that of a religious dimension and positive religion, is by announcing the demise of the latter to hasten that of the former, and in the void thus opened to allow both to reemerge solely and purely as a function and insignia of the existent.

IV

(In this last "fragment" follows, I restrict myself to speaking of the Christian religion and theology.) The preceding section is not meant to suggest that critical theory could restore positive religion to a position immune from criticism. On the contrary, formally, the challenge of a critical theory of society to religion is its critique of the abstraction "pure religion" which must be internalized within theology itself as the negative moment conditioning any positive retrieval of the Christian religious tradition. Critical theory must, then, become a methodological moment within theology as such and not merely a subsequent moment of application relegated to a discipline understood as ancillary to theology as such (i.e., social ethics, practical theology, moral theology, etc.). Further, critical theory poses a far more profound, material challenge to theology and Christianity's self-understanding. In the previous section, I suggested that there needs to be a "redistinguishing" of the moments of a critical theory of society and philosophy of history and a reversal of the latter insofar as it construed history as a whole as a new identity-system, not in the name of progress, but in the name of domination and catastrophe which is inscribed in the universal form of reason itself as identity-thought. However, there still remains the thesis of critical theory that in post-Enlightenment society there is an eclipse of history as the sphere of the "new" and a regression to myth in the automatic reproduction of the status quo. This regression, if consummated, would mean the eclipse and demise of Christianity itself in that the horizon of its meaning is history as a whole and as eschatologically valorized. The tendential thesis of the "end of ideology" which is premature and yet threatens to become reality challenges the meaning of Christianity insofar as it concretely erodes the objective condition of Christian faith, history, as well as the capacity of subjects for this presupposition. The most appropriate response of Christian theology to this challenge of critical theory and its interconnection of history and society is an explicitly political theology—the subject to which the remainder of this essay is devoted.

CHAPTER III

Johann Metz: Christian Faith and History as Society

> If a man wishes to come after me, he must deny his very self, take up his cross, and follow in my steps. Whoever will preserve his life will lose it, but whoever loses his life for my sake and the gospel's will preserve it.
>
> Mark 8. 34b-35

INTRODUCTION

This chapter treats the work of Johann Metz as an example of "political theology," i.e., a theology oriented to the world as history eschatologically valorized and socially mediated. One may speak of three "phases" of Metz's theological reflection to date: a first phase found primarily in the text *Christliche Anthropozentrik* where his theological reflection is stamped by the categories and method of Rahner's transcendental theology; a second phase which coalesces around his entry "Political Theology" in *Sacramentum Mundi* and the essays of *Zur Theologie der Welt* (roughly 1964-68) which initiates a break with the first phase in the turn to a "postmetaphysical" and "posttranscendental" theology, i.e., a political theology and a theology of the future; and a third phase initiated by the essay *"Politische Theologie in der Diskussion"* (1969) and continuing through the specification of the categories of political theology as a "practical fundamental theology" in *Glaube in Geschichte and Gesellschaft*.[1]

---

[1] The principle texts by Metz to be used in this chapter are: *Christliche Anthropozentrik* (Munich: Kosel, 1962); "The Theological World and the Metaphysical World," trans. Dominic Gerlach, *Philosophy Today* 10 (1966): 253-63; "Freedom as a

Given the focus of this chapter, it is the second and third phases of Metz' work which will be treated—an omission perhaps all the more acceptable insofar as there exist various expositions of Metz' earliest work.[2]

The two sections which follow roughly correspond to these two phases. A third section of critical reflections and questions concludes the chapter. A few observations on the genre, contextual and stylistic characteristics of Metz's work are, however, in order because they cumulatively set the parameters for my interpretation.

First, a glance at Metz's bibliography in Bauer or Widenhofer leaves one with the impression of an extensive and lengthy corpus of written works. Such an impression, however, is only adequate to a cursory glance. While Metz's output is by no means meager, a closer look at the bibliographies reveal a somewhat smaller "core corpus" of written works which has often been reworked, revised and republished under different titles. Indeed, eight of the thirteen chapters of *Glaube und Geschichte im Gesellschaft* were previously published and revised for that work.

Threshold Problem between Philosophy and Theology," trans. William Kramer, *Philosophy Today* 10 (1966): 264-79; *Theology of the World*, trans. William Glen-Doepel (New York: Seabury Press, 1969); "The Responsibility of Hope," trans. William Kramer, *Philosophy Today* 10 (1966): 280-88; "*Gott vor uns, Statt eines theologischen Arguments*," in *Ernst Bloch zu ehren: Beitrage zu seinem Werk*, ed. Siegfried Unseld (Frankfurt: Suhrkamp, 1965), pp. 227-41; "Political Theology," in *Sacramentum Mundi*, 6 volumes, ed. Karl Rahner (New York: Herder and Herder, 1970), 6: 34-38; "'*Politische Theologie'in der Diskussion*," in *Diskussion zur politischen Theologie*, ed. Helmut Peukert (Munich: Chr. Kaiser, 1969), pp. 267-301; *Faith in History and Society*, trans. David Smith (New York: Seabury Press, 1980); *The Emergent Church*, trans. Peter Mann (New York: Crossroad Publishing Co., 1981); *Unterbrechungen* (Gutersloh: Gerd Mohn, 1981); "*Zu einer interdisziplinär orientierten Theologie auf bikonfessionneller Basis: Erste Orientierungen anhand eines Konkreten Projekts*, in *Die Theologie in der interdisziplinären Forschung*," ed. Johann Metz and Trutz Rendtorff (Düsseldorf: Bertelsmann Universitätsverlag, 1971), pp. 10-25. Insofar as it is generally acknowledged that Metz has not been well-served by the translation of *Faith in History and Society*, I have also noted the page numbers of the original German text, *Glaube in Geschichte und Gesellschaft* (Mainz: Matthias Grunewald, 1977), in parentheses after the English citation.

[2] An exposition of what I have termed the "first phase" of Metz' thought can be found in Roger Dick Johns, *Man in the World: The Theology of Johannes Baptist Metz*, American Academy of Religion Dissertation Series, number 16 (Missoula: Scholars Press, 1976). A discussion of Metz's work up to the year 1974—and one which attempts to situate his work within the context of contemporary Continental theology—can be found in Gerhard Bauer, *Christliche Hoffnung und Menschlicher Fortschritt* (Mainz: Grunewald, 1976).

Second, while there is a relatively clear interpretive center within this core corpus—the attempt to articulate the agenda and categories of postmetaphysical, postexistential political theology—difficulties arise as one moves chronologically further into Metz's work. The first difficulty arises from the fact that even the "major" published "books" by Metz are collections of articles. The genre of the article tends to constrict the presentation and exposition of key terms, concepts and positions to either a highly schematic or highly focused form thus eluding a desired balance between the particular and the general. A second difficulty arises from the diverse genre's of Metz's writings along with their differing "implied audiences." Not only has much of Metz's writing been cast in the professionally "normal" form of articles and addresses to colleagues, it has also taken the form of devotional and meditational material, *laudatio*, commentaries on church documents, addresses to student groups and political seminars and "open letters." Thus, for example, one of the most complete expositions of the category of *imitatio* occurs within the short work *Followers of Christ*: a work whose theme is the contemporary relevance of "religious orders" within the context of the synodical statement *Unsere Hoffnung*.[3] Finally, potential difficulties arise from the tenor of Metz's rhetoric. Particularly in his latest work, Metz's arguments are critical-polemical. They resemble a sort of theological guerilla warfare which is decisive in what positions are rejected but less clear in what is being positively asserted. In short, his language and rhetoric becomes simultaneously more malleable by scholarly standards and brittle by common sense conversational ones.

Third, I suggest that these limits to any interpretation of Metz's most recent work are not accidental. They reflect a major goal of the third phase of his work: the attempt to rupture theology as a noetic identity system along with its institutional condition in the modern university. Metz's theology becomes through his rhetoric an evocative and provocative one and this is precisely its point: to remain noetically "unconcluded" because of the nonidentity of faith and history as a history of suffering.

---

[3] Johann Metz, *Followers of Christ*, trans. Thomas Linton (New York: Paulist Press, 1978).

THE ORIGINS OF "POLITICAL THEOLOGY"

The substance of the essays published in *Theology of the World* (1968) can be presented along three themes: the secularization (*Verweltlichung*) thesis, the "world" as history and hence the primacy of the future, and political theology. These three themes progressively represent a more concrete and determinate specification of the horizon of Christian theology and faith where each subsequent theme presupposes and incorporates the ones which preceded it.

The essays in *Theology of the World* are framed by the problem of the identity and relevance of Christianity in an age where the hominization of the world appears in its own self-interpretation as an undialectical protest against and emancipation from God thus provoking a crisis of faith and belief. Attempts at the preservation of the identity of faith through a socially restorative integralism and a positivistic theological dogmatism simultaneously provoke strategies which emphasize the relevance of Christianity through its accommodation to a secular and secularist culture and vice versa.[4] The essays of *Theology of the World* are apologetic ones—an attempt to defend theologically the "worldliness of the world" and its attendant ambiguity as well as the worldliness of the Christian faith. More specifically, they are an apologetics *ad intra* as a criticism of the church, of theology and of society and only thereby do they serve as an apologetics *ad extra*.[5]

The connotations which Metz gives to the term "secularization" are wider than that accorded to the term in social-scientific discussions. For him, the term refers to the emergence of "modernity." Included in this regard is the dissolution of the identity of *imperium* and *sacerdotum* at the twilight of the medieval period and the subsequent "setting free" of the former as "state" and "civil society" which assumes autonomous responsibility for the worldliness of the world apart from the "once for all" normative framework of the latter. Equally important is the rise of empirically- and historically- oriented sciences which challenge the normativity of all theological and metaphysical systems. Negatively, the world as secular may be described as a denuminized world, as a world which does not exhibit the *vestigia Dei* but only the *vestigia homini*: a world where the numinous does not lay immediately at hand in nature,

---

[4] The language of the "identity" and "relevance" of Christian faith is drawn from Jürgen Moltmann, *The Crucified God*, trans. R. A. Wilson and John Bowden (New York: Harper and Row, 1974), pp. 7-31.

[5] *Sacramentum Mundi*, 1968 ed., s.v. "Apologetics," by J. B. Metz.

but one where it provokes and demands a human self-recognition. Positively, the "world as secular" refers to the worldliness or the autonomy of the world and reason: a world where objective and immutable normativity gives way to creative growth and development, delivered over to the subjectivity in freedom of men and women and hence as given over to both a subjective and objective pluralism of consciousness, forms of life, areas of experience and modes of conduct.[6] As the hermeneuts of suspicion from the Enlightenment to our own time have asked, does not such an epochal shift reveal religion as a form of "inauthentic consciousness" even as it harbingers the "death of God?"

Metz's response to those who would see an absolute disjunction between the secularity of the world and Christian faith takes a "strong" form.

> The secularity of the world, as it has emerged in the modern process of secularization and as we see it today in a globally heightened form, has fundamentally, though not in its individual historical forms, arisen not against Christianity, but through it. It is originally a Christian event and hence testifies in our world situation to the power of the "hour of Christ" at work within history.[7]

The secularization thesis argues that not only is there no disjunction between Christianity and modernity as the secular of world—although "secularity" as a basic orientation and posture must be differentiated from "secularism" as a misinterpretation of secularity—but that the latter is an "effect" of Christianity.[8] More precisely, the secularity or the worldliness of the world is grounded in Christianity's witness to a transcendent Creator and the Incarnation.

Belief in a transcendent creator lets the world appear in its worldliness, its nondivinity and hence autonomy in that such a belief posits a

---

[6] Metz, *Theology of the World*, pp. 13-77 passim.

[7] Ibid., pp. 19-20. See, also, pp. 35, 39, 63.

[8] The distinction between "secularity" and "secularism" assumed here may be found in Ogden, *The Reality of God* (New York: Harper and Row, 1966), pp. 6-70, and Gilkey, *Naming the Whirlwind: The Renewal of God-Language* (Indianapolis,IN: Bobbs-Merrill Co., 1969), pp. 247-304. Metz's thesis, although emerging in the context of transcendental Thomism, parallels that of Friedrich Gogarten, *Verhangnis und Hoffnung der Neuzeit: Die Sakularsierung als theologisches Problem*, 2nd ed. (Stuttgart: Friedrich Vorwerk, 1958). For a response to this thesis and an attempt to argue that what characterizes the emergence of "modernity" is a rupture between it and the Christian tradition, see Hans Blumenberg, *The Legitimacy of the Modern Age*, trans. Robert M. Wallace (Cambridge: The MIT Press, 1983).

"difference" between the finite and the infinite, profane and sacred, the human and the divine. Belief in a transcendent creator-god in its difference from the world opens up and grounds the basic secularity of the world: "(w)e could say that where there is no faith in a transcendental creator, there is no genuine secularization of the world and no genuine availability of this world to men."[9] Yet alone and by itself, belief in a transcendent creator and the sheer difference of the divine and the world runs the risk of an ontological dualism.

It is the belief in the Incarnation which grounds the original divine liberating acceptance of the world in that women and men, the world, are accepted by the eternal Word in the hypostatic union as "different," where this difference emerges precisely due to its divine acceptance. Together, the symbols of creation and incarnation disclose that "God's divinity consists in the fact that he does not remove the difference between himself and what is other, but rather accepts the other precisely as different from himself"[10] thus making free the authentic, independent being of the nondivine. Together, these symbols thematize the "unity in difference" of God and the world which lets the worldliness of the world appear as nondivine yet not severed from the divine. The language of the hypostatic union, applied to the relation of God and the world, as a unity without confusion or mixture avoids the equally dangerous extremes of a monophysitic incarnational optimism— a redivinization of the world— and an ebionism which posits an unbridgeable difference between the divine and the world.

To be sure, this is not to identify the secularity of the world set free in Jesus Christ with the modern history of secularization. Precisely due to the former, there is also set free the possibility of the distortion, alienation, ambiguity and concupiscence of the latter in its shutting itself off from its origin. Yet this cannot drive the Christian towards an undialectical negation of the secularity of the world, but propels him or her into a recapitulation of that authentic secularity of the world which is described as an *imitatio Christi*:

> . . . the Christian's relation to the world is found in the faithful imitation of God's descent into the world, of the liberating acceptance of the world in Jesus Christ. The primary thing in the believer's attitude to the world is not

9   Metz, *Theology of the World*, p. 65.
10 Ibid., p. 26.

to close the gap with the world, but to accept it in faith, leaving the world its
secularity.[11]

Specifically, such an openness to and acceptance of the world is one of
openness to and acceptance of its ambiguity and suffering.[12]

The secularity of the world, however, points to a more primordial
change regarding human being's anticipative understanding of the nature of "world" as such. "The process of the growing secularization of
the world is governed by a worldview that is coming into being in history beneath the primacy of the future."[13] For Metz, the issue here concerns the primary analogue for the understanding of world as such: either "nature" and hence the world as a normative, a priori comprehensive framework of the cosmos or "history" and hence the world as fundamentally oriented toward the future and the new to which women's
and men's relation is not primarily contemplative, but operative. In this
sense, "history" signifies not something which merely "takes place
within" the world, as a moment within a more comprehensive whole or
totality which sublates it; rather, it signifies the world itself as that more
comprehensive whole which is not sublated, but which sublates other
moments within it. It is this understanding of the world which Metz
asserts is prethematically effective in and constitutive of modernity and
which grounds the secularity of the world.

Another formulation of that "turn" grounding the modern secularization of the world is the turn from a formal cosmocentricity to a formal
anthropocentricity with regard to an understanding of Being. "To see the
world not as cosmos, not as nature interpreting itself, but as history, to
see it in its relation to man, as mediated by him, means to interpret the
world in its formal anthropocentricity."[14] The terms and relations used
here are drawn from Metz's dissertation under Rahner, *Christliche
Anthropozentrik*, whose thesis is that in the explicit confrontation of Greek
metaphysics and Christian tradition in the work of Thomas Aquinas, it is
the formal anthropocentricity of the latter which emerges to the foreground over the former's formal cosmocentricity.

> Greek thought is, regarding its material content, i.e., ontically with reference
> to the hierarchy of beings, anthropocentric (=materially anthropocentric);
> formally, however, i.e., ontologically with reference to the dominant under-
> standing of Being, it is cosmocentric-objectivistic (=formally cosmocentric).

[11] Ibid., p. 42.
[12] Ibid., pp. 20-21.
[13] Ibid., p. 147.

Thomas' thought, in contrast, regarding its material contents, i.e., ontically with reference to the hierarchy of beings, is theocentric (=materially theocentric); formally, i.e., ontologically with reference to the dominant understanding of Being, it is anthropocentric and thus oriented to the peculiar mode of being of humanity (=formally anthropocentric). In short: the form of Greek thought is cosmocentric, that of Thomas, anthropocentric.[15]

The "effectivity" of this turn in the understanding of Being, rendered thematic in the theology of Aquinas, itself grounded in the founding biblical discourse of Christianity, constitutes modernity and the contemporary experience of the worldliness of the world as this shows itself in, i.e., the turn to the subject in theology and philosophy, the rise of the empirical modern sciences and technology and the impetus towards change in social and political forms. The effectivity of the formal anthropocentricity of the world as a letting-be of human subjectivity in freedom, actively oriented to the future as the "not-yet," grounds the secularity of the world as one which is denuminized, pluralistic, open to growth and change. Summarily stated: the turn to the formal anthropocentricity of the world as history (beneath the primacy of the future) gives rise to the secularization of the world as the hominized world.[16]

The transition from a formally cosmocentric and divinized world to a formally anthropocentric and hominized world illuminates for Metz at one and the same time the contemporary "crisis of faith" as well as the truth and aporia of modern atheism. Modern atheism views the Christian experience of God as inextricably bound to a divinized cosmocentrism which is waning and thus equates the transition from a formally cosmocentric to a formally anthropocentric world as unmasking the "meaninglessness of religion." This, however, is to claim too much.

> Because the world itself, as a result of its hominization, loses its numinous character, it does not follow that its connection with the numinous completely disappears. There simply appears a new, as it were "anthropocentric" place in which the numinous is experienced: no longer the comprehensive openness of the pre-given world, but the freedom that acts on this world; no longer all-embracing nature, but the history of this hominized nature, taken in hand by men, in its free futurity.[17]

---

14 Ibid., p. 53.
15 Metz, *Christliche Anthropozentrik*, p. 47.
16 Idem, *Theology of the World*, pp. 56-77, and "The Responsibility of Hope," pp. 280-88.
17 Idem, *Theology of the World*, p. 69.

Here, apologetics *ad extra* coincides with that *ad intra* and becomes "fundamental theology."[18]

In this exposition, one theme has been missing: the "primacy of the future." This omission was deliberate insofar as there is a curious shift in emphasis within the essays collected in *Theology and the World*. That shift may be denoted as from one which emphasizes the secularity of the world as coordinated with the understanding of the world as history to one emphasizing the world as history as presupposing the secularity of the world. It is with the latter that the emphasis on the primacy of the future becomes explicit. The shift is most apparent by noting the shift in "dogmatic loci": in the former, the doctrines of creation-incarnation ground the unity in difference of the secularity of the world and the divine and lead to what may be denoted as a "theology of the world"; in the latter, appeal to the doctrines of creation-incarnation recedes and virtually disappears, and eschatology which grounds the world as history *as* the primacy of the future leading to a political theology emerges to the fore.

It may well be asked at this point whether the initial difference of emphasis does not work itself out into a qualitative theological one. That this appears likely may be surmised from the virtual absence of the first line of reflection in Metz's later work as well as a tacit shift in his "method." Briefly stated, this first line of reflection appears to devolve into a form of "transcendental theology" à la Rahner which asserts that the categorical form of Christian revelation is the concrete condition of the possibility of a formally anthropocentric turn in history, noetically grounding, despite distortion, ambiguity and alienation, the identity of Christianity (through the "orthodoxy" of its dogma) and modernity as the worldliness of the world. Further, this categorical condition is also the condition for the anthropological (or "transcendental") experience of human subjectivity as freedom, thus grounding a form of "anonymous Christianity."[19] As I argue below, there are some grounds to question

18 The significance of the name-change from "apologetics" to "fundamental theology" is discussed by Claude Geffré, *"Zur neueren Geschichte der Fundamentaltheologie: Von der Apologetik zur 'politischen Theologie,'"* in *Politische Theologie*, pp. 96-120. More detailed discussions of the current "situation" of "fundamental theology" can be found in Peukert, *Wissenschaftstheorie-Handlungstheorie-Fundamentale Theologie*, pp. 17-71, 311-56; Tracy, *A Blessed Race for Order* and Fiorenza, *Foundational Theology* (New York: Crossroad Publishing Co., 1984), pp. 249-310;

19 Metz, *Christliche Anthropozentrik*, pp. 124-35; *Theology of the World*, pp. 23, n. 13, 47, and "The Theological World and the Metaphysical World," pp. 253-58. See, also, John, *Man in the World*, pp. 61-81.

whether this line of reflection has ever completely disappeared in Metz's latest work. Here, however, it may be asserted that this line of reflection clearly recedes in his turn to a postmetaphysical and posttranscendental theology under a retrieval of the eschatological horizon of Christianity correlated with the primacy of the future for the world as history. A corollary to this is his turn from the "abstract" anthropological ("transcendental") focus on subjectivity as freedom to the incarnate, "concrete" subject as socially mediated and situated. Henceforth, the focus on the secularity of the world becomes a focus on the world as history given the primacy of the future; the "theology of the world" becomes "political theology" even as the latter still presupposes the former in the world's unity-in-difference from God.

If previously secularity as the worldliness of the world was Metz's focal point for his understanding of "modernity," now he asserts, "(t)he modern man's understanding of the world is fundamentally oriented toward the future. His mentality therefore is not primarily contemplative but operative."[20] What is prethematically effective in modern man's experience of the world, what defines this horizon as a particular horizon of expectations and shapes the forms of experience,[21] what conditions this experience and horizon as a determinate appearance of the world is its orientation to the "new," the "not-yet" and the "never-having-been." With the past as past, modern men and women have a purely historical (*historisch*) relationship. With the future as the "open," the "indeterminate" and the new, their relationship is a historical-existential (*geschichtlich*) one. Under the impact of this primacy of the future, the relationship to history as the "having-been" is uncovered as abstract and to be sublated into a hermeneutical stance whereby interest in and consideration of the past arises from the questions and concerns of the present whose future possibilities it seeks to illuminate.[22]

It is this primacy of the future which discloses the world as history: "For the future is the constitutive element of history as history. . . . Only in relation to the future can the soul of all history, namely, freedom, be finally grasped."[23] This appearance of the world denotes not only a particular horizon of subjectivity, of how the world is spontaneously perceived and experienced, but also engenders a certain characteristic manner of comportment to the world. From the perspective of an open and

[20] Idem, *Theology of the World*, p. 82.
[21] Koselleck, *Vergangene Zukunft*, pp. 349-375.
[22] Metz, *The Responsibility of Hope*," pp. 280-281.
[23] Idem, *Theology of the World*, p. 99.

indeterminate future, the world appears not primarily as the object of contemplation bounded normatively by "what already is" and hence, tacitly, as "what has been and always must be"; rather, it is experienced as that which is open to the active intervention, formation and deformation of human freedom. Under this primacy of the future, the world is primarily something to be done, for which men and women, singly and collectively, must assume responsibility. Secularization as the worldliness of the world is now understood as the correlate of the primacy of the future which discloses the world as history.

> The phenomenon called "secularization" and the primacy given to the future are really of one piece.[24]

> The world appears in this horizon not as a fixed and sacrosanct reality in a pre-established harmony, but as an arising reality, which can be innovated towards its future through the historically free actions of men. This universal alteration and innovation of the world through the offensive of human freedom characterizes that process, which we call secularization.[25]

The anthropocentric turn receives its completion in the turn to the primacy of the future.

By rendering thematic the primacy of the future, Metz can make explicit the locus of the "new" paradigm of transcendence in the transition from a divinized, cosmocentric to a hominized, anthropocentric worldview. For the latter, transcendence, if it is to allow a true worldliness of the world which is more than a mere dualism, that is, if it is to allow a unity in difference between God and the world, can be conceived neither as a "world beyond the world" and hence as an undialectical negation of the world nor as a direct sacralization of some region of the world, but only as a transcendence "before the world, forward" as that future "which calls forth our potentialities to unfold themselves in history."[26] The locus of transcendence is that absolute future which calls

---

24 Idem, "The Responsibility of Hope," p. 281.
25 Idem, *Theology of the World*, p. 89.
26 Ibid., p. 89. See, also, his essay, "*Gott vor uns*" where Metz also speaks of "God" as the "power of the future." Two remarks are perhaps appropriate at this point. First, this expression is even less frequent in Metz's work than Pannenberg's. Second, however, insofar as Metz does have recourse to this manner of expression, the criticisms noted in the first chapter with regard to Pannenberg also apply here, i.e., that there is a confusion between two separate questions: the question concerning the temporalization of human self-transcendence as grounded in the horizon of the Christian totality of meaning, and the question concerning the temporalization of the

forth our experience of the world as history and the realm of the new. Indeed, similar to Pannenberg, Metz asserts that "(t)his orientation of the modern era to the future, and the understanding of the world as history, which results from this orientation, is based upon the biblical belief in the promises of God."[27] Here the same criticisms applied to Pannenberg in the first chapter regarding the assertion that the eschatological heritage of Christianity supplies *the* concrete condition of the possibility for the emergence of modernity and the horizon of the world as history apply to Metz, although the relative infrequence of this argument in Metz perhaps renders such criticism moot.

Minimally, however, this leads Metz to argue that the focus of theology is eschatology and to retrieve the biblical tradition of faith through a (schematic) theology of salvation history as the history of the promises of

---

Transcendent. At this point, recourse to "process theology" might appear appropriate in addressing the second question. Given the recent interest on the part of some process theologians in political theology, this might appear particularly attractive. In addition to Gilkey in *Reaping the Whirlwind*—and here it must be acknowledged that it is not especially accurate to refer to Gilkey as a "process theologian" insofar as his position is as much indebted to the thought of Paul Tillich and Rheinhold Niebuhr as it is to Whitehead—both Schubert Ogden in *Faith and Freedom* (Nashville: Abingdon Press, 1979) and John Cobb in *Process Theology as Political Theology* (Philadelphia: Westminster Press, 1982) have also suggested that dipolar or neoclassical theism is relevant to the project of a political theology. My own misgivings regarding this suggestion are simply that—misgivings and the issues raised here are beyond the scope of this essay. Therefore, I will simply enumerate them. My first misgiving is a fundamental-theological one. It concerns the possibility of a material knowledge of the divine which is in principle accessible apart from the positivity of religious traditions thus acting as a criterion of the adequacy of these traditions. Second, I am wary of process theology's tacit understanding of the task of theology, i.e., an elaboration of a metaphysics (Christian or otherwise) and more in agreement with Metz's position regarding theology's task i.e., an exposition of its foundational narratives. Third, I am perplexed by the relative lack of concern with "history" in "process theology." "History" more often than not simply appears as the ontological and temporal structure of finite entities or actual occasions "writ large." There is a curious gap in process theology between analysis of temporal occasions and generalizations concerning history as the history of "nations" or "epochs," with little attention being paid to whatever might mediate the former and the latter. Finally, and deriving from the third point, there is a divergence between the construal of the essence of Christianity in process theology and political theology: whereas the latter eschatologically valorizes the world as history in anticipation of the redemption of history, the former tends to construe the world as "nature" whose telos is the aesthetic completion of the divine life. In a real sense, the only object of redemption in process theology is the divine life itself for which actual entities provide the substance.

27 Ibid., p. 87.

God. Given the prethematically effective consolidation of the primacy of the future and the heuristic location of the paradigm of transcendence in the experience of history as the future, then the retrieval of eschatology, which was often relegated to the position of a postscript in traditional dogmatics, demands not its retrieval as a "region" of dogmatics and piety, but as the "root and marrow of every theological expression."[28] "Eschatology is not a discipline besides other disciplines, but that basic discipline which determines, forms and shapes every theological statement, especially those concerning the world."[29] Here, again, apologetics *ad intra* and *ad extra* coincide.

The retrieval of the biblical witness of faith, influenced by biblical theology of von Rad, occurs through the focus on revelation as "promise." "Their [the words of revelation] statement is announcement, their announcement is proclamation of what is to come, and therefore the abrogation of what is."[30] In such a manner the anthropocentric turn is accomplished in theology itself, and this leads to a criticism of the completeness of the anthropological turn in transcendental theology, i.e., Rahner and implicitly Metz's own earliest work.

> The transcendental pre-apprehension (*Vorgriff*) of Being as a whole is concerned with what exists (*Bestehendes*) and not with what develops (*Entstehendes*). In my opinion the problem of the developing history of the future cannot be solved with this theory of pre-apprehension.[31]

If the demand of an anthropocentric turn in theology is that Christian theology must be formally anthropocentric and materially theocentric, the transcendental theology of Rahner shows itself to be the reverse: formally theocentric and materially anthropocentric.

This critique of Rahner is part of a broader one regarding metaphysics per se and its adequacy in comprehending "the future."[32] First, the neglect of the future in metaphysics arises from its tacit identification of history with "the origin" and, thus, the present. The future becomes constricted to the repetition of "what is" or to the working out of that

---

[28] Idem, "The Responsibility of Hope," p. 284.

[29] Idem, *Theology of the World*, p. 90.

[30] Ibid., p. 87.

[31] Idem, *"Die Rede vom 'Ende der Metaphysik' und die Theologie"* (unpublished manuscript, 1966), p. 17; cited in Johns, *Man in the World*, p. 96. See, also, Lamb, *Solidarity with Victims*, pp. 116-52.

[32] "The Responsibility of Hope," pp. 281-83; *Theology of the World*, pp. 51-55, 98-100.

teleology present in the story of the origin of the present. Second, the occlusion of the future in metaphysics arises from its implied understanding of time. The priority and preeminence accorded to the "always at hand" gives precedence to that which presents itself to subjectivity in the mode of contemplation and representation. Yet the future as the realm of the "new" and the "never having been" escapes a contemplative mode of consciousness. Precisely as that which is not yet, it demands a "doing-mind" in which theory is subordinate to the priority of praxis realizing itself in freedom. Thirdly, the occlusion of the future in metaphysics is the occlusion of all history insofar as the future is the preeminent mode of history. In this, metaphysics betrays itself as primordially oriented not to history as the focal meaning of the world and reality, but to nature as that which is devoid of a future and, at best, has a teleology and hence can be contemplated once and for all in "what is."

> So long as history is considered in terms of the primacy of the origin and present, it can be conceived as a reality that has come about, that already exists, and hence again seen as nature and thus ontologized.[33]

Finally, it may be asked whether metaphysics in its orientation towards being as a whole, in its claim to totality, prematurely harmonizes and ideologically veils the relation between (the Christian) religion and society, divesting the former of its potential critical force. Metz's consolidation of the primacy of the future as determinative of history in his criticism of metaphysics is the first step towards an articulation of an explicit political theology.

The second step is Metz's criticism of "transcendental, personalist and existential theologies."[34] What unites these forms of theology as forms of a theological liberalism or neoorthodoxy is the attempt to respond to and internalize the moral, historical and metaphysical criticisms of Christianity which emerged during the period of the Enlightenment—as is seen in Bultmann's project of a demythologization of the gospel as the form of its retrieval. However, what is also common to these theologies is a systemic neglect of the social-political conditions which obstruct "enlightenment" as the realization of the autonomous subject and hence whose change is essential for the realization of enlightenment—the realization of the exigencies of reason in history as society as Kant, albeit

---

[33] Idem, *Theology of the World*, p. 99. Metz's criticism of "metaphysics" parallels Adorno's in "The Actuality of Philosophy" and *"Die Idee der Naturgeschichte."*
[34] See Peukert, *Wissenschaftstheorie*, pp. 23-71.

ambiguously, challenged in his essay "What is Enlightenment?" and as the "left wing" Hegelian tradition brought into focus. It is this latter tradition of Enlightenment which forms the starting point for Metz's theological critique in its assertion that the realization of reason is most concretely a practical, social-political one in which "theoretical, transcendental reason appears within practical reason, rather than the reverse."[35]

For Metz, this systemic aporia distorts the horizon of such theologies insofar as it leads to an abstraction of the subject and its subjectivity from its constitutive social matrix (i.e., as transcendental subject, as the subject defined through I-Thou relationships or as the subject defined by the *existentiell* categories of *Dasein*). It engenders a constriction of history from its social-political mediation to a function (i.e., historicity) corresponding to an abstract subjectivity. By this, such theologies fall behind the concept of the Enlightenment even while ostensibly confronting it in its critical claims and hence veils their own (potential) distortion as a mediation of the social whole which is operative as a *vis a tergo*.

> . . . so any existential and personal theology that does not understand existence as a political problem in the widest sense of the word, must inevitably restrict its considerations to an abstraction. A further danger of such a theology is that failing to exercise its critical and controlling function, it delivers faith up to modern ideologies in the area of societal and political theories.[36]

This foundational theological constriction of the horizon of Christian faith, which both reflects and reproduces "bourgeois piety" (see below), reverberates throughout the entirety of theological categories and constructions. Specifically, eschatology and history are eviscerated into the historicity of the subject who lives in the world as the sphere of the paradoxical coincidence of salvation and damnation and who lives before the "eternal now" which hovers above history, indifferent to it and only tangentially intruding into it through the kerygma. The world and history become that which literally has "no future" and is merely the stage setting for a salvation which subsists in the "interior" reaches of the self.

> The paradoxical idea of the world assumes that as far as the world is concerned we can speak only of salvation and damnation, of light and darkness, but never of salvation *or* damnation, of light *or* darkness. The historical struggle for salvation, for light, remains unimportant and outside salvation history. In this connection we could speak of a formal "historicalness" of salvation . . . but we could not speak of a real "history" of salvation with an

---

[35] Metz, *Theology of the World*, p. 112.

historical future of this salvation. In the light of the Gospel of scripture the world is not simply the place where there is a dialectical unity of salvation and damnation. In defining it we need the promise of a "new world." Part of its nature, then, is a future in which the world is either the one thing or the other, the world of absolute self-encapsulation or the world as the place of the presence of the promise. Thus a purely paradoxical theology of the world either does away with the eschatological structure of the history of the world, in which this world is not always both, but the one or the other, or it does away with the permanently historical and world structure of salvation, because it can conceive of the salvation of the world always only in a dialectical way, as salvation and damnation.[37]

The exigencies for a transformation, renewal and sanctification of the world come to lie in the private sphere of the subject as a self-contained monad. The promise of faith to the world is reduced to an extrinsic application, subordinate to the "essence" of faith and nonnormative in its claims or it becomes a "counsel of perfection" within a theological social ethic.

If Metz's call for a "postmetaphysical" theology is issued in an attempt to retrieve the eschatological dimensions of Christian faith in correlation with the primacy of the future for the world as history, his criticism of transcendental, personalist and existential theologies is an attempt to locate more determinately the sphere to be understood by the term "history" in its futurity. Negatively, this issues in the call for a deprivatization of theology; positively, the operative assertion is that the most concrete understanding of the subject and history is their constitution through their social and political mediation. Thus, in accordance with the turn to the primacy of practical reason in one segment of the tradition of the Enlightenment, there is the attempt to formulate a new postcritical theology: "Through the political understanding of the world (political in the broadest sense), a new possibility of historicizing the world has emerged. At the same time a new method of overcoming the hiddenness of the social relationships of our hermeneutical point of departure has been introduced."[38]

The central positive theological assertion, however, grounding a "political theology" as the most appropriate form of a Christian theology of the world as history is the assertion of the unity of the future of the

---

[36] Ibid., p. 111.

[37] Ibid., pp. 52-53.

[38] Idem, *"Glaube und Geschichte"* (unpublished manuscript, University of Munster, Winter Semester, 1965/66), p. 302; cited in Johns, *Man in the World*, pp. 125-26.

world and of God. The faith by which Christians live and believe cannot be separated into a supernatural and natural end which exist in mutual indifference to each other but must be conceived in their unity-in-difference by which both extremes of a direct politicization of the promises of God with the world and undialectical negation of the world are avoided. "[God's] promises are not an empty horizon of religious expectations; neither are they a regulative idea."[39]

> ... the hope which the Christian faith has in regard to the future cannot be realized independently of the world and its future, that this hope must answer, must be responsible for, the one promised future and hence also the future of the world.[40]

Given the anticipation of the unity of the future of the world and of God and the world as history, sociopolitically mediated, the description of the Christian, "his possible mode of being in the world," is that of a creative-militant eschatology: an engagement in and for the world which breaks through the separation of the public and private spheres as a "crucified hope for the world."[41] Such a stance is critically subversive of what is in that the promises of justice and peace become "a critical, liberating imperative for our present times. These promises stimulate and appeal to us to make them a reality in the present historical condition and, in this way, to verify them—for we must 'ver-ify' them."[42] Further, within this stance, the description of Christian being in the world becomes neither "orthodoxy" nor "authenticity" but "orthopraxis" which sublates the former two and demands that that which is believed be embodied, made incarnate not only within the parameters of the private sphere of interiority and interpersonal relations, but in the social-political worldliness of the world as oriented towards the critical and liberating promises of redemption, justice and peace disclosed in the Christ-story.[43]

Despite Metz's language which sometimes seems to place the promised future of God completely in the hands of men and women, thus collapsing the unity-in-difference of the future of the world and

---

[39] Idem, *Theology of the World*, p. 114. For a presentation of the position, in general not shared by most political and liberation theologians, that the "promises of God" are only regulative, see Alfredo Fierro, *The Militant Gospel*, trans. John Drury (New York: Orbis Books, 1977).

[40] Ibid., p. 150.

[41] Ibid., p. 93.

[42] Ibid., p. 114.

[43] Ibid., pp. 91-97.

God and transforming those promises into a regulative ideal or a deceptive total-utopia, the demand of orthopraxis is balanced by the affirmation of the "eschatological proviso":

> ... that man's history as a whole stands under God's eschatological proviso. She [the church] must stress the truth that history as a whole can never be a political notion in the strict sense of the word, that for this reason, it can never be made the object of a particular action.[44]

Christian theology as eschatology, in its orientation to the world as history under the primacy of the future and its stance of a socially creative-militant eschatology, is neither a "sacral" political program nor does it presume a utopian omniscience concerning the future. Political theology subsists largely as "critique." It is a negative theology of the future.[45]

In summary, three "moves" appear to be constitutive of Metz's articulation of theology as political theology. First, the identification of an effective worldview of the world as history under the primacy of the future which emerged in the period of the Enlightenment and has increasingly consolidated itself in (post-)Enlightenment (Western) modernity. In correlation to this is his attempt to retrieve the biblical tradition of the Christian faith through an eschatological focus as a theology of the "promises of God." It is this move which issues in the call for a post-metaphysical theology. Second, there is a critique of the privatization of Christian faith in post-Enlightenment transcendental, personalist and existential theologies which occurs under the operative assertion that the most concrete mediation of history is a social-political one—an assertion which is drawn primarily from the left-wing Hegelian tradition of Enlightenment along with its assertion of the primacy of practical (as social) reason. Finally, there is the assertion of the unity-in-difference of the future of the world and of God which grounds the stance of the Christian as one of creative-militant eschatology and which demands the unity of faith and praxis in negation of the separation of the public and private

---

[44] Ibid., p. 118. In Metz's latest work, influenced by the writings of Walter Benjamin, mystical solidarity with the dead becomes the limit which fragments a naive utopian activism.

[45] Ibid., p. 97. See, also, his essay, "Prophetic Authority," in *Religion and Political Society*, ed. and trans. in The Institute of Christian Thought (New York: Harper and Row, 1970), pp. 177-209. See, also, Jürgen Moltmann's essay, "The Cross and Civil Religion," in the same volume [pp. 14-46] for a presentation of the distinction between a "political theology" and "political religion."

spheres. "Every eschatological theology, therefore, must become a political theology, that is, a (socio)critical theology."[46]

"POLITICAL THEOLOGY" AS PRACTICAL FUNDAMENTAL THEOLOGY

Metz's theological work subsequent to the publication of *Theology of the World* is continuous with the project of that work or, more precisely, its last three chapters. While there is a refocusing of political theology in his later work, there remains, in my estimate, less of a *Kehre* between the second and third stages than between the first and second stages of which the first two essays of *Theology of the World* are an "echo." The work collected and published under the title, *Faith in History and Society*, less represents a new "stage" of theological reflection than a second phase of political theology. The "revisions" which emerge here derive less from a new start than from a response to criticisms of the original project of political theology, an intensification of themes which were marginal in the earlier work and a dialogue with the theology of the churches in the Third World. That refocused center by which the themes and motifs of political theology are reconstellated is, as Rebecca Chopp has argued, the "interruption of suffering,"[47] to which I would add Metz's own growing recognition of the dialectic of enlightenment as characteristic of that "piece" of history which is contemporary society.

Thus, for example, in *Theology of the World*, the primacy of the future as the "absolute future of the new" was the focal point for the discussion of human freedom and characteristic of political theology as a "negative theology of the future." This is "counterbalanced" by Metz's elaboration of the *memoria-These* in his 1969 paper "*Politische Theologie in der Diskussion.*"[48] As an attempt to specify the irreducible theological character of political theology, the *memoria-These* may be seen as a response to the criticism that political theology, construed as a tripartite critique of church, society and theology, risks becoming purely formalistic—an empty theological cipher of a conceptual negative dialectics of the future which might as easily dispense with its positive theological trappings as retain them. Further, the *memoria-These* as primarily a memory of suffer-

---

[46] Ibid., p. 115.
[47] Chopp, *The Praxis of Suffering*, passim.
[48] Metz, "'*Politische Theologie*' in der Diskussion," p. 248ff.

ing corrects the potential "optimism" of the future which laces Metz's earlier essays.

So also, in Metz's earlier work the emphasis on the "operative" character of modern men's and women's comportment to the world potentially lays itself open to being assimilated to the ideology of an anthropology of domination and subjugation. Significant in this regard is Metz's more dialectical treatment of secularity and modernity as *Freiheitsgeschichte* in his later work—a treatment which in general tenor as well as certain specifics parallels that of the "Frankfurt School" in their exposition of the dialectic of enlightenment. In short, the theological dialogue with the Enlightenment must be "post-Enlightenment," an "eating of the tree of knowledge a second time."[49] The theological consequence of this intensification is Metz's unmasking of the ironic triumph of Christianity as *bürgherliche Religion*.

Flowing from these two revisions, Metz's specification of the dialectics of "emancipation" and "redemption" as an elaboration of the "eschatological proviso" responds to implied objections to his earlier work, i.e., that in the unguarded language of *Theology of the World* with its emphasis on "doing" or "making" the truth of Christianity in the name of orthopraxis and a creative-militant eschatology, the impression is given of a complete anthropologization of the "subject" of history whose praxis definitively reconciles the nonidentity of history thus risking a regression to a direct politicization of faith and theologization of politics in the manner of "classical" political theology through an identification of *Freiheitsgeschichte* and *Heilsgeschichte*.

Methodologically too there occurs a refocusing of political theology. According to Widenhofer, "Political theology is, in its first phase, above all, eschatologically and future oriented, oriented to action and critical of society. At the same time, it understands itself as a critical corrective over and against the earlier German theology."[50] In its second phase, however, political theology is characterized by a

> ... growing 'theologization' and 'dogmaticization' of the theory-praxis relation, i.e., a theological widening of the concepts of 'theory' and 'praxis'. While the concept of theory is filled out ever more dogmatically, the sphere

---

[49] Idem, *Faith in History and Society*, p. 47 (29).
[50] Wiedenhofer, *Politische Theologie*, p. 21.

of praxis is also expanded so that it now encompasses the entire continuum of human existence.[51]

What Widenhofer perhaps infelicitously denotes as a theologization and dogmaticization of the theory-praxis nexus, signifies a real shift in political theology, i.e., making explicit the theory-praxis relationship within the foundation of theology itself. The central issue for Metz now becomes an articulation of the practical mediation of faith and the identity of the subject and the delineation of the "practical structure underlying the *logos* of Christian theo-logy."[52] Significantly, this shift is marked by a shift in the naming of such reflection: from "political theology" to "practical fundamental theology."

The preceding paragraphs briefly indicate the latest phase of Metz's work in relation to his articulation of political theology in the mid-1960s. What remains to be mentioned is what was called above, the "interruption of suffering." It is the concrete surd of suffering which fragments and fractures the noetic identity and truth of Christian faith and recoils back upon it as the question indicting its contents. No better articulation of this theological interruption can be found than Metz's own, published in an open letter to Walter Jens, "*Warum ich Christ bin.*"

> At the center of my theological interest in Christianity is the questionable religious-political treatment of the so-called 'theodicy question', the question of God in light of the experience of suffering. Autobiographically, this is all of a piece with the very drastic experiences of the war in my youth so that I slowly became aware of my Christian theological situation as a 'post Auschwitz' one and finally increasingly realized that the condition of suffering and oppression in the world poses a decisive question to us Christians. For me, Christianity deals with the foundation capable of supporting a universal solidarity and unconditional justice, i.e., a solidarity and justice even in the face of the victims and victors of history, for those burdened ones for whom we live and build our paradise but whose fate no passionate struggle of the living can raise a finger to change. The Christian belief in a God, before whom past suffering does not disappear subjectless into the abyss of an anonymous evolution, in my estimate vouches for the fixed standard of a universal liberation, of the ability-to-be-a-subject of all humanity, in the midst of unceasing conflict. Where our socially accepted wisdom lets itself be led exclusively by the imaginary totality of an unjust evolution, not only does 'God' become unthinkable, but consequently every selfless interest in a universal liberation also disappears. All dialectics of the emancipation of humanity in the end proves itself to be a trick of an indifferent evolution if

---

[51] Ibid., p. 50.

there does not exist a God who interrupts the graceless and apathy produc-
ing continuity of nature and before whom even the past is not fixed. This
God is, for me, the trustworthy foundation of any universal solidarity and
justice—not just now, by decree of the 'spirit of the age', but throughout the
history of humanity.[53]

The words "theodicy-question," "experience of suffering," "post-
Auschwitz," "situation of suffering and oppression," "universal solidarity," "unconditional justice" and the negation of those contemporary
identity-systems which negate suffering as the sublated prehistory of
progress define the space of Metz's theological reflections in this phase:
the nonidentity of history as suffering.

For Metz, the task, form and foil of contemporary theology is set by
history itself: those "theories" deriving from the Enlightenment, which
he calls the evolutionary-scientistic interpretation of reality and the his-
torical-materialist system.[54] What may at first strike one as odd, that theories are here identified with historical reality, is mitigated when one realizes that such theories are not "mere" theories but are effective in
structuring contemporary social-historical reality. They are both subjective and objective in that the objective structuration of social reality increasingly secures the subjective conditions for its reproduction thus
forming a synchronic totality. They are, further, theologically significant
insofar as they also represent metatheories of religion by which it can be
deconstructed and abolished as a form of false consciousness and inau-
thenticity, a prehistoric impediment to the *Mundigkeit* of men and
women. Finally, such theories function as quasi-religious ciphers for totality in a diachronic sense as metatheories of history which negate the
concrete subject of history and society in favor of an abstract subject of
history and society (usually some "common noun" as class, nation,
science, etc.). As both synchronic and diachronic totalities, these theories
have as their soul and telos the negation of the subject in its reduction to
a secured condition for the reproduction of a social totality. By this, such
totalities are "identity-systems" to which all its moments are immanent
in their automatic reproduction.

For Metz, the proper theological response lies not in the elaboration
of a further metatheory—a strategy which holds open the possibility of
an infinite theoretical regression—but a return back to the subject in a

---

52   Metz, *Faith in History and Society*, p. 51 (47).
53   Idem, *Unterbrechungen*, pp. 21-22.
54   Idem, *Faith in History and Society*, pp. 3-11 (3-12).

political theology which confronts the precariousness of the subject "defined by the social and historical situation with all its painful contradictions."[55] The question of the identity-formation of the subject in contemporary society and the question of the subject of faith are no longer external to one another, for the negation of the former is also the negation of the latter. Again, at this historic juncture, a return to the subject of faith is identical with a return to the social subject. The intersection between the two is the crisis of Christianity as *bürgherliche Religion*. Theology today, as a form of apologetics, is the evocation and description of a *praxis* of noncontemporaneity (*Ungleichzeitigkeit*), of interruption, of nonidentity in response to the socially effective totalities of identity in the name of the subject whose being-a-subject is threatened. Apologetics today can only be a practical fundamental theology.

> A theology which is theoretical because it is interested in justification must be apologetical. It cannot simply subordinate itself to the existing types of theory if it is to function as theology. If it is theoretical because it is interested in justification, then this theology must be practical and guided by a new dialectical tension between theory and praxis. It can only deal effectively with attempts at evolutionary reconstruction or to impose a total social conditioning of religion by adopting a praxis that breaks open these systems of interpretation.[56]

The first task is a theological enlightenment of the Enlightenment which names the "subject" of Enlightenment and modernity. It names the concrete, social-historical subject in the abstract, "universal" subject which, as rational and autonomous, has come of age. So also the crisis of Christianity today is the crisis of its (implied) subject which is embedded in that broader crisis which is the dialectic of enlightenment. ". . . there is an inner dialectical tension in emancipation, Enlightenment and secularization and that the Enlightenment has therefore given rise to problems over and above what it has itself raised to the level of a problem. . . ."[57]

---

[55] Ibid., p. 10 (11). I have argued elsewhere that Metz's procedure in reality continues the transcendental "turn to the subject" initiated in the theologies of Rahner and Lonergan and that Metz is mistaken in where he locates his disagreement with Rahner. Metz's disagreement with Rahner over the nature of the "subject" is itself a symptom of a *theological* disagreement, i.e., their differing conceptions of the "essence of Christianity." See, J.A. Colombo "Rahner and His Critics: Lindbeck and Metz," *The Thomist* (Forthcoming).

[56] Ibid., pp. 7-8 (8). For a full exposition of the notion of the *Ungleichzeitigkeit der Religion*, see *Unterbrechungen*, pp. 11-19.

[57] Ibid., p. 26 (25).

Metz traces this crisis as the crisis of tradition, authority and metaphysical reason. Indeed, these three crises are interrelated because in the Enlightenment the critique of authority was a critique of tradition and a critique of metaphysical reason made in the name of its subject, the propertied citizen (*Bürgher*).[58] Yet the dialectic of enlightenment is that movement by which this critique becomes the crisis of the very subject in whose name enlightenment was initiated.

The crisis of tradition refers not primarily to the critique of a particular tradition(s), but to its systematic erosion in what Gadamer has called the Enlightenment's "prejudice against prejudice."[59] Tradition as such is exorcised from the constitution of the identity of the subject and is reconstituted as that which stands over and against the subject: an historical object as a storehouse of information. To be sure, tradition continues to be effective in society. Yet now it is publicly reduced to a matter of "taste" in a society where taste has been emptied of all its cognitive claim and become decisionistic.

The crisis of authority follows that of tradition because the two cannot be separated. The Enlightenment criticism of authority was a criticism of authoritarian authority which appeared once authority was no longer universally convincing and socially plausible. Yet as with tradition, the consolidation of the Enlightenment threatens authority as such, including those authorities which might be a "precondition and inner aspect of critical and liberating reason."

> What is threatened, in other words, is that authority to which men give their consent when they affirm their own state as subjects or the possibility of others being subjects. This authority is the authority of freedom on the one hand and suffering on the other.[60]

The vacuum created by the dialectic of enlightenment is then constituted on its own terms: the pure self-transparency of instrumental reason, the ideology of professionalism and the politics of technocracy.

So also the crisis of metaphysical reason. In its origin in the Enlightenment, the criticism of metaphysical reason and its claim to an objective universality and normativity which occluded its own social,

---

[58] Peter Gay, *The Enlightenment*, vol. 1: *The Rise of Modern Paganism*; vol. 2: *The Science of Freedom*; 2 vols. (New York: Alfred A. Knopf, 1966-69); and Ernst Cassirer, *The Philosophy of the Enlightenment*, trans. Fritz Koelin and James Pettibone (Princeton: Princeton University Press, 1951).

[59] Gadamer, *Truth and Method*, pp. 241-45.

[60] Metz, *Faith in History and Society*, p. 40 (37).

political and ecclesiastical context was made in appeal to the subject and its praxis of liberation. The fundamental ambiguity of the Enlightenment, however, was that in its raising of critique to the level of cognition in the name of the subject and freedom, it tacitly "constricted" the subject to a new elite. The social cipher of the subject of enlightenment is the proper-tied citizen, the so-called bourgeois who is identified with the subject per se. Enlightened reason does not remain impermeable to its own historical subject and regresses.

> The characteristics of the middle-elite, however, also entered into Enlightenment reason itself and its concept of praxis and the subject. In the logic of this reason, praxis developed not as a praxis of liberation, but as a praxis of control . . . a control of nature in the interest of the market.[61]

A structural continuity threads the three crises of the dialectic of Enlightenment sketched above: the distinction between the public and private sphere by which a space was opened up for the emergence of the subject as *Bürgher*. Emancipatory in its inception, this distinction has become repressive insofar as the public sphere becomes identical with the hegemony of the market as exchange, the pursuit of profit and growth and the exigencies of instrumental reason. To the private sphere, to the sphere of mere taste, opinion, feeling and interiority are assigned "all other values, which may have had a decisive effect on society in the past, but which no longer directly contribute to the functioning of the middle-class society of exchange."[62] Tradition, the authority of a critical praxis of freedom and suffering and a reason of substantive ends rather than means become mere private opinion which a priori is excluded from the public sphere. Tendentially, the distinction—or better, the separation—between the two spheres is de facto abolished as the private sphere is reduced to an appendage of the public sphere to be systematically managed as a commodity. The fundamental irony of the dialectic of enlightenment is that the subject whose public identity is increasingly formed under the aegis of an anthropology of domination and subjugation must abolish itself in its own name. The secret of the dialectic of enlightenment is its totality of identity where the subjective and objective conditions of the reproduction of the social whole converge and difference disappears. In a cruel parody of the biblical injunction, the subject of enlightenment must lose its life *qua* subject in order to gain it.

---

[61] Ibid., p. 43 (40). See, also, *The Emergent Church*, pp. 35-37.
[62] Ibid., p. 35 (32).

Religion too does not escape the vicissitudes of the dialectic of enlightenment. Indeed, it has all too readily comported itself to it. Metz's argument parallels his call for a deprivatization of theology. There is a subtle shift, however, because the task now is not the corrective of a deprivatization of *theology*, but a naming of the implied *social subject* of that theology and recognizing its piety as enveloped in the dialectic of enlightenment. The task is an enlightenment of the Enlightenment in modern theology which implicates modern theology and its implied subject in the larger dialectic which it supports and mediates.

In the repressive separation of the private and public spheres lies the crisis of religion which is essentially consigned to the former. "Religion no longer belongs to the social constitution of the subject, but is added to it."[63] Not unlike the manualist separation between nature as *pura natura* and grace as a *donum superadditum*, enlightened Christian piety is, by and large today, bourgeois religion: the solace and comfort of the private reserve of interiority which is hermetically sealed off from the public sphere of the "real world." The price of the preservation of the self-identity and triumph of Christianity is its mutilation: it must divest itself of its messianic character which would negate the separation of the two spheres in the name of the unity of the future of the world and of God.[64] Bourgeois Christianity becomes a religion of mere "belief-in" which leaves undisturbed the identity of the self shaped through the public sphere of exchange.

> Our bourgeois Christianity is sickening from a sweet poison. The poison of a mere belief in faith and in the praxis of discipleship, a mere belief in love and repentance. All grace remains thereby in the realm of invisibility and intangibility. And we ourselves remain always unchanged, we go on defining ourselves by the trusted standards of bourgeois identity.[65]

In bourgeois religion, the fundamental realities of Christian faith, *metanoia* and discipleship, are constricted in advance: they are tolerated as the prerogative of the private sphere as long as they do not seriously threaten and disrupt the logic of the anthropological model of domination, subjugation and growth in the public sphere of the economy and politics.

[63] Ibid., p. 33 (30). See also, Metz, *The Emergent Church*, pp. 50-66.
[64] Idem, *The Emergent Church*, pp. 1-16.
[65] Ibid., p. 55.

From the above, it appears that for Metz the crisis of Christianity to-day is the crisis of bourgeois Christianity and its subject, both of which are related to the socially-effective dialectic of enlightenment. Thus Metz revises the *theological* agendas of liberal, neoorthodox and academic the-ologies which see the fundamental problematic of Christian faith in the cognitive dissonance between the contents of faith and the exigencies of the Enlightenment for the pure self-transparency of the concept. The cri-sis of Christianity is most fundamentally a social-political one to which the adequate response is a political theology of and for the subject.

> It is . . . clear from this that the so-called historical crisis of the identity of Christianity is not a crisis of the contents of faith, but rather a crisis of the Christian subjects and institutions which deny themselves the practical meaning of those contents, the imitation of Christ.[66]

The *metanoia* and discipleship of Christianity as messianic religion de-mand that religion becomes an interruption and disruption of the self-destructive identity-formation of modern society. Christian faith must take part in "the revolutionary formative process for a new subjectiv-ity"[67] as the harbinger of an "anthropological revolution" for "a basic change of direction throughout the church, throughout society and in world politics."[68] Christianity, which is not to reduce itself to an ap-pendage of "what is" and thus to betray itself, must seek, cultivate and evoke a new noncontemporaneity with the world mediated by a social praxis which interrupts the deconstruction of the subject in the identity-totalities of Enlightenment.

So also the question must be raised anew as to who is the "subject" of theology, given that the reversal of the crisis of Christianity is the praxis of interruption of messianic religion. This question is not merely a "speculative" one and is tied to Metz's growing interest in the signifi-cance of the "basic community churches" in the Third World.[69] Even as the church must become not a "church for the people"—with the as-sumptions of a hierarchical representation and paternalistic orientation toward the simple faithful—but a church "of the people" whereby their hopes, fears, sufferings and stories become the subject of the Church as the people of God, so also for political theology as a practical fundamen-tal theology there is a transposition of the subject of theology from that

66 Idem, *Faith in History and Society*, p. 165 (177).
67 Idem, *The Emergent Church*, p. 42.
68 Ibid., p. 9.
69 Ibid., passim.

subject who first and foremost is identified with the "professional theologian." Theology, its logic of argumentation and its telos of translating the narrative *Vorstellung* of the people into *Begriff* must be interrupted as critical theology takes on the function of a corrective while attempting to restore the religious subject as the subject of theology. Given what was said above concerning the nature of the crisis of Christianity, the form of an adequate theology for Metz is a practical restoration to "the people" of the capacity to do theology which has been expropriated by the professionalization of theology and the theologian.

> The critical interest of this theology, however, must always be governed by the conviction that the symbols, stories and collective memories of the people in the Church are absolutely necessary to any theology which wishes to avoid losing all foundation. Its critical attitude should not lead to direct criticism of the symbolic world of the people. It ought, on the contrary, to lead to making the people more and more the subjects of their own symbolic world. . . . It is possible to say that the main task of critical theology is not to eliminate the religious symbolic world of the people, but to correct a wrong evaluation of it and to give it the right address.[70]

Before proceeding to Metz's own construal of Christianity as a messianic religion interruptive of bourgeois religion, one further theme demands attention: the notion of suffering. It might seem odd that "suffering" is not singled out and treated separately in *Faith in History and Society*. Its treatment is, however, interlaced throughout the work where it modifies and intensifies all other categories and themes. Above all, suffering "is." With Adorno, Metz could assert "the need to lend a voice to suffering is a condition of truth. For suffering is objectivity that weighs upon the subject; its most subjective experience, its expression, is objectively conveyed."[71] The acknowledgement of and restoration of "suffering" to thought is the leaven of Metz's reflections and forms the focal point for the twofold critique which underlies his latest work: the critique of the totalities of identity which are effective in contemporary society and the noetic identities of Christian theology as system.

The synchronic totality of modern society eclipses both the objective witness of and subjective capacity for suffering in its quest for identity. It must do so to pursue its telos of automatic reproduction. Society exorcises suffering as that which tarnishes and questions its glistening stainless steel facade. The medicalization of death, the incapacity for mourn-

---

[70]   Idem, *Faith in History and Society*, p. 150 (133).
[71]   Adorno, *Negative Dialectics*, pp. 17-18.

ing and grief, the compulsive denial of aging in the light of a slick, youthful ideal of beauty and well-being, the trivialization of compassion into sentimentality are some symptoms of a society for which suffering and the capacity to experience it, despite its seeming omnipresent media coverage, remain something "other" and taboo. As a diachronic totality, the ideologies of modern society in the guise of an emancipatory, evolutionary progress and dialectical materialism, ignore and negate history as the history of the victims, the vanquished and the defeated. Marching into utopia, the victors (or survivors) must drink from the pool of Lethe even as the objective suffering of those nameless and forgotten ones who have preceded them are dismissed as "unavoidable prehistory." Christianity interrupts this identity-formation by restoring to and nurturing, in the name of the subject, the pathic structure of experience. "Christianity attempts to make men capable of experiencing the sufferings of others through their own capacity for suffering and in this way of being close to the mystery of Christ's suffering."[72]

If suffering is the concrete nonidentity of history which, albeit as suppressed and repressed gives lie to the modern totalities of identity, it also ruptures that form of theology which posits a noetic reconciliation of suffering in history. Here, suffering is always already comprehended and redeemed in the name of Christ Jesus and the God of love in advance. Christianity secures the identity of history through a supernatural teleology, one fixed firmly where the messianic future is the necessary end of the Christ event. It grounds a euphoria about "meaning" in history by which suffering is reduced to mere appearance.

> Wherever Christianity vigorously conceals its own messianic weakness, its sensorium for dangers and downfalls diminishes to an ever greater degree. Theology loses its own awareness for historical disruptions and catastrophes. Has not our Christian faith in the salvation achieved for us in Christ been covertly reified to a kind of optimism about meaning, an optimism which is no longer really capable of perceiving radical disruptions and catastrophes within meaning? Does there not exist something like a typically Christian incapacity for dismay in the face of disasters?[73]

Metz's most explicit and profound reflections of "suffering" and Christian faith/theology occurs in his confrontation with Holocaust. In the event of the Holocaust, reflection is confronted with the event which fractures thought and its quest for meaning.

[72] Ibid., p. 142 (126).
[73] Idem, *The Emergent Church*, p. 25.

> To confront Auschwitz is in no way to comprehend it. Anyone wishing to comprehend in this area will have comprehended nothing . . . it eludes our every attempt at some kind of amicable reconciliation which would allow us to dismiss it from our consciousness. The only thing "objective" about Auschwitz are the victims. . . . Under no circumstances is it *our* task to mystify this suffering! . . . Faced with Auschwitz, I consider as blasphemy every Christian theodicy and all language about "meaning" when these are initiated outside this catastrophe or in some level above it.[74]

In the shadow of this event—and not detracting from its uniqueness as a historical event—thought confronts that suffering which is "other," "outside" of that event spatially and temporally. The event of the Holocaust is the constitutive occasion for those who live and survive after it for reflection on the event of suffering as interruptive of the identity of history.

After Auschwitz, the transmutation of the sensuous dissonance of lived suffering into the intellectual consonance of noetic meaning is unmasked as blasphemous, the denial of suffering through its mystification. After Auschwitz, Christianity's abandonment of the messianic-apocalyptic praxis of discipleship and its all too shameful readiness to compromise itself with whatever social and political forces that exist cannot be avoided and ignored. After Auschwitz, the truth and identity of Christian faith, secured within the theological system, is seen to be a lie, a strategy for immunizing faith and thought from concrete reality.

> After Auschwitz, every theological profundity which is unrelated to people and their concrete situation must cease to exist. Such a theology would be the very essence of superficiality. With Auschwitz, the epoch of theological systems which are separate from people and their concrete situations has come to its irrevocable end.[75]

After Auschwitz, the "interruption" of suffering forces a fundamental reconsideration of the categories and foundation of Christian faith/theology—one which heeds the voice of suffering without relegating it to appearance and which realizes that while "there is a suffering that cannot be passed over in silence or transfigured by religion, [it] has to be combatted and transformed."[76]

---

[74] Ibid., p. 19.
[75] Ibid., p. 22.
[76] Idem, *Faith in History and Society*, p. 142 (126).

In light of Metz's specific construal of the crisis of Christianity as bourgeois religion, the crisis of the subject in the identity-totalities of post-Enlightenment society and the interruption of suffering as a theological datum, he offers the following "definition" of Christianity as a messianic religion of the praxis of discipleship.

> The faith of Christians is a praxis in history and society that is to be understood as hope in the solidarity in the God of Jesus as a God of the living and the dead who calls all men to be subjects in his presence. Christians justify themselves in this essentially apocalyptic praxis (of imitation) in their historical struggle for their fellow men. They stand up for all men in their attempt to become subjects in solidarity with each other. In this praxis, they resist the danger both of a creeping evolutionary disintegration of the history of men as subjects and of an increasing negation of the individual in view of a new, post middle-class image of man.[77]

What follows is a brief commentary on this "definition" by specifying the categories of practical fundamental theology: memory, narrative and solidarity; discipleship as *imitatio Christi*; the dialectics of emancipation and redemption and eschatology as apocalyptic.

The category of memory (*Erinnern*) first emerges in Metz's theological reflections in his 1969 article noted above under the rubric of the *"memoria-These."* Originally introduced to specify the theological character of political theology and to counter the criticism that political theology was essentially a negative dialectics of "pure" practical reason, operating from a formal, empty concept of the future—a form of *totale Kritik* à la Adorno—even a cursory reading of *Faith in History and Society* reveals that the category of "memory" is an overdetermined one, emerging in diverse contexts which enter into its meaning.

First, it should be noted that there is a certain productive ambiguity in the term itself. Memory spans the dichotomy between subject and object, referring both to the "object remembered" and the "subject remembering." Two common senses of the term, however, must be acknowledged only to be dismissed as alien to Metz's understanding: an understanding of memory as the object of "recall," that which exists merely as the "past" and hence separated from the activity of the subject recalling, and that understanding which would reduce memory to one faculty of the subject among others. Indeed, these two understandings of the term are opposite sides of the same coin. Even after excising such understandings of memory, however, Metz's explication of the term still remains

77 Ibid., p. 73 (70-71).

protean and global. Theologically, memory becomes coextensive with "faith," encompassing both the subjective and objective poles as *fides qua creditur* and *fides quae creditur*.

> Christian faith is thus to be understood like any other condition in which men and women remember promises which have been made and in view of these promises, living hopes, they bind themselves in their manner of living to these memories.[78]

Memory as "faith" refers, in this context, to the "traditioned horizon" of the subject where the term "horizon" refers to the constitution of the identity of the subject and "traditioned" to the intrinsic constitution of that identity and "reason" by history as tradition. More specifically, memory as faith, as the memory of suffering and hence as a "dangerous memory" points to that particular, effective fusion of horizons in political theology of the "Christian fact" and the present in the mode of a social-political interruption of the present age's one-dimensionality.

Second, the "privileged" object of memory is suffering. As the memory of suffering, memory is the originative occasion for the differentiation of "history" from "nature." In its particularity, memory resists the sublation of history to nature and its schema of teleology. It protests the reduction of suffering to the cliché of progress as the necessary condition of the self-realization of an abstract subject—be it *Geist*, class, nation or species. It throws into question the ontologization of suffering into an abstract universal which constitutes existence as such. In these positions, the "problem" of suffering is "solved" by silencing or noetically coming to grips with it, i.e., by rendering it into mere appearance through insertion into a "larger" context of meaning. In Metz's reflection, the history of suffering mediated by memory is *the* inner condition of a history of freedom. The former gives rise to the latter, the memory of suffering to consciousness of freedom. In this movement, the sphere of "history" appears such that the eclipse of the history of suffering into the present faceless mass best kept out of sight and into the "dead" past heralds the immanent collapse of the history of freedom, a congealing of "history" into "nature."

> The substratum of history, then, is not nature as evolution or a process without reference to the subject. The natural history of man is to some extent the history of his suffering. In that history, the absence of reconciliation between nature and man is not suppressed, but preserved—against all teleo-

---

[78] Idem, "'Politische Theologie,'" p. 286.

logical projection and all ontological generalization. The history of man's suffering has no goal, but it has a future. It is, moreover, not teleology, but the trace of suffering that provides us with an accessible continuity of this history. The essential dynamics of history consist of the memory of suffering as a negative consciousness of future freedom and as a stimulus to over-come suffering within the framework of that freedom.[79]

In this sense, memory as a memory of suffering is, thirdly, a "dangerous memory." The obvious question is "dangerous for whom and toward what?" If the second point suggested an inner link between memory of the history of suffering and the realization of the history of freedom, then the third point refers to the inner link between the identity of the subject and the social whole.

The notion of "dangerous memory" appears to be proximately drawn from the work of Marcuse, whom Metz often quotes in this con-nection:

Remembering the past can let dangerous thoughts arise and established so-ciety appears to be afraid of the subversive content of these memories. Remembering is one way to become detached from the 'given facts', a way which, for a brief moment, breaks through the almighty power of things as they are. Memory summons back to mind past screams as well as past hopes.[80]

The memory of suffering is dangerous towards the identity-totalities of Enlightenment and, insofar as the problem of the future is a social and political one, the remembrance of suffering breaks through the magic circle of what "is," is subversive of it and witnesses to a future which is more than a mere teleological refinement of what exists. Over and against the hegemony of an instrumental and planning reason in the public sphere, the memory of suffering is, in comparison, an "anti" or "pseudo" knowledge which shocks one from reconciliation to the facts and their "logic" with its implied notion of history as the history of the victors, of those who have prevailed and veiled the victims. The memory of suffering is a political act. It is, however, also dangerous for the subject insofar as it invests the subject with the burden of freedom in a society where freedom has increasingly taken on the status of mere appearance. Hence, such a memory is productive of a subjective identity of "contradiction" to and "noncontemporaneity" with what is. In theologi-

---

[79] Idem, *Faith in History and Society*, p. 108 (94-95).

[80] Idem, *"'Politische Theologie'"*, p. 287. See, also, Herbert Marcuse, *One Dimensional Man* (Boston: Beacon Press, 1964), p. 98.

cal language, the freedom of the memory of suffering is a "costly grace."[81] It is a grace and freedom which seeks to be costly by seeking out a solidarity with those marginalized in society and history and which as a *lebendbestimmend* faith leads to the praxis of discipleship.

Fourth, for Metz, the mediation of the memory of suffering is never purely or even primarily argumentative-theoretic; rather, it is narrative-practical, founded in the telling of liberating stories which fragment the equation of praxis with the domination of nature, society and self.

> Respect for the suffering that has accumulated in history makes reason perceptive in a way which—in the abstract contrast between authority and knowledge within which the problem of the autonomy of reason is usually discussed and to which our understanding of emancipation as the a priori interest of reason is apparently fixed—cannot be expressed. In this perception, history—as the remembered history of suffering—has the form of a dangerous tradition. It is . . . mediated in a practical way. It takes place in dangerous stories in which the interest in freedom is introduced, identified and presented in narrative form.[82]

Fifthly, a specific dangerous memory of suffering, practically mediated by narrative, which is interruptive of the identity-totalities of the Enlightenment and contradictory to all attempts to reduce history to an identity system on the analogy of the immanent teleology of nature, is determinative for the Christian faith. "Christian faith declares itself as the *memoria passionis, mortis et resurrectionis Jesu Christi.*"[83] The fundamental form of Christian faith is its memory of Jesus Christ: his suffering and death, from which his ministry of words and actions cannot be severed, and his resurrection. If the "practical structure of the idea of God is the reason why the concept of God is basically narrative and memorative,"[84]

---

[81]   Dietrich Bonhoeffer, *The Cost of Discipleship*, trans R.H. Fuller (New York: Macmillan Paperbacks Edition, 1963), pp. 45-60.

[82]   Idem, *Faith in History and Society*, pp. 195-96 (173).

[83]   Ibid., p. 111 (97). Metz's use of the category "memory" obviates the difficulties encountered in some christologies of the Latin American liberation theologies, i.e., their appeal to the "Jesus of history" as the criterion of contemporary christology. Yet it must also be acknowledged that the determinate memory of Jesus of Nazareth in Metz's thought is but one of many memories of Jesus of Nazareth: Metz's construal of the content of the memory of Jesus as the Christ has more in common with Marcan apocalypticism than Johannine *Logos* Christology. What must be acknowledged is the de facto pluralism of memories of Jesus in the Christian tradition. This issue will be indirectly addressed in the following chapter under the rubric of the "theological proviso."

[84]   Ibid., p. 51 (48).

then embedded in this narrated memory of Jesus, "God" is that "cipher" of the divine, that particular disclosive and transformative characterization of the divine who is the God not only of the passion of Jesus Christ, but of the entire history of human suffering, that is, as a God pledged, covenanted with the living and the dead. Indeed, one may well suspect that the above characterizations of the dangerous memory of suffering are all "abstract" moments constitutive of the concrete memory of Christian faith.

Thus, the noncontemporaneity of Christian faith and praxis is not founded in the dialectics of pure practical reason, but in practical reason mediated and formed by a particular dangerous tradition. Nor is its critical edge anticipative of an empty future—empty in the sense of Adorno's characterization of "redemption" in *Minima Moralia*; rather, in the memory of Jesus's passion "is grounded the promise of future freedom for all. We remember the future of our freedom in the memory of his suffering. . . ."[85] Interestingly enough *pace* Pannenberg and without further exposition, Metz adds, ". . . this is an eschatological statement that cannot be made more plausible through any subsequent accommodation, and cannot be generally verified."[86]

From what has been said above concerning the focal point of "suffering" for Metz's theological reflections, it appears clear that, lest it devolve into mere denial of reality, there is no *memoria resurrectionis* apart from a *memoria passionis*. In this, the Christian *memoria passionis* is an anticipative memory but the precise character of this anticipation as *memoria resurrectionis* is elusive in Metz's writings.

> The Christian memory of suffering is in its theological implications an anticipatory memory: it intends the anticipation of a particular future of man as a future for the suffering, the hopeless, the oppressed, the injured and the useless of the earth.[87]

"Resurrection faith" is expressed in the capacity of the subject to endure the history of suffering without resignation or despair or the specious attempt to forge noetically an ersatz redemption of that sensuous suffering which only negates it. As a universal solidarity of the living and the dead, *memoria resurrectionis* mediated by *memoria passionis* asserts that in history even the dead and vanquished are still at stake.

---

85 Ibid., p. 111 (97).
86 Ibid.
87 Ibid., p. 117 (103).

There is, no doubt, a certain "reserve" on Metz's part concerning the *memoria resurrectionis* and the universal anticipative character of the Christian *memoria passionis*. In my estimate, such a "reserve" is not accidental. First, there is the circumspection and care demanded by the reality of suffering not to blaspheme the suffering of men and women by imposing a noetic meaning upon it *even in anticipation*. Second, the *memoria resurrectionis* is an anticipative memory, a hope for those who have suffered, the vanquished and the silent. Hence it speaks of the "not present' and that which, due to its absence, cannot be directly spoken about: it remains the blank of anticipation within the text of the history of suffering which is different from merely being an empty space. The rage to fill in the blank or to convert the anticipated "not-present" into a concealed present (and hence only absent in appearance) falls under the suspicion of a negation of the claim of the memory of suffering and the attenuation of the danger of history. "Where the Redeemer nears, the danger also increases."[88] The anticipation of the redemptive future of God exists only fragmentarily—in the solidarity of men and women with one another in the present and the memory of that solidarity in the past. Similarly, the *memoria resurrectionis* undergirds *memoria passionis*: "Only where there is hope, is there also a sensorium for danger and decline."[89] The two are concretely mediated and made present in the praxis of solidarity and discipleship.

By way of conclusion, it may be stated that the category *"memoria"* is both protean as well as the center of Metz's latest theological reflections. A careful reading of *Faith in History and Society* leaves one puzzling to what degree Metz's formal reflections on memory are constituted and conditioned by his material retrieval of Christian faith through *memoria Jesu Christi* as a *theological* category. Be this as it may, and I suspect that the two aspects of Metz's reflections mutually interpenetrate and condition each other, it may be argued that these reflections are the nodal point of his reflections on the subject, society and history. First and at the most fundamental level, it is the memory of suffering which productively differentiates "the contrast between nature and history, teleology and eschatology"[90] and protests in the name of its own dignity all reductions of the latter terms to the former. The sphere of history as that which (may) have a future, if not a *telos*, is opened up by the memory of suffer-

---

[88] Idem, *Unterbrechungen*, p. 64.
[89] Ibid.
[90] Idem, *Faith in History and Society*, p. 107 (94).

ing as the spur of freedom. Second, the memory of suffering as a negative consciousness of future freedom mediates history as the history of suffering by constituting practical reason. Here, history takes the form of a dangerous tradition—much like Benjamin's reflections in his "Theses on the Philosophy of History."[91] Thirdly, this mediation is inherently "practical," that is, social and political as the stimulus to overcome suffering in the praxis of liberation and solidarity. Fourthly, the memory of suffering as the anticipative memory of freedom is the primordial form of the constitution of the identity of the subject as practical reason with its interest in freedom.

> The form of memory that is immanent in critical reason is the memory of freedom. It is from this form of memory that reason acquires the interest that guides the process by which it becomes practical. The memory of freedom is a definite memory . . . related to the traditions in which the interest in freedom arose. The traditions are, in the narrative characteristics, that is, as the narrated history of freedom, not the object, but the presupposition of any critical reconstruction of history by argumentative reason.[92]

What Metz is asserting is that there exists no "pure" practical reason constitutive of human being as such which is not always already mediated by those tradition(s) in which the interest in freedom becomes explicit and thematic. Finally, in the practical-narrative constitution of the subject, society and history by the memory of suffering, history assumes the form of a dangerous tradition which steers a middle-course between the purely affirmative and submissive attitude towards the past in hermeneutical theory for which the classical (and elitist) ideal of *Bildung* is constitutive and the wholly critical attitude towards the past in *Ideologiekritik* for which the self-transparency of the concept (as self, society and history) is constitutive.[93]

---

91 Benjamin, "Theses on the Philosophy of History," *Illuminations*, pp. 253-64. For a discussion of Benjamin's protean thought, see Terry Eagleton, *Walter Benjamin or Towards a Revolutionary Criticism* (London: New Left Books, 1978); Richard Wolin, *Walter Benjamin: An Aesthetic of Redemption*; Buck-Morss, *The Origins of Negative Dialectics*, pp. 136-84; and Habermas, "Walter Benjamin: Consciousness-Raising or Rescuing Critique," in *Philosophical-Political Profiles*, pp. 129-64.

92 Idem, *Faith in History and Society*, p. 195 (172-73).

93 The major texts in the so-called "Gadamer-Habermas" debate can be found in Jürgen Habermas, ed., *Hermeneutik und Ideologiekritik* (Frankfurt: Suhrkamp Verlag, 1971). The most thorough commentaries on this debate are Dieter Misgel, "Critical Theory and Hermeneutics: The Debate between Habermas and Gadamer," in *On Critical Theory*, pp. 164-83; Jack Mendelson, "The Habermas-Gadamer Debate," *New*

The second category of practical fundamental theology is "narrative." Already this category has been noted in the thesis that "memory" is constituted by a narrative structure. Even more, however, than with the category of memory, Metz's reflections on "narrative" remain fragmentary and suggestive rather than systematic. What is clear is the significance of his use of narrative as a category of fundamental theology. "Narrative" denotes the founding, effective and concrete transmission-communication of religious meaning and truth which ruptures the attempts to secure the meaning, truth and self-identity of faith in pure theory. What is at stake in Metz's use of the category is the *recognition* of the fundamental role of narrative and story in the transmission of religion and the formation of the identity of the subject and *not* the banishment of all argument and theory from faith and theology. The category of narrative acts as a critical corrective to transcendental and universal-historical theologies.

> There is no question of regressively obscuring the distinction between narrative memory and theological argument. It is much more a question of acknowledging the relative value of rational argument, the primary function of which is to protect the narrative memory of salvation in a scientific world,

German Critique, 18 (Fall 1979): 44-73; Ricoeur, "Hermeneutics and the Critique of Ideology," in *Hermeneutics and the Human Sciences*, ed. and trans. John B. Thompson (Cambridge: Cambridge University Press, 1981), pp. 63-100; and Fred Dallmayr, *Twilight of Subjectivity* (Notre Dame, IN: University of Notre Dame Press, 1980), pp. 284-93. Metz's position represents, I believe, an attempt to steer a middle course between the positions of Gadamer and Habermas. With Gadamer, Metz's emphasis on the category of memory acknowledges the active constitution by tradition of the subject whose interest in freedom in fact is grounded in a determinate tradition. With Habermas, Metz's emphasis on "dangerous" memories implicitly distances itself from Gadamer's elitist articulation of *Bildung* and its seemingly conservative social stance. Against Gadamer and much more in keeping with the hermeneutics of reception of Jauss, Metz's retrieval of apocalypticism attempts to recapture the negativity and distance of the Christian classic which shatters the "immediate" fusion of horizons of the Christian classic and contemporary times in the form of "bourgeois Christianity." Against Habermas, Metz wishes to maintain that the foundation of the interest in freedom arises from the interplay of subject and tradition—and religious traditions in particular—and not from a rational reconstruction of societal learning processes or the transcendental claims implied in speech acts. Indeed, in systematically overlooking such liberating traditions (as Habermas seemingly has by accepting Weber's notion of the irreversible *"Entzauberung"* as characteristic of the modern age), critical theory overlooks the very condition of its possibility and falls back into the seduction of the pure self-transparency of the concept. See, also, Hans Robert Jauss, *Toward an Aesthetic of Reception*, trans. by Timothy Bahti, with an introduction by Paul de Man (Minneapolis: University of Minnesota Press, 1982).

to allow it to be at stake and to prepare the way for a renewal of this narrative, without which the experience of salvation is silenced.[94]

Argument is the midwife of narrative.

For Metz, narrative remains the original and originative embodiment in language of faith. To dismiss it as "precritical" is already to divest faith—and indeed all experience—of cognitive significance and to marginalize it as merely "private" opinion. The erosion of narrative and story is of one piece with the extirpation of the subject insofar as the subject is fundamentally a subject formed by stories. Further, there is a performative and practical aspect of narrative. It is performative in that narrative can be characterized as "a linguistic action in which the unity of the story as an effective word and practical effect is expressed in the same process."[95] "Practical," in this context, refers less to the constitution of practical reason's interest in freedom as social and political—although this is the case with regard to the "dangerous" stories of the memory of suffering—than to the "extra-" theoretical role of narrative as constitutive of and foundational for the religious identity of the subject and the transmission of faith. The foundational stories of the Christian tradition, those of Jesus, "attempt to change the listening subject in the telling of the story and to make him ready to imitate Christ. Christological knowledge, then, is not handed down primarily as a concept, but in such stories of the imitation of Christ."[96] In a critical, postnarrative age, the claims of a narrative theology seem impotent, possessing more the character of an invitation than coercion. "There can, of course, be no a priori proof of the critical and liberating effect of such stories, which have to be encountered, listened to and told again."[97] More specifically, narrative as the dangerous memory of suffering is disclosive of history, interruptive of the contemporary social totality and transformative of the identity of the subject such that subject can truly be a subject and not an object.[98]

---

94 Idem, *Faith in History and Society*, p. 213 (190).
95 Idem, *Faith in History and Society*, p. 208 (185).
96 Ibid., p. 52 (48).
97 Ibid., p. 210 (187).
98 The ambiguity of the term "subject" in Metz's writings arises from the fact that the essential determination of the subject is "freedom." Yet "freedom" is most often used by Metz not to portray some positive picture of the "free subject," but in a negative sense as "the subject free *from* suffering." Insofar as there is no a priori determination of the systemic form or matrix of human suffering which can only be a posteriori recognized in history and society, so the notion of "subject" and "freedom" can only be specified in a negative and dialectical way. Metz's use of the two terms in this

Finally, in Metz's view, a narrative theology and soteriology meets the crisis of an argumentative soteriology occasioned by taking seriously the history of suffering which must mediate the nonidentity of history as suffering and faith. These strategies of argumentative theologies—most specifically, Rahner's transcendental theology and Pannenberg's hermeneutics of universal history—to form a new identity of meaning from the nonidentity of suffering and faith are "idealist": they lead to the loss of the concrete, i.e., social and political, subject and the spiritualization of history in which its catastrophic character and quality of danger is reduced to appearance, if not negated. "There is no way of making sure of meaning, either transcendentally or in a universally historical sense."[99] The concrete mediation of salvation and history, Christian identity and nonidentity of history is through the praxis of solidarity and discipleship, these latter themselves being mediated by narrative.

> As distinct from pure discourse or argument, narrative makes it possible to discuss the whole of history and the universal meaning of history in such a way that the idea of this universal meaning is not transferred to a logical compulsion of totality or a kind of transcendental necessity, as a result of which the mystical-political histories of individuals would be of secondary importance in comparison with the saving meaning of history as a whole and could only be incorporated subsequently into the framework of a definitive history dissociated from the subject. In the narrative conception of Christian salvation, history and histories—the one history of salvation and the absence of salvation of individuals—merge together without diminishing each other.[100]

Narrative mediates identity and nonidentity without that rage for identity which blasphemes the history of suffering by positing its noetic reconciliation and creates—and demands—the moment of a praxis of solidarity which is the concrete mediation of identity and nonidentity. Finally, I would suggest that Metz's *apologia* for narrative constitutes a "naming" of the crisis of Christianity and the theological-religious task in a post-Enlightenment age. This crisis is the enlightenment distrust and erosion of narrative and the theological task of a "retelling"—which is

---

manner closely approximates that of Horkheimer and Adorno and, more proximately, that of Paulo Freire in *Pedagogy of the Oppressed*, trans. Myra Bergman Ramos (New York: The Continuum Publishing Co., 1970).

[99]   Ibid., p. 168 (146).

[100]   Ibid., pp. 164-65 (147).

distinct from a theological reflection on the conditions of the possibility of such a retelling—of the *memoria Jesu* as a dangerous story.

The third category of a practical fundamental theology is "solidarity." Solidarity is by no means extrinsic to or the mere application of the other two categories, but must be conceived in unity with them. The dangerous memory of suffering and the narrative of salvation only become concrete and effective in the mystical and political praxis of solidarity. Conversely, the expression and communication of solidarity's structure cannot be accomplished without memory and narrative. Again, the precise meaning of the term remains elusive. Negatively, Metz rejects those understandings of the term which would equate it with the nostalgic romanticism of *Gemeinde* or the notion of (free) relations of (un)equal exchange or a community of "the rational" based upon a potential or actual argumentative competence. Rather, as formed by the memory of suffering, the recognition of the (threatened) subjectivity of the "other" is expressed in the recognition of the "other's" need and suffering.

For Metz, the solidarity of faith is both a mystical and political one:

> In a practical fundamental theology, the essentially twofold structure of solidarity is preserved. In other words, solidarity is seen on the one hand as mystical and universal and on the other as political and particular. This double structure protects the universal aspect of solidarity from apathy and its partisan nature from hatred and forgetfulness. It raises again and again the question: With whom should there be solidarity? What form should solidarity take?[101]

As universal and mystical, solidarity looks forward not only to utopia, but also backwards encompassing the defeated and vanquished, the nameless and silent ones. In this sense, solidarity posits a whole or unity of history which is critical of all totalities of identity in which the past is reduced to the instrument and means of the victors. Anamnestic solidarity as a care for the dead remains the crisis and indictment of all projects of emancipation and utopia. As political and partisan, solidarity heeds the present authority of the suffering of the "other" and gives a hermeneutical privilege to the oppressed whose broken lives give the lie to claims of the realization of truth, the good, justice and beauty in the contemporary world. In an age of the growing interdependence of all men and women, where the question of the future is preeminently a so-

[101]   Ibid., p. 232 (207).

cial-political one, a partisan solidarity takes the form of a worldwide solidarity in the political praxis of liberation. The tension between the two forms of solidarity cannot be abolished by argument or reduced to one or the other since they mutually penetrate and condition one another. Without the former, the latter becomes repressive and totalitarian: forgetfulness becomes the categorical imperative of practical reason oriented towards happiness. Without the latter, the former becomes purely interiorized and spiritualized: the dangerous memory of suffering becomes the merely believed-in dangerous memory.

"The Christian praxis of solidarity will always be directed towards the imitation of Christ."[102] Indeed, the statement can be reversed and it may be asserted that the imitation of Christ *is* the Christian praxis of solidarity and, hence, that imitation is both mystical and political. The centrality of the imitation of Christ as discipleship, for Metz, can be seen in his assertion that Christianity is essentially and primarily a praxis.

> Christianity is not first and foremost a 'teaching' which it is necessary to maintain as 'pure' as possible or a teaching to be interpreted so as to be on the cutting edge as much as possible. It is a praxis which must be radically lived. Without this, the intelligible and comforting power of its message remains strange and inaccessible. We Christians have a simple word for this praxis: 'discipleship'. Discipleship of the poor and the suffering, discipleship of Jesus.[103]

Within this context of the naming of Christianity as a praxis and faith as discipleship and *imitatio Christ*, praxis refers not to mere action, but to an intelligible activity, an incarnate meaning. The unity of the categories of memory and narrative, on the one hand, with that of solidarity, on the other, cannot be sundered into the relationship of "essence" and "application." While distinguishable, they are not separable: the former are abstract moments in-forming the latter as concrete. The categories of practical fundamental theology (memory, narrative and solidarity) can be viewed as attempts at a description of the praxis of Christians which is foundational for the contemporary identity-crisis of Christian faith and its continued transmission—a crisis which is all of one piece with that of (post-)Enlightenment society as a whole. More precisely, the categories, interpreted through the crisis of the dialectic of enlightenment and bourgeois Christianity, specify a political hermeneutic of Christian conversion

---

[102]   Ibid., p. 235 (210).
[103]   Idem, *Unterbrechungen*, pp. 22-23.

and discipleship in its orientation to the mediation of history by society which today threatens to regress to the rigidity of a first nature.

If, as Elizabeth Fiorenza maintains, "Jesus' *praxis* and *vision* of the *basileia* is the mediation of God's future into the structures and experiences of his own time and people,"[104] then today there is a need for an ecclesial mediation of the identity of the religious subject as Christian insofar as the Church exists *sub memoria Jesu*. It appears fair to Metz's position to assert that through the subject's incorporation into that ecclesia of the Spirit, normed by the *memoria Jesu* and the exigency of discipleship, those realities which the gospel proclaims are made present in a fragmentary form.[105] Such at least appears to be the corollary to Metz's assertion of the "practical" character of the idea of God.

> The Christian idea of God is a practical one: the stories of departure (Exodus), conversion and discipleship, of raised heads and of liberation belong to this idea. This idea of God cannot be achieved, justified or even disproved through an absolute reflection or a theoretical reconstruction. It is finally nothing other than an abbreviation for a reservoir of memories and stories which are not mere diversion but dangerous because they do not introduce one primarily to a 'thinking' but an 'acting' and because only in this praxis of discipleship is this idea's saving power revealed.[106]

In the mystical-political discipleship of Christ, the "divine" appears as the "God of the lowly, the helper of the oppressed, the protector of the forlorn, the savior of those without hope" (Judith 9.11).

Similarly, Metz also asserts that the primal intelligible power of christology lies neither in a metaphysics of the *Logos*, nor in an adjudication by critical-historical reconstruction of the dichotomy between the Jesus of history and the Christ of faith; rather, its power lies in the ecclesially mediated and fragmentarily present reality of God in the praxis of discipleship.

> Following Christ and christology belong closely together. . . . It is only by following and imitating him that we know whom we are dealing with. Following Christ is therefore not just a subsequent application of the

---

104 Elizabeth Schussler Fiorenza, *In Memory of Her* (New York: Crossroad Publishing Co., 1983), p. 121.

105 On the ecclesial mediation of redemptive reality, see the work of Farley, *Ecclesial Man* and *Ecclesial Reflection*.

106 Metz, *Unterbrechungen*, pp. 22-23.

Church's christology to our life: the practice of following Christ is itself a central part of christology.[107]

The dialectics of emancipation and redemption recapitulate *in nuce* the problem of the confrontation of the Christian tradition with modernity as *Freiheitsgeschichte*. "Emancipation" refers to the thematic emergence of human autonomy and its actualization in the movement towards self-liberation. It is "a universal, quasi historico-philosophical category of the modern history of freedom."[108] "Emancipation" names the prethematically effective experience of the world which has become thematic and concrete in the modern histories of enlightenment and revolution, and which has received exposition in both "liberal" and "Marxist" political philosophy. Modernity as the age of emancipation witnesses to the practical, concrete and social demands of freedom. "Redemption" refers to the

> . . . assured deliverance from the suffering of guilt and from the sinful self-degeneration of man . . . and as an assured deliverance from the suffering of finitude, of mortality, of that inner corroding nihilism of created being. . . .[109]

While the contemporary experience of emancipation brings into the light a social-political history of oppression, repression and violence, the Christian tradition of redemption brings into focus a history of destructive guilt and the fated destiny of all men and women through their finitude to death.

The question arises as to the relationship between emancipation and redemption. Are they mutually exclusive? Does the purported historical dependence of the modern history of emancipation on the Christian tradition of redemption recoil back upon the latter in its dismissal as irrelevant in a world come of age? Can the two be merely added together as, e.g., secular immanence and religious transcendence? Is redemption a mythological "dressing up" of emancipation or the "stop-gap" for its delay—the regulative ideal of a utopian projection? Or is emancipation as secular and profane, as directed toward the penultimate reality of discord in history, unmasked by faith in redemption through Christ as mere "appearance"? In raising the question of the relation of faith and history as society in this manner, the question of the relation of redemption and

---

[107] Idem, *Followers of Christ*, pp. 39-40.
[108] Idem, *Faith in History and Society*, p. 119 (104).
[109] Ibid., p. 124 (109).

emancipation becomes not merely *a*, but *the* question of contemporary theology.

Most particularly, Metz censures those, largely "liberal" attempts to gain a "theological foothold in the crevices of these dialectics of the history of emancipation" and which uncritically negate the claim to totality of emancipation.

> Concisely, I would assert that a theology of redemption does not become critical by assimilating the critical theory or by inserting itself into, or superimposing itself over that theory. Theology would thereby remain uncritically aware of the totality-aspiration at the origin of the modern history of emancipation. Only if theology takes the entirety of this history into account in its evolutionary version, can theology confront it in such a way that theology will neither regressively and undifferentiatedly fall short of the modern problem, nor from the very start, falsely seek to immunize its understanding of redemption from the criticisms of the history of emancipation through abstract and unhistorical distinctions, nor, finally, simply subordinate the logos of redemption to the logos of emancipative reason.[110]

What Metz appears to be protesting against are those strategies of a noetic reconciliation of emancipation and redemption which either mixes the terms or reduces one term to the other. The *social-critical* categories of critical theory, such as "redemption," "reconciliation" and the "resurrection of fallen nature," do not support a *theological* superstructure of a theology of redemption—although, at the end of the previous chapter, the religious aporia of critical theory raises a question concerning its own claims to totality. While eschewing a noetic reconciliation of the redemptive and emancipatory history of freedom, Metz suggests that the concrete mediation of the two histories takes place in the one history of suffering. The social-political history of suffering addressed by emancipation and that of guilt and finitude addressed by redemption are not merely separate or parallel histories but are moments mediating one another in the single concrete history of suffering. In short, the history of suffering is both political and mystical, calling forth a history of freedom as both emancipative and redemptive, and each to maintain the integrity of the other. Hence, Metz's strategy is not to play off the aporia of emancipation and redemption against one another, but to relate both to the concrete history of suffering which mediates them.

The aporia of emancipation with regard to the concrete history of suffering is twofold. First, the transposition of the "subject of history"

---

[110] Ibid., p. 122 (108).

from the divine to humanity as *homo emancipator* generates in its "liberal-progressive," "Marxist," and positivist-technocratic" forms [111] an "exonerating mechanism" which constricts the scope of emancipation rendering it abstract. If humans are the subject of the history of freedom, then so are they also the subject of the history of suffering. Yet the overwhelming reality of the history of suffering leads not to a recognition of the subject's own guilt and responsibility, but to the creation of new projected heteronomies of class, race, sex, or nature which act as those "transcendental subjects of history to which the dark side of emancipation, the history of guilt can be attributed without repercussions."[112] Where emancipation is cast as a universal historical totality and theodicy is transposed to anthropodicy, there emerges a bifurcation of the subject of history into the children of light and the children of darkness, where the former are the subject of the history of freedom and the latter that of the history of suffering.

> A universal theory of emancipation without a soteriology remains caught under an irrational mechanism of exoneration or guilt-repression. A history of emancipation without a history of redemption, faced with the concrete history of suffering, subjugates the historical subject to new irrational constraints and either man is forced into a transcendental suspension of his own historical responsibility or he is forced into irreconcilable enmity of finally to negate himself as a subject.[113]

Over and against the exonerating mechanism of the bifurcation of the subject of history in the modern movement of emancipation, the anticipative memory of a future for all in the Christian tradition asserts that God is the eschatological subject of history—an assertion which is anticipatorily and fragmentarily present in the utopian orientation of the liberative praxis of discipleship.

> In the memory of this [Jesus'] suffering, God appears in his eschatological freedom as the subject and meaning of history as a whole. This implies first of all that for this *memoria* there is also no politically identifiable subject of universal history. The meaning and goal of this history as a whole are instead—to put it very summarily—under the so-called "eschatological proviso of God." The Christian *memoria* recalls the God of Jesus' passion as the

---

[111] Ibid., pp. 124-28 (109-14), 115-18 (101-3). See also the recent "Symposium on Religion and Politics," *Telos* 58 (Winter 1983-84), pp. 115-57.

[112] Ibid., p. 125 (111).

[113] Ibid., p. 127 (112).

subject of the universal history of suffering, and in the same movement refuses to give political shape to this subject and enthrone it politically.[114]

In the Christian *memoria passionis et resurrectionis*, men and women are set free from the exonerating mechanism of the negation of guilt to assume responsibility for the history of suffering as well as that of the history of freedom.

The second aporia, already mentioned above, is the suffering of finitude and the suffering of the dead: "for the greater freedom of future generations does not justify past sufferings nor does it render them free."[115] In both "oversights," emancipation as a universal historical totality betrays itself as an abstract history of freedom whose vision of history is one of victory, success and triumph. The true subjects of history are the victorious survivors.

For Christian faith, in the light of the anamnestic solidarity with the *memoria Jesu*, however, it is the victim, the failure and the forgotten, the silent ones—those who would be surpassed and suppressed in emancipation as a historical totality—who are the interpretive key to history in which *all* women and men participate and who seek and call for a history

---

[114] Ibid., p. 117 (102-3). The understanding of the category of the "eschatological proviso" remains one of the dividing points between political theology and the Latin American theology of liberation. The force of this category for the former is the acknowledgement of the nonfinality of all "utopias" as well as a caveat that no penultimate qua human subject be made into the subject of history as such. On such an understanding of the eschatological proviso, the theological task is largely one of "negative criticism" of political ideologies and the social whole. The objection from the theology of liberation is that in such an understanding of the "eschatological proviso," political theologians have unwittingly placed all strivings for social change in Hegel's proverbial "night when all the cows are black." Over and against this understanding of the eschatological proviso and its relativization of all social totalities as qualitatively different from the eschaton and the reservation of the theological task to a negative-critical stance, the theology of liberation wishes to maintain the reality within history of partial anticipations and incomplete realizations of the *eschaton* which are not simply equatable with one another and as a corollary to this the need for theological reflection to enter into the evaluation of concrete, positive political, economic and social proposals. My suggestion here is that such positions are not mutually exclusive, for real partial advance in anticipation of the eschaton is *real* advance. Such "advance," however, if not qualified by the proleptic assertion of God as the "subject of history" potentially betrays itself into a forgetfulness and indifference towards the dead. Yet, as I will briefly indicate in the following chapter, the assertion of "God" as the "subject of history" is rendered no less questionable by the character of that history as a "history of suffering."
[115] Ibid., p. 128 (114).

of redemption. To see history in this fashion is, in Bonhoeffer's words, "to see the great events of world history from below, from the perspective of the outcast, the suspect, the maltreated, the powerless, the oppressed, the reviled."[116]

Yet this redemption too has its aporia. There is no argumentative soteriology which can definitively ground a history of redemption and God as the eschatological subject of history. An argumentative soteriology, shorn of its apocalyptic sting, in the affirmation of the definitive and present—albeit perhaps "concealed"—reality of men's and women's reconciliation and redemption in Christ is a strategy of immunization which negates both "the risk and suffering of the non-identity of historical existence."[117] History as the history of suffering is thus negated, fostering an objective cynicism or indifference to history to which an ahistorical objective being or time is counterposed. The dialectics of emancipation and redemption vis-à-vis the concrete history of suffering cannot be solved noetically or argumentatively. The resolution is practical-rhetorical: the need is for finding "another way of expressing a real and effective redemption in the non-identity of the age of suffering."[118] The need is for the recognition of the nonsublatability of narrative into the concept and for a renewal of the narrative witness of faith within the context of an emancipatory praxis of discipleship. Hence the dialectics of emancipation (modernity) and redemption (Christian faith) itself points back to the categories of memory, narrative and solidarity as the practical-effective mediation of the identity of faith in contemporary society.

The final theme to be considered is Metz's intensification of eschatology in his reflections on apocalyptic time and consciousness. Such reflections constitute a summary of the stance of Christian faith as interruptive of "what is" in acknowledgement of the danger of history. "Apocalyptic time and consciousness" is the summary-category of practical fundamental theology which specifies Metz's projective retrieval of the Christian faith. Not without significance, however, such reflections are *literally* fragmentary and in Metz's own words "critical correctives." What becomes clear in these reflections is the elusiveness and difficulty of a rhetorical articulation of the mystical and political dimensions of faith which breaks through the language of both liberal and (neo)orthodox articulations of the identity of Christian faith and discipleship which

[116] Dietrich Bonhoeffer, *Letters and Papers From Prison*, ed. Eberhard Bethge (New York: Macmillan Paperbacks Edition, 1972), p. 17.
[117] Ibid., p. 130 (116).
[118] Ibid., pp. 132-33 (118).

threaten to swallow up and assimilate the concerns of a practical fundamental theology into its own agenda, language and concerns.

Apocalyptic time and consciousness is, above all, interruptive of that timeless time—itself a part of the dialectic of the enlightenment—by which history and society as a second nature come to resemble first nature. Under the guise of a "scientific" evolutionary logic—which in its ideological functioning is no more rational than the time symbols of other "religions"—which holds both objective and subjective sway, history and society is reduced to a natural entelechy. This understanding of time—"whatever is, was; whatever will be, is"—in its "optimistic," "pessimistic" and "realistic" versions is modeled on the analogy of the potential existence of the telos in actual substance. Suffering too is assigned its place of comprehensible meaning, while hope and expectation are replaced by a faith in reformism or resignation to "more of the same."

Yet to leave the timeless time of evolutionary logic to itself is "abstract" and a form of "false consciousness." As "empty time," the time of a "bad infinity" devoid of "surprise," it is also a social, historical time: the time of the victors, the comfortable. It is bourgeois time: the time of those who "have" time and hence have no need of time. Bourgeois Christianity, in its attenuation of its eschatological orientation or its constriction to the fate of the individual soul/monad in the four last things comes to play its role herein: it is the grease on the gears of a repressive and oppressive totality and the anesthetic balm on the open wound of the telos of history to which in forgetfulness of its own apocalyptic sting it conforms.

> All the prevailing versions of modern eschatology—both present and future-oriented versions—seem to have been successfully adapted to an evolutionary understanding of time that is alien to them. This understanding has compelled the Christian imminent expectation (if it has not already been dropped in advance) to become extremely privatized—to the death of the individual—and has induced it either to think of the future of God as strictly timeless or to project that future on to an evolutionary scheme with the help of a transcendental or universally historical teleology.[119]

---

[119] Ibid., p. 174 (154). Both in genre and in content Metz's reflections on "timelessness" and apocalyptic as imminent expectation follow Benjamin's "Theses on the Philosophy of History." "History is the subject of a structure whose site is not homogeneous, empty time, but time filled by the presence of the now [*Jetztzeit*]" which is not only a time of (possible) fulfillment, but the moment of danger" [Theses on the Philosophy of History," p. 261]. Here it must be admitted that Metz's fragments—originally written to honor Ernst Bloch—are more provocative than system-

Apocalyptic time is also a social time. It stands for the hermeneutical privilege of the oppressed. It is the time of the hungry, those in flight, the desperate, the suffering for whom time is "crisis," the time of the expectation of the fullness of time or the time of the final capitulation to despair: the time of the *Jetztzeit* (W. Benjamin) in which the Messiah—or the Antichrist—might appear. Apocalyptic time is also the time of Christian faith as a messianic religion: the time of anamnestic solidarity, together with its sensorium for danger and catastrophe, in the shadow of the *memoria Jesu*. It is the time of a "conversion" to suffering, to those who do not "have time." For Christian faith, apocalyptic time as a form of consciousness is the mystical counterpart to the lived political reality of oppression and suffering in the imitation of Christ. Indeed, for Metz, these two belong inextricably together:

> The Christian idea of imitation and the apocalyptical idea of imminent expectation belong together. It is not possible to imitate Jesus radically, that is, at the level of the roots of life, if "the time is not shortened." Jesus' call: "Follow me" and the call of Christians: "Come, Lord Jesus!" are inseparable.[120]

If, for Metz, the "shortest definition of religion is interruption,"[121] then apocalyptic time and consciousness as immanent expectation which is inseparable from a sensorium for danger and catastrophe, together with the praxis of discipleship as *imitatio Christi*, is the reflective explication of that Christian "interruption." Rather than rupturing the motivation for practical action in history through a dualistic quietism, apocalyptic restores the urgency of time which enters into all social praxis.

> To live Christian hope on the basis of the imminent expectation of the second coming does not mean sacrificing its social and political responsibility but the reverse: injecting the urgency imposed by time and the need to act into a responsibility that has been robbed of its tension by extending the expectation of the second coming to infinity —one that has been diluted and deferred.[122]

---

atic, even while his major point is clear: that the "original" apocalyptic temporal matrix of following Christ has been co-opted into a timeless view of time, free of anything which might disrupt it and thus abandoning "history" as the sphere of a possible redemption or catastrophe.

120   Ibid., p. 176 (155).
121   Ibid., p. 171 (150).
122   Idem, *Followers of Christ*, p. 79.

The intensification of eschatology as apocalyptic represents a polemical attempt to rupture the grip of timelessness in piety and theology and to restore the social and political dimensions of time to Christian faith. In this, the "corrective" of apocalyptic is a protest against the constriction of eschatology and expectation to the "existential time" of the subject which abstracts from the time of the social and political world. It protests against those forms of eschatology whose parameters are set by an existential balance between an (already) realized and a (not-yet) future and against those eschatologies which view the future as that utopia brought forth from what is. Against these, apocalyptic time and consciousness in the praxis of discipleship asks the questions "How much time do we still have?", "To whom does the world belong?", "To whom does its time and suffering belong?"[123] for which a political theology of the subject, directed towards history and society, is less an "answer" than the delineation of an orientation (piety) and task.

A concluding "note" on Metz's use of the term "praxis" is appropriate here. What follows here is an initial attempt to situate the meaning of the term and its significance for Metz's theology—a more comprehensive determination of the term exceeds the context of this chapter. Without exaggeration it may be affirmed that Metz's use of the term "praxis" is elusive. Nowhere does the term become the focus of thematic attention as with the categories of memory, narrative and solidarity; rather, it is the background against which all these are explicated. In this, Metz does not differ from many other contemporary theologians who have recourse to this term.

To a large degree, the elusiveness of "praxis" derives from the diversity of intellectual traditions in which its use is embedded: most particularly, the Aristotelian, Hegelian-Marxist and American pragmatic traditions.[124] To raise the question of the meaning of praxis for each of these traditions is, to a large degree, to raise the question of these traditions' mutual relations as a whole. What is the nature of "practical reason" and the relation of praxis to such reason? What is the nature of

123 Idem, *Faith in History and Society*, p. 178 (157).
124 For an overview of the diverse traditions of reflection on the notion of praxis and its relation to theory, see Richard Bernstein, *Praxis and Action* (Philadelphia: University of Pennsylvania Press, 1971); Nicholas Lobkowicz, *Theory and Practice* (Notre Dame, Indiana: University of Notre Dame Press, 1967); Hans Georg Gadamer, *Reason in the Age of Science*, trans. Fred Lawrence (Cambridge: The MIT Press, 1981); and Habermas, *Theory and Practice*. For an attempt to map out the contemporary theological terrain along the axis of the relation between theory and practice, see Lamb, *Solidarity With Victims*, pp. 61-99.

"theoretical reason" and the relation of theory to such reason? What is the relation of the four terms to each other? What is the relation of these to nature and/or society and of nature to society and society to nature?

The situation is no less bewildering in Metz's use of the term. Throughout the pages of *Faith in History and Society*, the term praxis is used alone and by itself. It is more determined in references to "moral praxis" and "social praxis." It is theologically determined as the "praxis of discipleship," the "praxis of solidarity" and "interruptive praxis." References are made to the new relation between theory and praxis—references which ostensibly occur in relation to the left-wing Hegelian tradition. Yet thematic attention is rarely given to any of these. What then may be said of the use of the term praxis by Metz? What I wish to suggest is that the most concrete and common use of the term praxis by Metz occurs within a specifically theological context. Given the absence of a "pure" practical reason and the narrative structure of subjective identity, "praxis" refers first and foremost to religious praxis or what, in the Christian tradition, has been called conversion and discipleship, which is constitutive of the subjectivity of Christians and which founds a moral/social praxis of liberating and liberated solidarity with the victims of history and society. Such social praxis is not merely an application of religious praxis as conversion and discipleship, but is an inner constitutive moment of it as can be seen in Metz's description of religious praxis through the categories of memory, narrative and solidarity. Further, such religious praxis is foundational for, as well as interruptive of, all theological noetic identities and forms the concrete mediation of the self-identity and relevance of faith. In this, what is at stake is not only a new agenda for "doing theology," but more fundamentally and importantly, the demand for a particular form of piety as incarnate, embodied meaning.

Two contexts determine Metz's use of the term "praxis." The first is the dialectical relation of praxis to theory. If, following Matthew Lamb,[125] theory is the movement of the "subject toward objectivity" and praxis as the movement of the "subject toward subjectivity," then, for Metz, the primacy of praxis refers to the "intelligible force of praxis itself"[126] in contradistinction to subordinating praxis to theory as the latter's application and foundation. Further, the primacy of praxis asserts that not only is praxis the goal of theory, but that theory is not "self-grounding" except as a *proton pseudos* and, hence, that praxis is the foundation of theory.

125 Lamb, *Solidarity With Victims*, p. 62.
126 Metz, *Faith in History and Society*, p. 50 (47).

The second context is "praxis'" essential reference to the sphere of the social and the political. Axiomatic here is that the (moral) praxis of the subject as an individual is never socially neutral and politically innocent. Moral praxis is socially conditioned—Kant as corrected by Marx—even as, for the Christian, social praxis remains morally conditioned in that this social "praxis cannot lead to an abstract or violent negation of the individual."[127] The most concrete determination of the subject is as the historical, that is, social subject. Together, the two contexts specify the intrinsic connotations of the identity of faith in the concrete conversion and discipleship of the subject and the social-political interpretive retrieval of Christian identity in an explicit political hermeneutic of the Gospel.

CONCLUSION: THE NEED FOR A "CORRECTIVE"

To summarize, I begin with Dorothea Sölle's definition of "political theology" in *Political Theology*:

> There are no specifically Christian solutions for which a political theology would have to develop the theory. Political theology is rather a theological hermeneutic, which, in distinction from a theology that interprets reality from an ontological or existentialist point of view, holds open a horizon of interpretation in which politics is understood as the comprehensive and decisive sphere in which Christian truth should become praxis.[128]

If it is correct to affirm that in the second phase of his work, Metz's focal point was an *apologia* for a political hermeneutic of Christianity, then it may be said that, in his later work, he has proceeded to an elaboration of those fundamental categories, concepts and themes which specify more concretely the form and content of a political hermeneutic of the Gospel. More specifically, his interpretation is focused by his characterization of the contemporary world under the rubric of the "dialectic of enlightenment" and the crisis of Christian identity as "bourgeois religion." The interruption of the former, which threatens the existence of the subject as subject and hence also as religious subject, is brought about through the renewal-retrieval of the messianic roots occluded by the latter, which helps to restore the identity of the subject. Simultaneously, however, the

---

[127] Ibid., p. 56 (53).
[128] Dorothee Sölle, *Political Theology*, trans. and with an introduction by John Shelley (Philadelphia: Fortress Press, 1974), p. 59.

rescuing of the subject and the interruption of the hegemonic identity-totalities of the Enlightenment is not in the name of a (pure) social criticism. In this there remains a decisive difference between "critical theory"
and "political theology." Such reflection is undertaken as a *theological*
hermeneutic of Christianity focusing on the practical universality of a
solidarity made present in the dangerous memory of Jesus Christ. In this,
theological hermeneutic and social-political interruption are inseparable
and define theology as a *political* theology.

The thrust of Metz's theological reflections is towards a description
of the religious praxis of Christians revolving around the foci of
"conversion" ("anthropological revolution") and discipleship. Together,
these are not only the concrete mediation of the identity of Christian faith
and the foundation of theology, but they are also a social-political mediation given, to use a phrase from Metz's earlier work, the unity of the
future of God and the world. Further, it is the noetic identities of theology and its rage for identity which are ruptured by the "interruption of
suffering." To suffering the only appropriate response is not its negation
or noetic reconciliation but a mystical-political solidarity which acknowledges suffering in the memory of the defeated and vanquished and
which incarnates a partisanship with the oppressed, thereby leaving to
suffering the "dignity" of its existence without reducing it to mere
"appearance." The themes and categories described above—memory,
narrative, solidarity, the dialectics of emancipation and redemption and
apocalyptic time—all converge on and approach from different perspectives the single issue: "What is it to *be* a Christian today?", i.e., a description of the foundational reality of (Christian) conversion and discipleship.

The protean nature of Metz's reflections and style leaves the reader
with a bundle of "loose ends" which open up a space for further critical
reflection. In part, this arises from his penchant for "assertions" with little or no explanatory warrants, e.g., the relation of theory to praxis as
indicated above. So, also, Metz's assertion, that narrative/tradition forms
the foundation of practical reason with an interest in freedom, raises
questions regarding the relation of practical fundamental theology to
contemporary hermeneutical theory and critical theory. Other questions
arise concerning a fuller explication of the themes and categories treated
by Metz, e.g., his reflections on narrative, on his own admission, leave
open many questions as even a cursory glance at the growing literature
on narrative demonstrates. Other questions arise concerning the plausibility and extensiveness of certain characterizations of contemporary so-

ciety as used by Metz, particularly those of "instrumental reason" and an "anthropology of subjugation and domination" which were subjected to critical scrutiny in the previous chapter on the Frankfurt School. Still further questions may be raised concerning Metz's evaluations of the social-political as well as theological role of the "people's church" in the Third World as the paradigm for a renewal of the church in Europe and the United States. This brief list could, no doubt, be lengthened. I mention them only to set such questions aside: not as unimportant, but as too expansive for this essay. In pursuing an immanent critique of Metz's work, I wish to address three issues. First, what questions does Metz *not* raise in his practical fundamental theology? Second, what is the relationship between religion, religions and Christianity in Metz's thought? Third, what are the "empty spaces" in Metz's thought, i.e., the *conspicuously* "unspoken" which emerges against the background of what is said and spoken about?

With regard to the first question, a comparison of Metz's foundational theological agenda with that of Pannenberg is instructive. As suggested in the first chapter, the focal questions for Pannenberg concern the nature of religion, the "senses" of religious discourse, the "reality-referent" of religion, its *traditio* as the history of the transmission of tradition (*Überlieferungsgeschichte*) and the dialectic of the history of religions. For Pannenberg, these questions constitute the space of fundamental theology—and with this I am in full agreement. What is noteworthy is that such questions receive little sustained consideration in Metz's practical fundamental theology. Indeed, while such questions have never been of great importance for Metz's work, their importance has seemingly become more attenuated in the progression of his thought from *Theology of the World* to *Faith in History and Society*.

Nevertheless, throughout the latter work, Metz continually uses the common noun "religion." Here, religion is generally characterized by its "interruptive" function and its existence as a "reserve" for the identity-formation of the subject. Thus, for example,

> If we are to achieve a postbourgeois and postindividualist "rescue of the human subject," religion seems to me to be indispensable. Without religion, I see the barbarism of a blind negation of the individual breaking out within a postbourgeois society. Without religion, the end of bourgeois society threatens to become the very "end of the human subject".[129]

---

[129] Metz, *The Emergent Church*, p. 70.

Metz's "definition" of religion has less to do with what makes religion religion than with its "function" as interruptive of the identity-totalities of Enlightenment. My point is not to raise anew the (false) dichotomy between "substantive" and "functional" definitions of religion. I also recognize that definitions of religion are as numerous as they are slippery. However, as more or less adequate—and I consider Pannenberg's to be more adequate than less—they are indispensable as heuristic devices for the preunderstanding of any particular religion and are *in fact* always operative either as thematically reflected or prethematically effective in theology. The question is, "Can practical fundamental theology in its intention to explicate the concepts and categories of a practical (social-political) mediation of Christianity with the contemporary world not address these "abstract" questions regarding the nature of religion, etc., *even* in acknowledgement that such reflections are abstract?" I think not.

Metz himself would seem to concur. He is neither "unaware" of such questions nor "in principle" set against such reflections as misguided. Quite to the contrary, he wrote:

> We theologians do not especially like to talk about this 'claim to universality' although there is obviously no 'talk about God' which is not at least implicitly an (anticipative) discourse about the whole of reality.[130]

Presumably, Metz himself belongs to that "group" of theologians who do not like to speak of the universality-claim of religion. What is remarkable, however, is that this statement reproduces *in nuce* the core of Pannenberg's fundamental theology. The second issue follows from the first: does a lack of sustained reflection on the questions which are the focus of Pannenberg's foundational theological agenda affect the relations of religion, religions and Christianity in Metz's theology?

In his assertion that religion is inextricably connected with the identity-formation of the subject, Metz writes,

> I could not appeal to a transcendental theology of the subject which presented man *a priori* as absolutely transcendent. I can, however, go beyond the developed ideas and refer to a historical anthropology based on the history of religion. This historical anthropology is certainly able to support the idea that man did not transfer his state as a subject to God in human history seen as a history of religion, but that he only acquired identity as a subject

---

[130] Idem, "Zu einer interdisziplinär," p. 21.

and became the subject of his own history through religion, that is, in his relationship with God.[131]

Three comments are appropriate. First, it is interesting that in a footnote to the paragraph quoted immediately above, reference is made to the work of Pannenberg. Second, what is even more remarkable is Metz's appeal to a "historical anthropology based upon the history of religion." To the best of my knowledge, Metz has not chosen to pursue the "logic" of such historical anthropology of the history of religions in any of his published writings. Third, while Metz speaks a great deal about religion used as a common noun and a particular religion, Christianity, he shows little concern for other positive religions. The only exception is Judaism which is treated in the context of the shadow of Auschwitz.[132] Yet even here, his concern is less the difference between Judaism and Christianity as religions, than an *apologia* for a "coalition of messianic trust." To be sure, his essay a powerful indictment of the messianic weakness and political acquiescence of Christianity. What is occluded, however, is the fact of the *religious* difference between Christianity and Judaism— a difference which is not peculiar to these two religions, but appears *prima facie* generalizable to many other positive religions.

Metz's silence regarding positive religions other than Christianity is connected with his ambiguity concerning "religion" used as a common noun. Earlier, I quoted a passage from *The Emergent Church* where Metz asserted the connection between the identity of the subject, the societal whole and religion. In the same volume, he restates the same point with a difference.

> Christians are convinced that such a moral change of heart cannot be kept going unless it is supported by religion. They start from the assumption that when religion disappears, not only among the so-called enlightened sections of the population but even among the people as a whole, so that among them as well the rumor of God's existence is no longer believed, then the "soul" of humanity itself dies and in the end there is only the apotheosis of banality and hatred: the individual will become a machine, a new kind of animal, or the inevitable victim of totalitarian tyranny. It is precisely for these reasons, and within this critical situation which we have described, that Christianity, with its moral reserves and its capacity for conversion, is called to stand the test of history. It is my view that nothing is more needed today than a moral and political imagination springing up from a messianic

131 Idem, *Faith in History and Society*, pp. 68-69 (66).
132 Idem, *The Emergent Church*, pp. 17-33.

Christianity and capable of being more than just a copy of already accepted
political and economic strategies.[133]

Here, "religion" as interruptive of the social-historical totalities of
Enlightenment is predicated specifically of Christianity and, further, it is
not "religion" as such but messianic Christianity which is denoted as a
bulwark against an asubjective barbarism. Indeed, it is not an overstatement to suggest that when Metz speaks of "religion" in *Faith and History
and Society*, the term may be replaced by "Christianity," whose specific
political hermeneutic supplies the warrants for those statements concerning "religion" in general. The following questions arise, then, concerning
Metz's use of the common noun "religion": "Is there not a tacit constriction of 'religion' to 'messianic religion' at work in Metz's latest work?"
"In focusing on the social-political interruption of messianic religion,
does not Metz forget to question whether the form of a particular religion's interruption of what is might differ from that of Christianity as
oriented to history as eschatologically qualified?" "Is Metz's use of the
common noun 'religion' covertly converted into the specific noun
'Christianity'?" "Does not Metz tacitly presume, by his silence on 'other'
positive religions and his seeming equation of religion as such with
Christianity, that to be a subject is to be a (Christian) subject?" To these
questions, the answer appears to me to be "Yes."

Confirmation of this can be found in the earlier work of Metz. In
Theology of the World, he writes,

> This involvement with the secularity of the world (letting it go its own
> course) is actually already an unthematic (as it were, "transcendental") reli-
> gious act, which always stands concretely within the framework of the
> Christ event, *for it is only in terms of the, latter* that this secularity can be faced
> without distortion, without its being over-painted, sublimated and secular-
> istically done up in a veiled cult of profanity. Basically, *only the Christian can
> take secularity fully seriously*, by accepting it as what it is of itself, without in-
> filtrating into it or throwing an ideology over it, thus destroying its sober,
> objective, almost sightless factuality. . . . For through the Christ event the
> world had achieved such a radical form of secularity, and has become in it-
> self so God-like because of God's liberating acceptance of it, that *man today
> can face it openly only out of the power of this event*, without invoking new gods
> of his understanding of the world.[134]

---

[133] Idem, *The Emergent Church*, p. 10.
[134] Idem, *Theology of the World*, p. 47, [Italics mine].

What Metz asserts here is a form of "anonymous Christianity" where Christianity is the definitive categorical form of a transcendental revelation which simultaneously grounds the secularity of the world and the subjectivity of the subject, to which "other" religions are subordinately related. To be a subject in the contemporary world is to be a Christian, even if only anonymously. In his later work, shorn of the transcendental framework of Rahner, this tacit assumption still appears to be operative in that only the specific messianic form of Christian religious interruption can fracture the (destructive) secularity of the dialectic of enlightenment. The identification of religion as such with Christianity and hence the occlusion of the claim to universality of other religious totalities of meaning serves to form a tacit "anonymous Christianity" in the latest work of Metz. What Metz risks is the formation of a new "identity-system" of modernity and Christianity as a messianic religion which is no less a "universal-historical" schema than Pannenberg's which he censures. It negates, by its silence, the claim to universality of "other" positive religions—something which must be regarded with a certain irony for a *political* theology given the bloody and shameful history of the Christian mission. The validity of the nonChristian religion's claim to universality which Pannenberg negates through both formal and material arguments, Metz as effectively negates by consigning these religions to the realm of silence and through his tacit equation of religion per se with Christianity or messianic religion, of the interruption of religion as such with the mystical-political interruption of a messianic Christianity. "Anonymous Christianity" emerges once again in Metz's work, this time by default. What I wish to suggest at the close of this second line of reflection is that Metz's inadvertence to those questions concerning the nature of religion, the senses of religious language, etc., corresponds to the occlusion of those positive religions other than Christianity in his latest work. In this, both Pannenberg and Metz attest to a dis-ease with "nonidentity": the nonidentity of positive religions as witnessing to a nonidentity of manifestations of the divine.

The third line of criticism is more fragmentary than the first two. It draws attention to what is not spoken about by Metz, suggests why this is the case and tentatively evaluates whether such silence is the silence of evasion or the silence which witnesses to that which cannot be spoken about. Specifically, I am concerned about Metz's silence concerning the "future," "history," "God" and "truth." The first two terms are significant because they are major parameters of political theology; the third, because it is ultimately *the* subject of Christianity; and the fourth, because it is a central topic of fundamental theology.

I have already noted Metz's "silence" concerning the eschatological future when discussing the *memoria resurrectionis*. Fundamentally, adverting and holding firmly to the interruption of suffering engenders a reservation towards that not-present which if directly spoken about risks reducing suffering to mere appearance. At the root of the resurrection faith of Christians is the anticipation that suffering is "not the last word." Yet to speak of that which is not-yet as that which is hiddenly already present is ideologically suspect of being an opiate which defuses the urgency of a liberating solidarity and by mere belief negates the witness of suffering to something which is, at best, a regrettable penultimacy.

Metz's silence concerning the eschatological future represents a sort of "negative dialectics" within the core of Christian theology. Much like Adorno's characterization of "redemption" in *Minima Moralia*, the eschatological orientation and horizon of Christian faith enables the Christian to view reality from the perspective of redemption and thus to view things in that light which unmasks them as unessential. Yet, unlike Adorno, for Christian faith, such a perspective is not only a regulative ideal. In the anticipation of a particular totality of meaning it is affirmed as constitutive of the being of all men and women. However, to assert it as constitutive appears to negate the concrete surd of suffering. What results is a horizon which acts as a regulative ideal, but which is nevertheless asserted to be constitutive in that provisional *modus* by which all religious assertions are characterized, i.e., as an *anticipation* of a totality of meaning which cannot be mediated noetically—vis à vis both the pluralism of religions and the history of suffering—but only practically in conversion and discipleship. Only through the recognition that the claim of a totality of meaning is anticipatory and hence provisional can that totality be asserted as constitutive of reality without negating either the pluralism of religions or the history of suffering.

Another "silence" is Metz's lack of explicit attention regarding "history"—curious given the title *Faith in History and Society*! Indeed, "history" received more explicit attention in *Theology of the World*. In the later work, reflection on history revolves around the Enlightenment and post-Enlightenment ideologies of history, and society as the concrete mediation of history. What Metz is silent about—and what I believe is nevertheless presumed in his discussion of *memoria passionis* and the dialectics of emancipation and redemption—is that notion of history which was the focus in his earlier work: "history" as, to use the language of

Pannenberg, the horizon of a specific totality of meaning which is implicit in the mystical-political discipleship of Christians.

Again, it is the interruption of suffering which appears to lead to Metz's silence. His reticence concerning history as a totality of meaning appears to arise from the "idealist" connotations of such speech, i.e., to speak of history as a totality of meaning appears to transmute the meaninglessness of suffering in history.

> The often careless use of the category of 'meaning' in theology should be subjected to scrutiny. 'Meaning' has become the darling of theologians and has quickly become, like all other darlings, spoiled and overrated. Even if theology cannot renounce this category (not even in its general form), it should not forget that it deals with a risky meaning and that the theme of meaning should not become the outward show by which we only pretend there are dangers and declines. The theological treatment of the question of meaning should not be seduced into reifying meaning and simply ignoring the problem of rescuing meaning, i.e., ignoring the historical threats to meaning and, being unconscious of apocalyptic, forget that in that on which the Christian expectation of meaning is based, the eschatological speech of the bible, He comes not only as the perfecter of the Kingdom of God but also as the conqueror of the antiChrist....[135]

Yet the category of a totality of meaning still appears, even in Metz's own estimate, to be indispensable for religious speech even if there is no certainty regarding a specific totality of meaning in either a transcendental or universal-historical manner. An alternative to this silence is the emphatic recognition that "history" as the determined horizon of the Christian totality of meaning itself stands exposed and at stake in history as the practical mediation or transmission of the Christian tradition. What emerges more firmly into view, I believe, is its fragmentary character, its quality as an *anticipated horizon* of meaning. Thus, like the eschatological future, speech concerning the anticipated totality of meaning is circumscribed by the interruption of suffering and only made concretely present in the mystical-political solidarity of Christians.

The third "silence" is the most interesting because it is the most fundamental: his silence concerning "God." I am assuming here that Christian theology is a theo-logy, a discourse about God. That "God" also is the subject-matter of "political theology"—and in this political theology differs from, i.e., critical theory—is acknowledged by Metz.

---

[135] Idem, *Unterbrechungen*, p. 64.

> In this process, the God of this dangerous memory does not secretly become
> a political utopia of universal liberation. The name of God stands rather for
> the fact that the utopia of liberation of all human subjects is not a pure pro-
> jection, which is what that utopia would be if there were only a utopia and
> no God.[136]

Yet precisely the absence of a theo-logy in Metz's work inevitably raises
the question of whether the implied counterposition to the above is not
true. If God is the subject-matter of political theology, then the silence
about this leads one to wonder whether it really is the subject-matter at
all.

The issue is complex because I have not been totally fair to Metz. One
might argue that, for him, speech about God is christologically refracted
through the category of *memoria passionis et resurrectionis*. The proper
question to pose, therefore, concerns the relationship between christology and theology, speech about "the Christ" and speech about God. My
own basic convictions can be stated in two parts. First, there is no generic
theological language since there is no generic religion as either a
"religion of reason" or a least common denominator of positive religions.
The only religious statements which enter into fundamental theology
which are not conditioned by the determinations of the positive religious
traditions are those statements concerning humanity's self-transcending
orientation towards a horizon of mystery which may be called the
"divine." Like Pannenberg and Metz—and for reasons which have
emerged in this and the first chapter—I am skeptical of the turn to transcendental analyses as found, for example, in Ogden in order to secure
the religious identity of the human subject or the substantial content of
statements about the "divine." Nothing can be deduced about the
"character" of the "divine" without revelation, without recourse to the
witness of the positive religions which are nonidentical to one another.
Speech about the "divine" per se is empty speech since humanity's orientation to the divine is an abstraction. For these same reasons, I find both
"classical" and "neoclassical" metaphysical theologies questionable in
their claims that as metaphysics they secure the truth of positive religion
which in reality grounds them.

Second, I would maintain that the theo-logical focus of Christianity is
christologically determined. The God of Christianity is preeminently the
God "known" in Jesus Christ. In Christianity, men's and women's orientation to the divine is made concrete and specific through the significant

---

[136] Idem, *Faith in History and Society*, p. 67 (65).

particular of Jesus as the Christ—christology mediates theology. Yet men's and women's orientation to the divine is a necessary condition for the intelligibility of christological language as indirect speech concerning the "character" of the divine—theology mediates christology.

What then may be said of Metz's "silence"? It is that his discourse about "God" is incomplete insofar as it solely focuses on christology mediating theology. Again, I suspect that the interruption of suffering is a decisive in this regard. All too often, speech about God has been the *proton pseudos* par excellence which acts as the guarantor of meaning in history and human existence thus reducing the interruption of suffering to penultimacy. Trinitarian theologies such as those of Rahner, Moltmann and Pannenberg thematize as "always already" in the *ordo essendi* what in faith is only anticipated in the *ordo cognoscendi* and thus, without vigilance, mask the anticipative character of Christian theological speech. Shorn of this character, however, speech about God cannot not nullify the nonidentity of suffering in history and the nonidentity of positive religions.

If acknowledging the formal anticipative and provisional quality of speech about God is a necessary condition for Christian God-talk today, it is not sufficient. A far more disturbing crisis is provoked by the *theological* significance of the witness of suffering which indicts traditional Christian God-talk (i.e., God as love, as omnipotent, etc.). This is, I think, the more proximate reason why little is said concerning "God" in Metz's work, and when something is said, it is refracted christologically as *memoria passionis et resurrectionis*. For the reasons mentioned above, however, such an exclusive christological refraction appears "incomplete." Christians *do speak* of *God* as Father, Creator and Redeemer. Yet it is the traditional way of speaking of God as Father, Creator and Redeemer which the witness of suffering interrupts indicting it as a "false projection" and which cannot be completely sublated by christological language insofar as this language always already refers to the whither of human self-transcendence. Metz's silence draws dangerously near to a christolatry which risks depriving itself of its own *religious* significance. If the *memoria Christi* is the concrete condition of the Christian understanding of God, and if "there is no 'talk about God' which is not at least implicitly an (anticipative) discourse about the whole of reality," then the theological language implied in the *memoria Christi* cannot be left unaddressed.

The last "silence" of Metz's work which I would like to note concerns "truth." The question of truth is not a focal concern for Metz and is not a category or theme of practical fundamental theology. Indeed, the most substantive passage in which Metz raises the issue of truth, raises the question only to give a cryptic "answer."

> What, in other words, is the position of truth in a practical fundamental theology? Is truth in this context not simply made subordinate to praxis? Is truth not reinterpreted as relevance? And does this reinterpretation not simply conceal (because it is in fact a semantic deception) what really happens, namely the liquidation of the concept of truth, insofar as a truth that is oriented towards praxis is no longer truth? In a practical fundamental theology, the difference between truth and relevance is in no sense simply a matter of personal discretion. In such a theology, the idea of truth without reference to subjects is irrelevant and even dangerous, with the result that truth and relevance are bound to converge to the extent that truth becomes the type of relevance that applies to all subjects . . . truth is what is relevant to all subjects, including the dead and those who have been overcome and conquered.[137]

After lucidly posing the question of "truth," Metz's response seems anemic. As is perhaps all too common with his work, Metz is more specific as to what he rejects than to what he wishes to assert: "truth" is not the correlative of "pure" reason or the product of an absolute reflection. Indeed, this appears to be the thrust of the conjunction of truth and "relevance." What I suggest is that reflection on the "abstract" questions concerning the nature of religion, etc.—precisely those questions which Metz chooses not to address—may provide a context for the understanding of the claim to truth of religion.

To my mind, Metz is quite correct in joining the issue of the truth-claim of religion to the issue of its "relevance" to the subject. There is a basic ambiguity in that conjunction, however, because the "relevance" of religion can be understood in two ways. First, the truth of religion becomes "subjectively" relevant in that its appearance is dependent upon the experience of the power of the significant particular (Pannenberg) or the disclosive-transformative experience of the religious classic (Tracy). Second, the truth of religion is "objectively" relevant insofar as religion intends a "totality of meaning" and what is intended is that which in one way or another is relevant to all that exists. Thus one may say that the objective truth of religion as a totality of meaning which is relevant for all that exists becomes subjectively present in the appearance of the divine in the experience of the significant particular. Further, given the non-

---

[137] Ibid., p. 59 (56).

identity of religions and hence the nondefinitive appearances of the divine in history, both the subjective and objective aspects of the claim to truth of religion have an anticipatory and provisional character.

What Metz's "political theology" corrects in Pannenberg's "theology of history" is the latter's understanding of the transmission of religious traditions. Over and against Pannenberg's understanding of history as the transmission of tradition qua primarily the transmission of an "concept" whose social-political mediation is accidental or extrinsic to the concept as such, Metz argues—correctly, I think—that the fundamental mediation of Christianity is both practical and social-political, i.e., Christian conversion and discipleship, and this alone secures the "identity" of the Christian faith and holds open a "space" for a continued traditioning and experience of the Christian significant particular, the gospel of Jesus Christ. I would add that what Metz has raised to a reflective level—the social-political mediation of the transmission of the tradition—has not only been operative throughout the history of the Christian tradition but is, in fact, the generalizable form of the transmission of all religious traditions.

What remains to be added regarding the claim to truth of Christianity as an anticipation of a totality of meaning is that it may be regarded as *provisionally* and subjectively true in the praxis of conversion and discipleship but its objective truth as a *totality* of meaning is at stake in history as the dialectic of the history of religions where the transmission of religious traditions is most fundamentally both practical and social-political. Indeed, to recognize that the truth of Christianity—as any other religion—is anticipatory is to recognize that such an anticipation may indeed be wrong. The mystical-political solidarity of Christians in imminent expectation of the coming of their God which bears its own fruits within the present amidst all hardships, defeats and worldly incredulity makes the claim to truth of Christianity credible and plausible as a particular religious anticipation today. Yet the disclosive-transformative experience of mystical-political solidarity with the Christ is an anticipation of a totality of meaning—history as eschatologically valorized and the redemption of men and women, nature and history—and is founded upon this. The former does not guarantee the latter and is, therefore, exposed to defeat and negation in history.

This last section indicated what I take to be major lacunae in Metz's work. In a sense, I can understand Metz's reticence on these issues: to raise such questions is to risk opening the door for that "idealistic" and "bourgeois" theology which political theology attempts to interrupt. If, however, Metz is earnest in his assertion that "I do not intend to be regarded as a reason for the exclusion of argument from theology. There is no question of regressively obscuring the distinction between narrative memory and theological argument," then that risk must be accepted and the door opened.

CHAPTER IV

Identity, Nonidentity and a Christian Theology of History

The Metaphysical only, and not the Historical, can give us blessedness.
— J. G. Fichte

This final chapter is divided into two parts. The first part (1) describes the theological "space" of this essay, (2) states the thesis for which the preceding chapters stand as warrants and (3) continues the critical reflections of the previous three chapters. The second part makes explicit three "corollaries" which together set forth three parameters for political theology as a Christian theology of history. These parameters materially represent an attempt to recognize, abide with and defend the theological relevancy of "nonidentity" in the form of the nonidentity of religion, the nonidentity of tradition and the nonidentity of history. Recognition of each form of nonidentity places a "limiting condition" or "proviso" on political theology as a theology of history—respectively, a confessional, a theological and an eschatological proviso. Finally, corresponding to each form of nonidentity and its proviso, there is a brief exploration of their relevancy to Christian theology, i.e., on the hiddenness and manifestness of God, the category, "essence of Christianity," and suffering and God-talk.

POLITICAL THEOLOGY AND A CHRISTIAN THEOLOGY OF HISTORY

The preceding chapters may strike one as a theological fruit salad—a mixing together of apples, oranges and pears. Where in the topography of theology does this essay stand? What is its theological "space"?

Langdon Gilkey describes the task of philosophy of religion as re-flection on

> (1) the relation of religion to the methods and results of the special sciences: physical, social, psychological and historical; (2) the relations of religious traditions to one another, of say, Buddhism to Christianity; (3) the relation of religion and theology to philosophy itself, that is, to linguistic, logical, epistemological and metaphysical issues; (4) the relation of religion to other areas of cultural life, to morals, politics, the arts—the theology of culture and of society.[1]

Philosophy of religion reflects on religion per se and its relation to other aspects of human action and knowledge. In doing so, it sets the terms and relations which supply a context for understanding any specific re-ligion. If to this list of topics one adds a fifth—(5) a delineation of the "essence of Christianity"—then, I suggest, the philosophy of religion be-comes fundamental or foundational theology as a part of Christian the-ology.

Three comments should be made here regarding fundamental theol-ogy. First, the understanding of theology implicitly appealed to is Schleiermacher's. The "assemblage of scientific elements" becomes theo-logical "only by virtue of their relation to Christianity." By the addition of (5), the philosophy of religion teleologically becomes fundamental theology.[2] Second, the category, "essence of Christianity," is used in Troeltsch's understanding of the term.[3] Third, the definition of the essence of Christianity is the bridge between two distinct tasks. On the one hand, articulations of the essence of Christianity always take place against more or less explicit positions on those issues which Gilkey has described as belonging to philosophy of religion. How one understands religion in general conditions how one understands a specific religion, Christianity, and every reflective understanding of the latter will pre-suppose some set of positions on the former, even if only implicitly. On the other hand, the articulation of the essence of Christianity points to-wards systematic theology if this is to be more than a mere collection of historical or philosophical details. If systematic theology is to mediate the

---

[1] Langdon Gilkey, "The Philosophy of Religion in Our Time," in *Society and the Sacred* (New York: Crossroad Publishing Co., 1981), p. 15.

[2] Schleiermacher, *Brief Outline on the Study of Theology*, trans. with an introduction and notes by Terence Tice (Richmond, VA: John Knox Press, 1970), p. 19.

[3] See, Troeltsch, "What Does 'Essence of Christianity' Mean," in *Ernst Troeltsch*, pp. 124-79 and the section "The Nonidentity of Tradition" in this chapter below.

Christian tradition for one's own time and place, then some attempt must be made to specify the point of Christianity as a whole which acts as the preunderstanding for a more detailed consideration of the diverse parts of Christian faith. It is within this "space," fundamental theology, that this essay is located. To be sure, not all the questions of fundamental theology have been addressed in this essay—only those directly relevant to understanding the essence of Christianity as a "historical religion" have been raised.

The thesis is that there exists a correlation between a theology of history and political theology. A theology of history implicitly constitutes the horizon of "political theology." Second, political theology represents the most appropriate embodiment of a theology of history. Further, given that the subject-matter of religion concerns a totality of meaning, the theology of history implied in Christianity must be a theology of history "as a whole" or a theology of "universal" history. In other words, because a claim to universality is constitutive of the claim to truth of religion per se and because the *Sache* of Christianity is one oriented to a God active in and convenanted to history, Christian theology cannot avoid talk of history as a whole. A Christian theology of universal history which could already be written would, however, be an obscenity: the forgetful repression of the objective and ultimate claim which history as a history of suffering places on the Christian. Thus the "gesture" towards totality, towards universal history on the part of Christianity is just that, a gesture, which is fragmentary, provisional and anticipatory, i.e., a "horizon."

A necessary condition for this thesis has been presumed throughout this essay: the validity of a determination of the *Sache* of the Christian faith in the direction of "history." Some warrants for this have been offered in the first and third chapters. Such reflections, however, were more incidental than thematic. This has been unavoidable inasmuch as the only fully adequate warrant for construing the essence of Christianity in this manner lies in the material discourse of systematic theology. This essay deals only with prologomena—what does it mean to speak of a Christian theology of history and what is the "cost" of defending such a position?

"What does it mean to speak of a Christian theology of history?" Christianity is a positive religion whose totality of meaning is formally oriented to history as a whole, eschatologically qualified and materially characterized by its christological focus as anticipating the redemption of history. As oriented to history as a whole, eschatologically qualified,

Christians proleptically experience this redemption as the community normed by the *memoria Jesu* and his God in their mystical-political conversion and discipleship where neither the term "mystical" nor "political" overwhelms the other. To acknowledge this practical foundation of Christian faith is to affirm that the most concrete understanding of the subject is "the subject embodied in a social totality" such that through this practical foundation is given the mediation of the historicity of the subject and an orientation whose horizon is universal history.

My agreement with Pannenberg's fundamental theology is extensive. I find questionable, however, two positions. First, his attempts to noetically secure the provisional claim to truth of Christianity strike me as mistaken. Neither eliding "history" as the formal process of the transmission of traditions with "history" as the material specification of the horizon of Christianity nor the defense of the resurrection as a verifiable historical event are plausible. At the heart of both these positions is a denial of nonidentity: the nonidentity of the material claims of the nonChristian religions and the nonidentity of history as a history of suffering.

Second, the foundation of the provisional claim to truth of Christianity, as well as every other religion, is given in the event of the powerful appearance of the divine, i.e., in the practical and prereflective transmission of religious traditions. In my estimate, Pannenberg often appears to locate the foundation of religion's provisional claim to truth in the theory-theory correlations of the reflective enterprise of theology. Theology, however, is a derivative enterprise. Its reflective mediation of religion lives off of the effectiveness of religion's prereflective and practical mediation or transmission. "Faith" is not simply *fiducia* and its illuminative—or, in Tracy's terms, "disclosive-transformative"—moment is not merely the event of clearing away prejudice and bias. It is the concrete, real and effective demonstration and mediation of a religion's own power in the ongoing process of history as the transmission of traditions. Given these substantial criticisms of Pannenberg, what remains of a Christian theology of history?

The transition from the first to the second part of the thesis, i.e., the more proximate determination of a theology of history as political theology, is problematic insofar as the latter as concrete cannot be deduced from the former as abstract. A middle axiom is necessary: the concrete mediation of history is society.

The warrants for this axiom are "soft" and were indirectly supplied by the example of Horkheimer and Adorno. The material diversity of their reflections embody the exigency of a *metabasis eis allos genos*, i.e., the turn of an "innocent" or "pure" theory into a critical theory of *society* which recognizes that the "history" which is most near to human beings is not the *existentiell* of the temporality of *Dasein* but the more mundane social, political and economic mediation of the subjectivity and objectivity of human existence by social totality. Particularly for Adorno, the turn to fundamental ontology and its focus on the historicity of *Dasein* together with the reduction of "society" to a categorical determination of *Dasein* was an abstraction which represented an ideological false consciousness.[4]

This recognition appears "self-evident" to me. The heralding or lamenting of the "end of history" as the twilight of subjectivity and the recognition of the myth of progress as a "broken" myth are themselves effects of the dialectic of enlightenment and indirect witnesses to the mediation of history as society in the inability amid the carnage, atrocities and contradictions of our era to recognize history as "our own." If "premodern" men and women queried "What has God wrought?" and "modern" men and women, "What have we wrought?," the emerging "postmodern" man and woman stands in frustrated silence struggling to name the subject of that question as history threatens to take on the silent, immutable necessity of a "first nature." Perhaps the only thing which is transparent today is the nonself-transparency of history as a totality of meaning. "History" is no longer the unthematic, but effective presupposition of thought and action. Indeed, the idea of history as a totality of meaning is all too questionable today—the victim of our recent history which ironically witnesses to the concrete mediation of history as society.

---

[4] The critique of "existential philosophy" and the fundamental ontology of Heidegger was a constant theme in the work of Adorno. It was implicitly treated under the categories of "myth" and "nature" in *"Die Idee der Naturgeschichte"* and continued through to *Negative Dialectics* and *The Jargon of Authenticity* [trans. Knut Tarnowski and Frederic Will, with a Foreward by Trent Schroyer (Evanston, Illinois: Northwestern University Press, 1971)]—the latter work originally conceived as a part of *Negative Dialectics*. The critique of "existential" and "transcendental" theology on the part of European political theologians such as Metz, Moltmann and Soelle parallels Adorno's criticisms of Heidegger: in focusing on the existential or transcendental aspects of human existence, what is an "abstraction" is mistaken for the "concrete" (human being as mediated by society) and in this the latter is mystified as accidental or penultimate to what is wrongly construed as "that which is most near to us."

The question directed to Christianity is, "Is its talk about history really talk the negation of history into 'nature,' 'myth' or the 'metaphysical' which stands imperturbably beyond history?" There is a new twist today to Lessing's "ugly ditch" between the facts of history and the convictions of Christian faith where the former takes the form of the dialectic of enlightenment and the latter the confession of a definitive redemption accomplished once and for all in Christ Jesus. Does not the Christian affirmation of the final and comprehensive meaningfulness of history repressively deny history as a history of suffering which confronts all men and women, including Christians, as a present challenge and shameful heritage?

It is questions such as these that Metz's "political theology" explicitly addresses. It shifts the problem of "Christian faith and history" from a confrontation with the canons of the historical-critical method to the social-political mediation of the identity of Christian faith in the praxis of discipleship. Metz's political theology correctly disputes the possibility of a Christianity which can ascertain its identity in itself vis-à-vis the "world" or, opening its own horizon onto the "world," is able to confirm its identity through a noetic reconciliation of itself and the world; rather, the identity of faith and theology cannot be attained apart from the concrete, practical mediation with that with which it is nonidentical, that is, the world as history and society in the full array of its complexity and determinations as a history of suffering.

At the core of Metz's political theology lies this obstinate abiding with the interruption of suffering such that this becomes the focal *religious* and *theological* issue in retrieving the "point" or "essence" of Christianity—a refocusing which becomes thematic in *both* the formal categories and content of political theology. In other words, Metz's practical fundamental theology is already marked by his own particular interpretation of the essence of Christianity.

As distinct from the ideal of a fatalistic, passive suffering all too often extolled in the classical and popular Christian religious traditions—an ideal often associated with an "otherworldly" piety whose conjunct was, at worst, a contempt towards or, at best, a resignation with regard to "this" world—the response of political theology to the interruption of suffering is a militant creative suffering of solidarity with the victims of history, normed, provoked and sustained by the *memoria Jesu*. It is this which grounds the orientation to the horizon of the world as history seen from the perspective of its victims and creates a sensorium for suffering which, embodied in the praxis of discipleship, is "dangerous" vis-à-vis the status quo.

In brief, Metz's position recognizes that the concrete mediation of history is society and that Christianity which orients itself to history as a whole must also reference itself to society as "messianic religion" because only thereby does it truly witness to the redemption of history as a whole. The identity of faith is thus not given "in itself" but is gained in what is "other" than itself, i.e., history as a history of suffering.

Over and against Pannenberg, I agree with two central positions of Metz's theology. First, Metz's recognition of the practical-social mediation of Christianity as the foundation of its provisional claim to truth "corrects" Pannenberg's understanding of the "transmission of tradition" as the mediation of the "concept" whose provisional claim to truth is secured in the reflective enterprise of theology. Second, I think Metz's more or less explicit interpretation of the essence of Christianity, i.e., Christianity is a historical religion in that it abides through the praxis of discipleship with the interruption of suffering, is persuasive.

Yet Metz's political theology is nevertheless a truncated one. While Pannenberg provides a context for and argues persuasively with regard to the first part of the thesis and Metz with regard to the second, each overlooks the concerns of the other. For Metz, Pannenberg's reflections on the nature of religion, etc., are suspect as already traveling down the slippery slope of bourgeois theology in an attempt to secure a noetic reconciliation of faith and history. Pannenberg's exposition of a "hermeneutics of universal history," however, can be separated from those questions and issues discussed in the first chapter. Metz's negation through silence to those same *questions* threatens his political theology in a twofold manner. First, there is the risk of forming in Metz' theology a new repressive identity-totality where religion equals Christianity and the subject equals the Christian believer. Second, the claim of Christianity as religion, its claim to totality, threatens to become impotent because it is consigned to silence.

Essentially, it is the perspectives of *both* Pannenberg and Metz *together*, along with the reversals of their positions indicated in the first and third chapters which appear to me to form the foundation for a Christian theology of history.

THE NONIDENTITY OF RELIGION, TRADITION, HISTORY
AND THE QUESTION OF CHRISTIAN THEO-LOGY

A Note on the Language of Identity and Nonidentity

The terms "identity" and "nonidentity" are, perhaps, unfamiliar ones. Their proximate source is Adorno, where these terms signify the dialectic of reason as "identity thought" and "nature" which, in its manifold forms, is the source of the dialectic of enlightenment.

> The prehistory of reason, that it is a moment of nature and yet something else, has become the immanent definition of reason. It is natural as the psychological force split off for the purposes of self-preservation; once split off and contrasted with nature, if nature in reason itself is forgotten, reason will be self-preservation running wild and will regress to nature. It is only as the reflection of nature that reason would be above nature.[5]

My reservations towards a critical theory of society which becomes a philosophy of history have been set out in the second chapter. The project which the terms point to, however, is worth preserving and transposing to a theological plane.

The categories of identity and nonidentity are heuristic categories. There is no "identity" without reference to "nonidentity" and no "nonidentity" without reference to "identity." Further, the categories only receive a concrete meaning from the specificity of their subject matter which they seek to approach. The term "identity" refers most fundamentally to the unitative function of reason, to what Adorno names in its most pathological form "identity-thought" in its "rage for a system." It is the ordering function of thought which seeks to capture reality in thought. The shortest definition of nonidentity is that which remains undigestible to this ordering function of thought: like the burning bush, it is that which thought envelopes but does not consume; it is that which escapes, fragments, fractures and thus stubbornly refuses the transformation of thought thereby convicting the gesture of the self-sufficiency of thought as self-deception. The legacy of the idealist tradition which formed the horizon of Adorno was its perception of the dialectic of identity and nonidentity. Its fate was to collapse the latter into a moment immanent to the former. What is exemplary in Adorno's work is that he sought to lay open and present the tension of identity and nonidentity

---

[5] Adorno, *Negative Dialectics*, p. 289. [Trans. amended]

according to the subject matter at hand in order to let thought abide therein.

If "nonidentity" is the residue of thought, the undigestible which refuses the transformation of thought into thought, it must nevertheless be distinguished from mere "difference" as, to use B. Lonergan's phrase, "the already out there now real."[6] Nonidentity takes its reference from the category of identity (reason) which seeks to gather up the manifold of mere difference into a unity. Yet nonidentity is that which resists and refuses sublation qua negation into thought and its consummation in the ideal of the "system." Nonidentity is that which escapes and eludes the seductive although empty unity of "abstract nouns," e.g. religion, the divine, history, tradition, classic, which, following the lead-string of the repressive forgetfulness of thought, passes over into action and sensuously negates that which has already been noetically negated. The task of thought for which the categories of identity and nonidentity are decisive is the laying open and the abiding in the tension of the two, while resisting both the alternatives of a noetic rage for identity and that of a resigned, skeptical and ultimately repressive tolerance for mere difference. The noetic mediation of the dialectic of identity and nonidentity is the rescuing attempt on the part of thought to restore to itself and to preserve that which is "other" to thought.

If the original inspiration of materialism was the insight that identity is always already mediated by nonidentity and the original inspiration of idealism was the insight that nonidentity is continually generated as a moment immanent to identity, then Adorno's reflections represent an attempt to view both insights as a unity in unraveling the weave of modern society as embedded within the dialectic of Enlightenment while maintaining the objective priority of materialism over idealism in the priority of the social totality over consciousness and the preponderance of the object over the subject.

In an age when the demise of the great theological systems appears to be already accomplished, perhaps this is not so much due to the absence of its subjective condition—those great "geniuses" of the tradition—but is, rather, elicited by the objective conditions of our history. The turn and preoccupation of theologians to questions and issues of methodology bears witness to the poverty of theology in the form of a "system." My hope is that such a situation does not demand the aban-

6 Lonergan, *Insight: A Study in Human Understanding*, pp. 154, 157, 160, 251-52, 412-25.

donment of theological reflection as such. It does demand, however, an *askesis* of thought. The theological habit actualizes itself today by becoming commensurate with its tradition in critique, in the rescuing of nonidentity in the face of the rage for identity. What Adorno asserted as the fate of philosophy today also pertains to theology:

> Philosophy rests on the texts it criticizes. They are brought to it by the tradition they embody, and it is in dealing with them that the conduct of philosophy becomes commensurable with tradition. This justifies the move from philosophy to exegesis, which exalts neither the interpretation nor the symbol into an absolute but seeks the truth where thinking secularizes the irretrievable archetype of sacred texts.[7]

That the dialectic of identity and nonidentity may give way to a chastened rhetoric of faith which incorporates dialectic is the final cause which drives a theological negative dialectics. From its own standpoint, the demand for praxis unmasks the pretensions of thought—even dialectical thought—to self-sufficiency. Yet perhaps at a time where the objectivity of society as history threatens to suffocate the subject, the subjective actualization by which the disinterest of the dialectic is resolved into the confession of faith and the praxis of discipleship is an objective condition breaking subjective affirmation gone wild.

Christian Faith and the Nonidentity of Religions

Justin Martyr—sometimes regarded as the first Christian theologian—is justly remembered for his reflections on the *Logos* and the *Logos spermatikos* which addressed the issue of the relation between the nascent Christian religion and "other" religions. Under the rubrics of "fullness" and "deficiency" he sought to vindicate the completeness of revelation in Jesus of Nazareth vis-à-vis the "pagan" religions and Judaism, and to demonstrate the harmony between Christianity and the "empire." That he was not quite successful may be gleaned from the name by which he is remembered today. In the following centuries, the issue initially addressed by Justin was transformed into the "sifting" of pagan culture and the repression of Judaism. Since that time, the number of Christian theologians who have addressed the question of the truth claims of "other" religions in a sustained fashion as an issue for Christian theology appear

---

[7]   Adorno, *Negative Dialectics*, p. 55.

to be few: Cusanus, Schleiermacher, Troeltsch, Tillich, Cobb, and Hick to name the most obvious.

In our own century, the silence of theologians regarding this question arises, in large part, from the heritage of neoorthodoxy and, in particular, the influence of Barth and Rahner in the former's distinction between "religion" and "revelation" and the latter's theorem of "anonymous Christianity." It should be asked, however, "Does this not represent, like Justin, a rage for the identity of Christianity as 'religion' which negates the existent nonidentity of religions?"

Pannenberg's attention to the dialectic of the history of religions provides an opportunity to recognize, without sacrificing either religion's claim to truth or leveling the differences between religions, what has been forgotten in our own time—the insight which Schleiermacher forcefully conveyed in the second and fifth speeches of his *Speeches*: the locus of revelation is religion and religion concretely exists only as the ensemble of positive religions. This recognition ruptures Christianity's definitive claim to be the "true religion" and forces a recognition of that claim's anticipative and provisional status which cannot be further mediated noetically. Indeed, it may be asked whether the reflective rage for identity on the part of Christian theologians, either by explicit argument or silence, and the political deed of the annihilation of the "other" by many Christians are not unrelated. Again, perhaps Christian theologians and believers have never truly forgotten, but only badly repressed, the de facto nonidentity of religions and the provisional character of their own claim to truth which, as Rosemary Reuther correctly suggests, is, in part, the reason why anti-Semitism has been continually a fellow-traveler of the triumph of Christianity.[8]

In this first reflection on nonidentity, I wish to suggest that the recognition and preservation of the nonidentity of religions is crucial to a political theology as a theology of history. The religious dimension of human existence, variously named as a "sense and taste for the Infinite," "*Weltoffenheit*," "*excessus ad esse*," "the pure and unrestricted desire to know," "the dialectic of centrality and exocentricity" or, more simply, as an "intimation and inclination towards transcendence," is empty, abstract and indeterminate and only becomes thematic, concrete and determinate in religion. "Religion" itself, however, is an abstraction and exists only in the determinate forms of the "positive religions." The unity

---

[8] Rosemary Reuther, *Faith and Fratricide: The Theological Roots of Anti-Semitism*, with an introduction by Gregory Baum (New York: Seabury Press, 1979).

of "religion" as a noetic category gives way to the unity of the history of religions as the ongoing history of the transmission and interaction of religious traditions. With respect to this process, the truth claim of every religion as articulating a determinate totality of meaning is provisional and an anticipation of the "end" of this process itself. If the "truth is the whole," then the definitive truth of a religion's claim to speak truthfully about a totality of meaning is only given in the "end" of history.

The passing over of the noetic unity of religion to the unity of the history of religions as a unity of nonidentical religions circumscribes all attempts to collapse such a factual nonidentity into a noetic identity. There is no material phenomenological "essence" of religion which is both "constitutive of" as well as "common to" all religions as their "least common denominator." There is no "pure" religion of "pure" reason which, in the manner of the Enlightenment ideal, stands as the criterion of positive religions. The plurality of religions is not reducible to a definitive genetic progression (usually ending in the triumph of the religion of the speaker) as the secret cipher of the Absolute. Finally, there is no ontological *"tertium quid"* with reference to which positive religions function as more or less adequate or decisive "representations" of an ontological *Sache*. Amidst all these strategies, the nonidentity of religions abides effectively unmasking them as futile.

In fundamental theology, the nonidentity of religions cannot be negated. In fundamental theology, the unity of the nonidentity of religions can be mediated no further than the actual history of the transmission of religious traditions in their interaction with one another and their prereflective and reflective reality-testing. It is with respect to history as the transmission of traditions and the continuing experience of the illuminative power of the "significant particular" of a tradition that religious belief stands as an anticipation of a determinate totality of meaning amidst other nonidentical determinate totalities of meaning. In Christian systematic theology, the nonidentity of religions qualifies all systematic theological assertions as provisional, an anticipation that Christianity's provisional claim to truth is definitive. To be sure, this does not deny the possibility of an interaction of traditions resulting in a decisive modification in any particular religion. Totalities of meaning are not windowless monads existing in absolute self-identity. Perhaps there will be a second Great Assimilation of Christianity and the religions of the East—as

Gilkey intimates[9]—comparable in its significance to that of the once fledgling Jewish sect and its Hellenic environment. Nor is this to assert that the characterization of Christianity as a totality of meaning oriented towards history as a whole and eschatologically qualified—that projection of the "essence of Christianity" which I have sought to explore— may not expire under a growing inability to recognize history as "our own" rather than as a near mechanical and immutable "second nature." The point is to recognize what the mature Hegel acknowledged: the owl of Minerva flies at dusk and the transmission of a particular religious tradition largely occurs behind the backs of theologians. The unity of the nonidentity of religions is only given a posteriori and amidst that nonidentity, "theology," as constructive theological reflection and as ineluctably grounded in a determinate totality of meaning stands under a "confessional proviso." Its own assertions are qualified as the anticipatory claims of a determinate totality of meaning—claims which are revealed as anticipatory in the nonidentity of religions.

On the Hiddenness and Manifestness of "God"[10]

If the nonidentity of religions is recognized in fundamental theology as setting a parameter for systematic theology, then what consequences does this have concerning the theme of religion as a totality of meaning: the "divine?" These consequences are best understood in Christian theological terms under the rubric of the "hiddenness and manifestness of God." Here, all I wish to suggest is that the recognition of the nonidentity of religions continues yet radicalizes this theme which is already recognized in Christian theology.

There are at least three relatively distinct frameworks within the Christian tradition concerning the hiddenness of God. The first is exemplified today in the theology of Karl Rahner and the theme of God as the abiding Holy Mystery. The *locus classicus* for this framework is the issue of the limits of God-talk. Represented in the Roman Catholic tradition by

---

[9] Gilkey, "The New Watershed in Theology" and "The Mystery of Being and Nonbeing," in *Society and the Sacred*, pp. 3-14, 123-38.

[10] I am heavily indebted to B. A. Gerrish's article "'To the Unknown God': Luther and Calvin on the Hiddenness of God," in *The Old Protestantism and the New* (Chicago: University of Chicago Press, 1982), pp. 131-49, for the distinction between the second and third framework. An expanded version of this section with reference to the question "Who is the subject of salvation in history?" can be found in my essay, "God as Hidden, God as Manifest," *Journal of Religion* (Forthcoming).

such neo-Platonic theologians as Pseudo-Dionysus and Eriugena, the hiddenness of God is manifest in the incommensurability between human language and understanding and the divine reality resulting in the recommendation of a *via negativa* as the most appropriate vehicle for God-talk. Even for Aquinas, where the procedure of "analogy" would seem to secure a middle position between univocity and equivocity securing a reserve of "proper" God-talk, there is still the limit axiom that "God in his essence is ineffable" (S.T. Ia, 12, 7).[11] So also for Rahner, especially in his later work, there arises the theological exigency of a *reductio ad mysterium* of all speech concerning God in recognition of the incomprehensibility of the Abiding Mystery as the whence and whither of human self-transcendence.[12] Constitutive of this line of reflection is the awareness of and a self-consciousness commitment to the preservation of the "moreness" and "density" of the experience of God against which the language of piety and theology pales. Even as manifest in its revelation, God remains the Known Unknown; in its nearness in grace and the Incarnation, it yet remains Abiding Mystery. Such a line of reflection while sublating, does not negate the biblical and creedal affirmations of faith—affirmations whose retrieval is described according to an *analogia entis* or an *analogia fidei* which repudiates the presupposition of an ontotheology and acknowledges that the reflective language of theological analogy arises from the focal meanings of a religion's significant particulars and narratives. Yet the hallmark of this framework is that the hiddenness of God as its abiding ineffability and incomprehensibility reveals itself in the very glowing core of its manifestness as the God of Christian faith, thereby fracturing all human language and enjoining on the believer the final posture of an "everyday mysticism": the trusting silent doxology of love.

---

[11] This insight is also operative in the "linguistic turn" in recent discussions of analogy where the question of analogy, tied for Aquinas to an ontology of participation, is now connected to the issues of metaphor and "focal meaning." See David Burrell, *Analogy and Philosophical Language* (New Haven: Yale University Press, 1973), Roger Hazelton, "Theological Analogy and Metaphor," *Semeia* 13 (1978): 155-76, David Tracy's defense of analogy as a language of ordered relationships expressing similarity-in-difference in *The Analogical Imagination* and Paul Ricouer, *The Rule of Metaphor*, trans. Robert Costello with Kathleen McLaughlin and John Costello (Toronto: University of Toronto Press, 1977).

[12] See, for example, Karl Rahner, "Reflections on Methodology in Theology," *Theological Investigations XI*, trans. David Bourke (New York: The Seabury Press, 1974), pp. 101-14.

The second framework focuses on the *Deus revelatus in Christo*. Unlike the first trajectory which focuses on the ontological incommensurability of human language and understanding and the divine reality as Abiding Mystery, the focus of this second trajectory is the Christological paradox that God is hidden in *this one* in whom it is revealed, Jesus as the Christ. In a trajectory which moves from the "messianic secret" in the Gospel of Mark, through Luther's *theologia crucis*, Kierkegaard's *Philosophical Fragments* and *Training in Christianity*, and represented today by Jürgen Moltmann's Trinitarian theology of the cross, the specificity of the story of Jesus as the one who was despised, reviled and ultimately rejected becomes paramount.

> In Christ, God works in a paradoxical mode *sub contrariis*. His wisdom is hidden under folly, his strength under abject weakness. He gives life through death, righteousness to the unrighteous; he saves by judging and damning. The hidden God is the God incarnate, crucified, hidden in suffering (*deus incarnatus, deus crucifixus, deus absconditus in passionibus*).[13]

The hiddenness of God coincides with the specificity of the christological reference of Christian faith, i.e., God manifests itself precisely in that place which Christianity qua Christianity acknowledges as the primary focus of revelation: the scandal of the folly of the cross before the wisdom of the world.

These two distinct trajectories tend to "pull away" from one another in the tradition. If the framework for the first is ontological-cosmological in the broadest sense of the term, that of the second is biblical and christocentric; if the focus of the first is the "gap" between the divine and the human even in the former's presence to the latter, that of the second is the paradox of the immanence of the divine in a particular human being and the particularity of his story, of a God who is *sub contrariis*.

During the period of the Reformation, a third framework for the hiddenness of God became thematic—one which since Augustine had remained somewhat subliminal to theological discourse. If the second framework emphasized the hiddenness of God *in* Christ, this one emphasizes the hiddenness of God *apart* from Christ. While no definitive or final lines may be drawn between the two trajectories of reflection—since they often occur within the thought of the same person, i.e., Luther—the latter stands to the former as the penumbra to the core: a penumbra

---

[13] Gerrish, "To the Unknown God," p. 134.

which emerged in reflection on the concealed and dreadful will of God as crystallized in the question concerning "double predestination."

Against the background of the nominalist distinction between God's *potentia absoluta* and *potentia ordinata* and the reopening of the debate concerning grace and free will, both Luther and Calvin noted the dissonance between God's ordained will as *Deus revelatus* for the redemption of all in Christ and both the empirical and scriptural warrants concerning those that heard, but did not heed the gospel. While the nominalist distinction raised the terrifying specter of a breach between *Deus revelatus* and *Deus nudus*, the answer to the question of the relation between grace and free will issued in what seemed tantamount to a radical curtailment, if not outright negation, of the latter in order to affirm the sole sufficiency of the former with regard to salvation. Together, these two factors led reflection in the direction of the God who hides himself beyond his revelation, of the ineffable and inscrutable will of God beyond the figure of Christ, of the Void surrounding the Word. "The God who hides himself outside of Christ, whether in nature, history or the eternal decree, does not move me to trust."[14] The threat and the anxiety of the hiddenness of God as the unknown God beyond the Word (*Deus nudus*) threatens to overwhelm God's manifestness in his Word. Towards this threat, the Reformers saw a practical solution which entered into the immanent constitution of Evangelical and Reformed piety: the constant renewal of faith in a resolute clinging and conforming to the Word as *Deus revelatus*, who himself was not spared the experience of the hiddenness of the Father's inscrutable will.

The dialectic of the history of religions continues reflection on the hiddenness and manifestness of God. The recognition of the positivity of religion which arose with the advent of historical consciousness is the obverse side of the recognition of the synchronic and diachronic nonidentity of religions. If one takes this positivity of religion seriously and hence takes their nonidentity seriously by acknowledging the "intratextual meaning"[15] of a religion as specific if not unitary, then there is a radicalization of the hiddenness and manifestness of God, not as an intra-Christian dialectic (as is the case in the first three trajectories), but as an extra-Christian one—though one which I suspect has more in

14 Ibid., p. 140.
15 On the "intratextuality" of religious meaning and its relation to a cultural-linguistic approach to religion versus an experiential-expressive model, see George A. Lindbeck, *The Nature of Doctrine* (Philadelphia: Westminster Press, 1984).

common at the level of experience and piety with the third trajectory than with the other two.

The recognition of the nonidentity of religions, i.e., religions raise an identical formal claim regarding totality of meaning but materially differ on what totality of meaning is definitive, raises the possibility that Christianity may be misguided in its anticipatory characterization of the divine as covenanted with men and women as their destiny, its orientation to history as eschatologically valorized and its proclamation of authentic existence as faith (trust) working in suffering love in and for the world. The universality of the truth claim of Christianity and hence the specificity of its God-talk is jarred by a similar, yet nonidentical truth claim of other religions. In the dispute of religions regarding the definitive totality of meaning, the foundational powerful experience of the divine and the derivative demonstration of a totality of meaning's coherence with nonreligious understandings of reality are but provisional verification of a religion's truth claim. Here, in the midst of history as the dialectic of religions, there arises as in the third trajectory the specter of a *Deus nudus*, of the divine apart from Christ and the specificity of all Christian God-talk. It is this dispute regarding the truth of a religion's totality of meaning which discloses "history" in its formal sense as the transmission of traditions and the claim to truth of Christianity as provisional and anticipatory but which nevertheless emerges from reflection on Christianity as a positive religion. What has been said here of Christianity's characterization of the divine certainly applies to each and every other positive religion and hence to all positive religions as a whole. The hiddenness of the divine here appears as the Void in relation to which a determinate religion and its talk about the divine are relativized. All material God-talk, dependent as it inevitably is upon a determinate religious totality of meaning —and this would include, I suspect, most Western philosophical God-talk as more or less explicitly derivative from the residue of Judaism and Christianity—stands against this penumbra and hence takes on against it and "other" religious totalities of meaning, the quality of a "confessional proviso": the confession which does not seek to annihilate the nonidentity of religion either noetically or politically, but which acknowledges the anticipatory character of its faith, i.e., the wager, permeable to reality-testing, that its totality of meaning is ultimately the one most adequate to the *Deus nudus*.

The Nonidentity of Tradition

There is a seductiveness to the noun "tradition." The sense of identification and participation, conveyed by phrases as "the Western tradition," "the great Tradition" and "the Christian tradition" glosses over the fragility of what the term denotes. While I am persuaded by the arguments of Gadamer that the finitude of "understanding" is that it always already is constituted by "belonging to" (*Zugehörigkeit*) tradition, I am uneasy with the noun itself and what it conceals.

"Tradition" is an abstraction. What exists are "traditions" of evergreater determinacy. To be sure, one may speak of the identity of a "tradition" but only while simultaneously recognizing the nonidentity of the subject matter to which the noun points. Throughout this work, I have referred to Christianity as a "totality of meaning"—which may be tacitly equated with "tradition"—which is nonidentical with other religious totalities of meaning. While this seems legitimate to me, it only takes a little further reflection to ascertain that "Christianity" is not a homogenous whole. It includes a host of distinct confessions and denominations with more or less distinct liturgical, creedal and theological emphases which, in turn, tend to define distinct ways of "being Christian." As Ernst Käsemann has suggested, this pluralism is unavoidable and rooted in the pluralism of the *norma normans non normata* of Christian faith.[16] Thus there is not only a nonidentity of Christianity as a totality of meaning vis-à-vis other determinate totalities of meaning but also a nonidentity of Christianity itself as a pluralism of relatively determinate traditions each of which more or less tolerates a certain pluralism among its members. As a reflective enterprise, the differences among Christian theologies make this pluralism explicit and thus reflect the nonidentity of the Christian tradition.[17] Inasmuch as theological pluralism is the one most easily accessible for examination, further reflection in this section on the nonidentity of tradition refers to this explicit pluralism.

It may seem odd to point to an irreducible theological pluralism at a time when there seems to be a consensus regarding the criteria of theological discourse. For example, many theologians would accept Paul

[16] Ernst Käsemann, "The Canon of the New Testament and the Unity of the Church," in *Essays on New Testament Themes*, trans. W.J. Montague (Naperville, IL: Alec R. Allenson, 1964), pp. 95-107.

[17] This is not to assert that "pluralism" is solely a phenomenon of second-order theological discourse. Even the first-order discourse of piety is always already marked by a tacit and prethematic construal of the "essence of Christianity" and hence exhibits the same pluralism to be found at the second, reflective level.

Tillich's "method of correlation" as accurately describing what in fact most theologians do when they do systematic theology.[18] The theologian must articulate the "question(s)" of the age and formulate the "answer(s)" of Christian faith. To be sure, there is a circle here because both the articulation of the question and the formulation of its answer are never accomplished in isolation from one another. Further, there is the rather grey area of discourse where the theologian attempts to persuade her audience that the "answers" are truly answers to questions which are truly "questions."

It would be facile to indict this characterization of the method of theology as simply "liberal." While one might make such a case with regard to Tillich's own theology, it seems to me that the method of correlation covers the procedure of a wide array of theologians. However, even with a relatively adequate accounting of the method of theology, there still remains a great deal of room for pluralism. After all, theologians may still find themselves in disagreement on what "counts" as the relevant question and/or answer.

More recently, David Tracy has attempted to reformulate Tillich's method of correlation in terms of the "adequacy" and "appropriateness" of theological discourse: "adequacy" in relation to "common human experience" and "appropriate" in relation to the "Christian fact."[19] In Tracy's estimation, this formulation represents an advance on Tillich's since it specifies not only the correlation of Christianity's "answers" with the "questions" of the age; it also allows for the play between the questions *and* answers of the age with those of the Christian tradition. Yet amidst all this, a nagging question remains: do we know in advance what will count as a good argument or as a decisive criticism against a conjecture? Apparently not. Thus, Tracy's discussion of the criteria of theology is complemented by a metamethodological construction of the various "models" of theology.[20] The decisive point appears to be that the specification of the criteria of adequacy and appropriateness which moves beyond the formalism of the terms already presupposes the material "filling out" of those categories in a tacit interpretation of the Christian tradition and contemporary human experience. Theology, which as an intellectual enterprise gestures towards clarity, is haunted by the chimera of an always elusive pure self-transparency. Yet as

[18] Paul Tillich, *Systematic Theology*, 3 vols. (Chicago: The University of Chicago Press, 1951-63), 1:59-66.

[19] Tracy, *A Blessed Rage for Order*, pp. 43-56.

[20] Ibid., pp. 22-34.

Gadamer has accurately observed, "we are more than we know" and hence seem to be abandoned in a morass, for while there may be some overlap in the definition of the problems, the elaboration of the concepts and the specification of the criteria of theology, the operative word is "some." There are two questions which arise here. First, does the recognition of theological pluralism entail a relativism regarding what "counts" as Christianity? Second, is there anything "theological" about theological pluralism? Are the differences between Christian theologies simply the reflection of differences regarding non-religious matters, i.e., differences in philosophical starting points and positions. My suggestion is that the cluster of issues which the first question poses and which have become important in the postempiricist philosophy of science have already been endured by theology in its attempt to answer the second question in the seemingly passé discussion concerning the "essence of Christianity."

The concept of the "essence of Christianity" first assumes a central role in the work of Schleiermacher where it defines the task of apologetics: the description of the distinctive nature of Christianity which can be apprehended neither in a purely speculative fashion nor in a strictly empirical one.[21] The explication of the essence of Christianity is a necessary condition for dogmatics as *Glaubenslehre* which is the culmination of historical theology. Yet the term "essence of Christianity," for all its indebtedness to Schleiermacher, is most notoriously associated with Adolph von Harnack whose *Wesen des Christentums* (1900) was one of the most popular texts of its day. Further, it appears plausible to suggest that Harnack's subsequent debates with Alfred Loisy and Karl Barth are substantially debates concerning the formal role and content of the essence of Christianity—the first at the symbolic close of 19th century theology in 1903, the second as the opening shot of 20th century theology in 1923. The finest exposition of the issues, however, was given to none of these parties but should be reserved for Ernst Troeltsch and his essay "What Does 'Essence of Christianity' Mean?" (1913)

For Troeltsch, the "essence of Christianity" functions simultaneously as a "critical principle," a "developmental principle," and an "ideal concept" which mutually condition one another. These are not three separate essences but three distinct functions of the one essence. Because the essence of Christianity is always also an ideal concept, its definition "is no longer merely a judgement about history but is itself a piece of his-

---

[21] Schleiermacher, *Brief Outline*, pp. 29-36.

tory."[22] Because of this function of the essence of Christianity, Troeltsch affirmed that the "definition of the essence is the crown and at the same time the self-abrogation of historical theology, it is the unification of the historical element in theology with the normative element or at least the element which shapes the future."[23] For the same reason, Troeltsch specified the second and third tasks of a Christian dogmatics as the specification and delineation of the essence of Christianity.[24] While Harnack seems to acknowledge the definition of the essence of Christianity as a critical and developmental principle in the first lecture of *Wesen des Christentums*, he seems less aware that the definition of the essence of Christianity

> . . . is itself a living, individual historical formation which joins the series of those which lie in the past. It is nothing other than a formulation of the Christian idea in a manner corresponding to the present, associated with earlier formulations in laying bare the force for growth, but immediately allowing the latter to shoot up into new leaves and blossoms.[25]

Harnack, rather, seems to speak of the definition of the essence of Christianity as an "inductive-empirical" task of discovering "something which under differing historical forms, is of permanent validity."[26] If Troeltsch is correct—and I think he is—then the definition of the essence of Christianity signals the normative and practical dimension of theological reflection which is a necessary condition for constructive theology where the resources of the past are explicitly and reflectively mediated into the present in the light of the future. Theological pluralism has a theological foundation and the differences which define the nonidentity of tradition are, above all, religious and theological ones, i.e., differences regarding the essence of Christianity.

That the category "essence of Christianity" has fallen on hard times is due to the victory of Barth and the turn to "revelation" in 20th century

22 Troeltsch, "What Does 'Essence of Christianity' Mean?" p. 161.
23 Ibid., p. 164.
24 Ernst Troeltsch, "The Dogmatics of the *Religionsgeschichtliche Schule*," *The American Journal of Theology* 17 (January 1913): 11-21.
25 Idem, "What Does 'Essence of Christianity' Mean?" p. 162.
26 Adolph von Harnack, *What is Christianity*, trans. Thomas Bailey Saunders, with an introduction by Rudolph Bultmann (New York: Harper Torchbooks, 1957), p. 14. G. Wayne Glick has persuasively argued [*The Reality of Christianity* (New York: Harper and Row, 1967)] that Harnack's understanding of the term, outside of the text *Wesen des Christentums*, acknowledged its function as an ideal concept and, indeed, constituted the "regal function" of the historian.

theology and, more importantly, the aporia of historicism in which the concept seemed irreducibly embedded.[27] Against the backdrop of the implied Cartesianism of historicism, the transition to systematic theology—an aspect of practical theology for Troeltsch—appears as "second best": a departure from *theoria* as scientific knowledge which devolves into a decisionism dependent on the prejudices and value judgments of the theologian.[28] Once again, the issue is, to use the title of Richard Bernstein's book, whether the circle of relativism and objectivism can be overcome.[29]

To connect this sketch of the essence of Christianity with that which preceded it, one might say that materially at the heart of the method of correlation is a more or less explicit definition of the essence of Christianity. As a critical principle, developmental principle and an ideal concept, such a definition is not a "theoretical" one. It is neither the discovery of an eternal or immutable "idea" nor spontaneously results from the collection of historical facts. It is a normative and practical definition. It specifies the "point" of Christianity and lays open the normative-practical dimension of theological reflection where the *tradita* becomes *traditio*. It is the point where speaking *of* the "tradition" becomes speaking *for* the "tradition." It is that point where, to use Gadamer's

---

[27] That Troeltsch himself remained captive to the Cartesianism of historicism can be seen in his denial to "dogmatics" of a "scientific" status and his assignment of it to the field of "practical theology:" "A dogmatics of this sort presupposes scientific conclusions and methods; it is, however, not a science; it is rather a confession of faith and a systematic exposition of this confession for the guidance of preaching and of religious instruction. . . . The decisive affirmation of the Christian conception of the world and life is due to a personal choice. The definition of an "essence" of Christianity, valid for the present, is no less a matter of personal intuition. . . . Thus dogmatics is a part of practical theology and is not essentially a scientific discipline. . . . As over against it the philosophy of religion and the history of Christianity bear a purely scientific character" ["The Dogmatics," pp. 16-17].

[28] On the Cartesianism of historicism, see Gadamer, *Truth and Method*, pp. 153-341. For an exposition of *Glaubenslehre* in the thought of Schleiermacher and Troeltsch, see Terence Tice, "Schleiermacher's Theological Method" (Th.D. dissertation, Princeton Theological Seminary, 1961); Gerrish, "Continuity and Change: Friedrich Schleiermacher on the Task of Theology," in *Tradition and the Modern World* (Chicago: University of Chicago Press, 1978), pp. 13-48; Walter Wyman, *The Concept of Glaubenslehre: Ernst Troeltsch and the Theological Heritage of Schleiermacher*, American Academy of Religion Dissertation Series, number 44 (Chico, California: Scholars Press, 1983) and Gerrish, "The Possibility of a Historical Theology: An Appraisal of Troeltsch's Dogmatics," in *The Old Protestantism and the New*, pp. 208-29.

[29] Richard Bernstein, *Beyond Objectivism and Relativism: Science, Hermeneutics and Praxis* (Philadelphia: University of Pennsylvania Press, 1983).

language, the unity of "understanding," "interpretation," and "application" becomes explicit. Pluralism is inherent in the very process of traditioning tradition. Is this admission tantamount to admitting a covert form of relativism?

The issues which cluster around the epistemic status of essence of Christianity as a necessary condition for systematic theology are formally similar to the issues which have arisen in the "postempiricist" philosophy of science, i.e., the questioning of a pervasive Cartesian self-understanding of science and rationality which reduces praxis to a moment of application external to the exercise of rationality itself, the discovering of the social, intersubjective and dialogic character of the foundations of "understanding," the recovery of the unformalizable aspects of inquiry and rational "explanation" and the questioning of the very possibility of the ideal of a "unified science." The debate unleashed by Thomas Kuhn's *The Structure of Scientific Revolutions* and Peter Winch's *The Idea of a Social Science* has forced a reconsideration of the Cartesian self-understanding of science and rationality in both the natural and social sciences.[30] In particular, Kuhn's distinctions between "normal" and "revolutionary" science, and observations on what "counts" as facts within a determinate paradigm—observation statements as theory-laden—and the unformalizable parameters in the application of criteria i.e., accuracy, consistency, scope, simplicity and fruitfulness, appear to rent the seamless garment of scientific rationality. What comes into view is the unformalizable dialogic-agonistic praxis of reason which shatters the naive verificationist and falsificationist theories of science of the previous generation.

What Kuhn has suggested of scientific paradigms also applies, I believe, to the various definitions of the essence of Christianity. The reflective consideration of what one is doing when one defines the essence of Christianity points to the same issues which have emerged for the philosophy of science: the unformalizable aspect of reason as well as the social- practical constitution of thought. These also are effective in constituting theological reflection as a *vis a tergo*. For example, is it specifiable in advance what is theologically appropriate or adequate? or, what is the spiritual situation of our age? or, what is the contemporary situation's "question" to which Christian faith (already constructively interpreted and appropriated) is a potential "answer"? The adjudication of these criteriological issues point, I suspect, to an always already, more or less

---

[30] Thomas Kuhn, *The Structure of Scientific Revolutions*, 2d. ed. enl. (Chicago: University of Chicago Press, 1970) and Peter Winch, *The Idea of a Social Science and its Relation to Philosophy* (London: Routledge and Kegan Paul, 1958).

explicitly formulated construction of the point of Christianity which prethematically guides the thematic answers to these questions—what a few generations earlier was called the "essence of Christianity."

Theologically, given the nonidentity of the Christian tradition and the practical character of the traditioning of tradition, descriptions of the "essence of Christianity" are "incommensurable" to one another. My use of the term follows its etymology and thus is more precise in what it negates than what it asserts. Felicitously, Richard Rorty has captured the meaning of the term "commensurability" which the negative form of the term denies:

> By 'commensurable' I mean able to be brought under a set or rules which will tell us how rational agreement can be reached, on what would settle the issue on every point where statements seem to conflict. These rules tell us how to construct an ideal situation, in which all residual disagreements will be seen to be 'noncognitive' or merely verbal, or else merely temporary— capable of being resolved by doing something further. What matters is that there should be agreement about what would have to be done if a resolution *were* to be achieved.[31]

To assert the incommensurability of descriptions of the essence of Christianity is to deny a Cartesian understanding of the self and knowledge which seeks to secure the sure and certain knowledge of the subject who is separate from the object of its contemplation through specific, permanent rules, maxims or methods which are a necessary and sufficient condition for warranting a particular belief as "scientific knowledge." Further, from the position which Bernstein calls "objectivism," the recognition of the incommensurability between definitions of the essence of Christianity appears as a capitulation to relativism and irrationalism. However, as Bernstein has argued, the key issue at stake in the postempiricist philosophy of science is not "rationality" versus "irrationality," but a self-understanding of rationality adequate to the unformalizable dimensions of "scientific rationality" itself. While the incommensurability of rival understandings does acknowledge their logical *incompatibility*, this does not entail their *incomparability* but points to the informal, practical character of rationality itself: the role of choice, deliberation, conflicting variable opinions, and the judgmental quality of rationality as intersubjectively constituted.

---

[31]   Rorty, *Philosophy and the Mirror of Nature*, p. 61.

My point in this broad-stroked presentation is to point to the non-identity of tradition which explicitly manifests itself in theology in the definition of the essence of Christianity. This can be summed up in three statements. First, the nonidentity of tradition as theologically reflected arises from the unavoidability of a definition of the essence of Christianity which stands as a necessary condition for systematic theology. It is the execution of this task, often not explicitly adverted to by theologians which gives rise to what is theological in theological pluralism. Second, differing theologies as reflected units of "tradition" as both *tradita* and *traditio*, continue the ongoing nonidentity of tradition and, insofar as these stem from differing projections of the essence of Christianity, are incommensurable with one another, i.e., their differences cannot be settled through appeal to an algorithm of objective and universal reason. Methodological reflection (i.e., the formulation of the "method of correlation" or of the criteria of "adequacy and appropriateness") and metamethodological reflection (i.e., the construction of theological "models") do not negate but only formally categorize the nonidentity of tradition as reflected in theology. Finally, the acknowledgement of the incommensurability of theological constructions arising from nonidentical projections of the essence of Christianity does not entail irrationalism, relativism or decisionism at the foundation of theological understanding. It points, rather, to that informal and unformalizable rationality, to the primordial conversation which we always already are and which is carried forward at a reflective level in the ongoing dialectic of questions and answers and in the openness of the theologian to the interjections of the "other" from both the present and the past.

The definition of the essence of Christianity operative in this essay—Christianity is an eschatological religion oriented to the redemption of history in its memory and solidarity with Jesus as the Christ—simultaneously delimits Christianity from both other positive religions and other interpretations of the essence of Christianity within the Christian tradition. The definition of the essence of Christianity is thus focused in two directions roughly corresponding to Schleiermacher's division of philosophical theology into "apologetics" and "polemics": the delimitation of Christianity as a totality of meaning vis-à-vis other such totalities and a normative-practical actualization of the Christian totality of meaning-tradition which continues it through its critical appropriation.

Do differences between different definitions of the essence of Christianity make any difference at all? I think so. How the theologian or religious believer implicitly or explicitly construes the point or essence of Christianity cannot not affect the material content of Christian God-talk insofar as the description of the essence of Christianity functions to specify the "grammar" of theo-logy, talk about God. Thus, parallel to the nonidentity of religion and the "confessional proviso," the nonidentity of tradition must also be acknowledged through the category of the "theological proviso." The category of "theological proviso" which is not confined to the sphere of theology but encompasses all explicit religious speech makes explicit the constructive, normative and inherently practical dimension of the transmission of tradition which breaks the spell of a Cartesian understanding of theory by recognizing the practical telos of *traditio*.

Insofar as one can find in the various forms of the Christian fact—not only theological writings but also mystical writings, spiritual diaries, catechetical and liturgical texts, paintings and sculptures, devotional tracts and creeds—a variety of descriptions of the essence of Christianity and hence a variety of conceptions of God and "sorts" of God-talk, the theological proviso points to the "wager" which attends every mediation of the tradition at the theological level in the interpretive circle of reflection on the Christian fact and human experience. Indeed, every act of *traditio* is not only a "retrieval" of past "tradition" but is also always already a consignment of a determinate portion of it to the "dead past."

The projection of the essence of Christianity operative in this essay which conditions the "grammar" of its "God-talk" represents, I believe, both an adequate and appropriate articulation of the Christian faith. It is not, however, the only way its point may be plausibly construed. I suspect, for example, that the understanding of the essence of Christianity of political theology as a theology of history would not be shared by James Gustafson or John Cobb whose own theologies also claim to be authentic actualizations of the Christian tradition. Inasmuch as these differences cannot be adjudicated by an impartial algorithm but represent differing circles of interpretation of the Christian fact and human experience in a practical-constructive mediation which is *traditio*, the only recourse is to dialogue, the isolation of differences and the ongoing exchange of questions and answers which, of course, presumes the goodwill of the parties involved. What remains decisive is that insofar as such differences are real differences arising from different projections of the essence of Christianity, differences in the conception of God and the form of God-talk are also real and not merely accidental ones—their unity in the Christian "tradition" notwithstanding. At this level, the provisionality of theological discourse within a specific construal of the point of a provisional and anticipatory totality of meaning becomes apparent in the irreducible and ongoing nonidentity of that totality of meaning itself.

The Nonidentity of History

This last defense of nonidentity concerns the nonidentity of history and society as suffering. If Christianity is a religion oriented to history as a whole, eschatologically valorized and if the concrete mediation of history is through society, then a Christian political theology which attends to the nonidentity of suffering in history and society cannot not affect the way its horizon, "history as a whole, eschatologically valorized," is conceived in relation to "God." As the last part of this section suggests, the focal issue for Christian God-talk today and one that demands a theological *askesis* by positing an "eschatological proviso" is the fact of suffering which calls into question not only the secular identity of history as the history of the victors—both in its "liberal" form as "progress" or its Marxist form as the socialist revolution—but also calls into question religious and theological attempts to attenuate the nonidentity of history as suffering through the noetic identity of "salvation history."

The point where the nonidentity of history as suffering becomes theologically relevant and interrupts the claim of the identity of Christian faith, i.e., history as salvation-history, can be denoted as a "turn to suffering," a "conversion to suffering" or a practical and intellectual "abiding with suffering" which refuses to negate or sublate it through any noetic schema of meaning. It is here that Christian theology directs a pressing question towards all projects of secular utopia: is the secret cipher of all such utopias forgetfulness—the forgetfulness of broken hopes, betrayed promises and the sensuous suffering of past victims who are relegated to the mere stuff of a prehistory out of which the future utopia is forged. The scandal of Christian faith for such utopias is the scope of its solidarity in hope—an imminent expectation for those who appear irredeemably unredeemable: the forgotten, the nameless and discarded victims of history. This anamnestic solidarity—a hope for something more than anamnestic solidarity—is grounded for Christianity in the narrated memory of the cross and resurrection of Jesus.

Yet the nonidentity of history as suffering not only questions the various projections of a secular utopia; it also poses a challenge to Christianity and Christian theology. The narrated history of salvation proclaimed and celebrated in Christianity must lose its political innocence if it is to be something other than false consciousness. Indeed, at the heart of political theology is an attempt to restore the concrete history of men and women in its social, political and economic mediations to the center of a theological reflection whose proclamation is the God who has covenanted itself with men and women in history as their destiny. The interruption of suffering, however, not only poses a challenge regarding the form of Christian theology. It also challenges and interrupts the very substance of Christian theology, its God-talk.

What this means as well as the scope of this challenge can be made clear through a contrast. What Arthur Cohen has termed the caesura of the Holocaust marks the occasion for the recognition of the nonidentity of history. Much of contemporary Judaism—its literature, poetry and theological reflection—is marked by this *tremendum* as a negative revelation whose claim to universality is no less than the claim to universality of the Exodus-Sinai event. It is asked, "What words can there be after the Holocaust which do not betray it?" Even more, "What religious words can there be which do not skip over and through this event?" For a significant portion of contemporary Jewish thought, the event of the Holocaust cannot be blasphemed—above all, this is *the* categorical imperative for thought which seeks to engage history—by being ignored, reduced or sublated into a schema of identity of faith and history or reason and history. For theologians such as Emil Fackenheim, Arthur Cohen, Irving Greenberg and Richard Rubinstein, the possibility of theological language—and that possibility is by no means tacitly conceded in advance, as is often the case with those that raise the question of the "possibility" of theological language—only lies through this event.

On the whole, however, I think that the urgency and depth of this event and the question which it directs regarding God-talk has not found its counterpart in *Christian* theology. For many within the Christian community even today, the Holocaust remains a "Jewish question"—a procedure which, by relegating *this* event (as well as perhaps every other) to the dung heap of "atrocity," dissolves this (as well as perhaps every other) event of suffering in its claim upon humanity hence rendering it manageable. To be sure, there are a number of Christian theologians who have addressed the "meaning" of the Holocaust as an event for Christian faith and theology, but the fact that they can be identified as a "specialist group" co-opts this event and the fundamental questions it raises into the all too familiar academic division of labor. The nonreception of the Holocaust as a *Christian* negative revelation renders plausible Metz's implied judgment that

> ... wherever Christianity victoriously conceals its own messianic weakness, its sensorium for dangers and downfalls diminishes to an ever greater degree. Theology loses its awareness for historical disruptions and catastrophe. Has not our Christian faith for the salvation achieved for us in Christ been covertly reified to a kind of optimism about meaning, an optimism which is no longer capable of perceiving radical disruptions and catastrophes within meaning? Does there not exist something like a typically Christian incapacity for dismay in the face of disasters?[32]

That Metz raises such questions by reflecting on the meaning of the Holocaust for Christianity is not extraneous to the questions themselves and cannot be reduced to an autobiographical idiosyncrasy, but dwells in the subject matter itself. The loss of a sensorium for danger and the betrayal of history in indifference to its past catastrophes and present and future threats is simultaneously the loss and betrayal of Christianity's eschatological orientation to history. The question is whether Christian theology in that it inevitably and ineluctably raises a claim towards totality is condemned to always already negate the nonidentity of history as suffering?

As mentioned above, the leaven of the turn to history in political theology is a conversion to "suffering." Encoded within Metz's political theology is the recognition of the claim to ultimacy of suffering as the decisive witness to the nonidentity of history with Christianity's totality of meaning. This conversion includes both the stance of a practical solidarity with those who suffer and a disavowal of those noetic attempts "to come to grips" with it. The task, rather, is to abide with suffering as an "in itself" without definitively referencing it to a schema of identity which surreptitiously transmutes its meaninglessness into "meaning," thus depriving it of its claim to ultimacy. In this, it is crucial to preserve the concrete polyvalent meaning of the abstract noun "suffering" without succumbing to the temptation to hypostasize *a* particular form of suffering as the *proton pseudos* of all other forms of suffering.[33]

---

32 Metz, "Christians and Jews After Auschwitz," p. 25.

33 In this I am suggesting that the pattern of liberation theology should imitate Adorno's method of "constellation" as a way of preserving the relative autonomy yet interrelationship of the manifestations of suffering in history, thus resisting the method of causality which posits *a* form of suffering as "really real" and hence implicitly occludes all other forms as "mere" secondary manifestations.

To be sure, this position does not lead to a negation of the insights of twentieth-century fundamental ontology or neoorthodox theology regarding "suffering" as guilt and its connection with the historicity, finitude and temporality of human existence and, for theology, the connection of finitude with anxiety and "sin" as idolatry and pride. Yet human historicity as finitude and temporality in the anticipation of one's own death, to use Heidegger's language, and the events of human inhumanity and barbarism, are irreducible to one another. To collapse either into the other is to lose an essential determinant of thought concerning history as the history of suffering even as these two conditions mediate one another. The historicity of men and women in their finitude and fate as "death" is never merely that bare abstraction, but a finitude and death of a particular sort mediated by history and society. Conversely, the utopia of the realm of freedom, even if realized, shatters upon the aporia of anamnestic solidarity framed by the finitude of human being. The "suffering" of finitude, captured in the anticipation of one's own death and the experience of guilt, pride and idolatry and the "suffering" of history as the socially mediated inhumanity of men and women towards one another cannot be thought apart lest in the preoccupation with the first, one falls into the fallacy of misplaced concreteness and history as society is ignored as accidental to the historicity of human being, or, in preoccupation with the second, the specter of a moralistic, triumphalistic and ultimately forgetful utopianism arises which unburdens itself of a completed—as surpassed—prehistory of suffering. In this abiding with the claim to ultimacy of suffering, the *motus* of political theology and the various forms of ideology-critique converge: "thought follows the direction determined by pain, and trauma, and compassion and outrage."[34] Christian theology ought not to contrive some "answer" to the "question" of theodicy so as to be done it; rather, by brushing history against the grain, it should allow the question to stand forth at the core of its own talk about God. To resist transmuting the dissonance of suffering into the consonance of meaning, to allow meaningless suffering to stand as a broken, sensuous "in itself" yet referenced provisionally and proleptically to the eschaton is an imperative for any Christian theology of history today. This turn to eschatology in recent Christian theology, however, is not unproblematic.

---

[34] Susan Griffin, *Pornography and Silence* (New York: Harper Colophon Books, 1981), p. 211.

Can one articulate Christian faith today, and most particularly its understanding of "God," and not negate the suffering of history by transmuting it into mere appearance? Positing this "eschatological proviso" attempts to address this question in a twofold manner. First, the eschatological proviso, by inscribing within Christian theology the claim to ultimacy of history as a history of suffering, implies that formally Christian theo-logical discourse is most appropriately realized in a dialectical rather than analogical discourse. Second, the eschatological proviso posits God as the "subject of history." The question is: can the second assertion be held without compromising the first and vice-versa? Does the gesture towards "totality" which is implicit in talk about God thwart the *askesis* of thought which seeks to abide with history as the history of suffering? As suggested in the previous chapter, Metz's silence on "God," "history" and the "future" may well be connected with this but simultaneously risks surrendering the claim which makes Christianity a religion. My suggestion is that the turn to eschatology in political theology as a theology of history is best realized in a form of a "negative dialectics" which recognizes the "silence of the Father" in history.

Talk about analogical relations between God, the world and humanity is unavoidable in Christian theology. By analogy, I mean

> a language of ordered relationships articulating similarity-in-difference. The order among the relationships is constituted by the distinct but similar relationships of each analogue to some primary focal meaning, some prime analogue. A principal aim of all properly analogical languages is the production of some order, at the limit, some harmony to the several analogues, the similarities-in-difference, constituting the whole of reality. The order is developed by explicating the analogous relationships among various realities (self, others, world, God) by clarifying the relationship of each to the primary analogue, the meaning chosen as the primary focus for interpreting reality.[35]

For Christianity, this primary analogue is the narrative witness to Jesus of Nazareth. A necessary analogical moment is introduced into all Christian discourse and experience through the disclosive-transformative remembrance and retelling of the story of Jesus of Nazareth whereby the "order," and "harmony" qua reconciliation of God, the world and humanity is described.

Yet it this analogical claim that is circumscribed by the negation of the nonidentity of history, the claim to ultimacy of suffering. Properly

---

[35] Tracy, *The Analogical Imagination*, p. 408.

speaking, analogical relations between God, the world and humanity as construed by Christian faith will only overcome dialectical ones in the advent of the Messiah and the Kingdom of God. Only the advent of the Messiah, towards which thought points, could redeem the sensuousness of suffering. Only the advent of the "Kingdom of God" would permit a direct and affirmative use of such talk about analogical relations constituting the truth of reality as a whole. Until that time, in the midst of history, speech of analogical relations is used dialectically in recognition of the claim to ultimacy of the nonidentity of history as a history of suffering. In other words, analogical talk is used in a negative, critical and regulative manner even while the believer, holding and acting upon such language regulatively, anticipates its constitutive validity. These dialectical relations of God, humanity and the world as the history of suffering cannot pass through the negation of the negation into a noetic reconciliation, but only be remembered and rendered present in the praxis of discipleship as an indictment of the present. Analogical relations between God, humanity and the world in Christianity are thus always proleptic ones, the object of anticipation or hope which cannot be converted into an already present reality.

Does this position willfully constrain Christian talk about God into an alien mold, i.e., that of an "negative dialectics." I think not. A plausible case can be made—and has been made by Pannenberg—that the narrative witness to the primary analogue of the Christian tradition, Jesus of Nazareth, points away from itself to the Kingdom where analogically ordered relations between God, men and women and the world will actually obtain. The primary analogue refers by its own material content to that which is "not yet"—a "not yet" whose locus is the world as history construed in a specific manner. The force of what this "not yet" means can perhaps be made most clear through a contrast with another in which the negation of the "not yet" also comes into play.

And yet the constant presence of apocalyptic negations, the "not-yet," throughout the gospel's narratives reminds the sensitive reader not to transform the radical importance of individual decision into the myopic concern of individualism—even for salvation. The "not-yet" of this eschatological Kingdom proclaimed by Jesus, the "not-yet" of the future transformation proclaimed in the narrator's confession of Jesus Christ in the narratives own non-end reminds the Christian that no Christian can turn this call to radical personal decision, to real and authentic individuality, into a compulsive concern with myself and my salvation, into the false security of an already present salvation. The *no* of that not yet, like the yes of the command to love the neighbor, is a no to all that: an enabling *praxis* to real, active concern with the other, indeed with all the living and the dead, especially the "privileged" ones of the Christian gospel and the ancient prophets—the underprivileged, the outcasts, the repressed, the tax-collectors and sinners, the oppressed. Only when that *all* comes will the total hope and the radical promise of these narratives be fulfilled. Only then will the story end.[36]

There is a certain ambiguity about the "not yet" of Christian faith in the quote above—an ambiguity which is symptomatic of many Christian theologians. Tracy's comments clearly suggest that the eschatological "not yet" functions negatively vis à vis the individual believer, i.e., as a call for the deprivatization of faith. I do not dispute that this is in fact correct. It must be asked, however: what is this "future transformation" which parallels the reference to the "Kingdom of God?" Is it the future transformation of the individual, society, the world? What is this provocative "all" which renders the Christian story one with a "nonend?" Both Pannenberg's polemic against neo-orthodox theology and Metz's against the eschatological attenuation of apocalyptic consciousness suggest that the "not yet" refers to something "more" than Tracy indicates: a hope for the world and *therefore* an imperative on Christians in the midst of history. As I have sought to suggest throughout this essay, the specification of the "not yet," of the "all" which Christian faith anticipates finds its "place" not in the historicity of the individual, but only in the world as history and thereby in the historicity of individual men and women. "Only then the story will end." Indeed, with the advent of the "all" the story *will* end; but it *may* also end in the nonarrival of this "all," although then the "ending" will be of quite a different sort—one where reality outstrips the Christian totality of meaning. Construing the essence of Christianity as referring to the world as history is, to be sure, a risky procedure because it exposes the truth-claim of Christianity to what seems most fragile in our own age: history itself.

Precisely in being delivered over to the sphere of history, the Christian exists in the recognition of the nonidentity of history as the history of suffering and holds to a "hope against hope": the hope that that negation is not the final verdict upon the "other" as victim. In its care for the dead, founded in the memory of Jesus of Nazareth, is imposed the task of considering posterity: to eradicate the conditions which lead to suffering even while acknowledging that this does not redeem the suffering of the dead past. The modality of Christian existence in and for the

---

[36] Tracy, "A Response to Father Metz," in *Theology and Discovery*, ed. William J. Kelly (Milwaukee, WI: Marquette University Press, 1980), p. 186.

world as history is to be immersed in the transformation of the present, through the anticipation of a specific future, in fidelity to and care for the past, where no one part overwhelms the other: that the enormity of past suffering causes resignation in the present before the future; that the anticipation of an eschatological future relieves one of the struggle for the transformation of the present in complacency towards the past and future; and that absorption in the demands of the present leads not to ignorance of the nonfinality of all utopias and the forgetfulness of past suffering. All three modes must be present at once: solidarity through memory with the past victims of suffering, liberative praxis in the present and a hopeful anticipation in that future by which all may be new.

The force of the category of the "eschatological proviso" therefore is to lay open, within the space of a discourse presupposing a particular construal of the essence of Christianity, that such analogical relations are in the midst of history proleptic ones in acknowledgement of the claim to ultimacy of the nonidentity of history as a history of suffering.

But this analogical moment in Christian experience is also at "stake" in that other religions raise nonidentical material truth claims concerning the ordered relations of the divine, the world and humanity. To this extent, not only is the analogical moment of Christianity eschatologically qualified, it is also confessionally qualified. The mediation of the eschatological and confessional proviso lies in the interpretation of the "essence of Christianity" as oriented to "history as a whole, eschatologically qualified and anticipating the redemption of history." Yet this constellation of the point of Christian faith and modernity is no "fact," but a theological judgment where understanding, interpretation and application mutually determine one another and hence the two provisos are mediated by a third, the "theological proviso."

The eschatological proviso, however, also serves a second function, i.e., it proleptically posits "God" as the "subject of history." But does this not negate the claim to ultimacy of suffering in history? My suggestion regarding this question begins with an assumption. When Christians speak about "God," that speech ineluctably contains a threefold reference to the "Father," "Son," and "Spirit." Properly speaking, Christian talk about "God" is unavoidably Trinitarian talk where the relations between Father, Son and Spirit are articulated in the originating narrative-witness to the memory of Jesus. Recently, various theologians—most notably, Jürgen Moltmann—have argued that the hallmark of Christian trinitarian talk about "God" is the inscription of suffering within its very being.[37] An explication of Moltmann's work lies beyond the scope of this essay, but Metz's critical reservations regarding Moltmann's theology of the "crucified God" point to the difficulties regarding "God"—even the Trinitarian God—as the subject of history.

In two extended comments, Metz tries to differentiate his position from Moltmann's:

> Jürgen Moltmann's concept of an eschatological hermeneutics of Christian praxis is very close to my own ideas about a political theology and for this reason I am bound to point to a clear difference. His book, *The Crucified God*, was in many respects quite splendid, but since its publication Moltmann has used the concept of praxis increasingly to describe a theology in which the history of the suffering of the Son and the world is rooted within the Trinity. Praxis, which can only prevent the danger of a speculative gnosis in such an approach, is no longer an intelligible principle in Moltmann's theology. On the other hand, this intelligibility is required in the attempts made to find a narrative and practical approach to Christology and soteriology and indeed in the idea of a practical fundamental theology as such.[38]

> The third attempt is a solution [of an argumentative soteriology], which is at present claiming a great deal of attention in the German-speaking countries will be discussed here in more detail and called by name. To begin with, it does not treat soteriology as purely precise nor does it see redemption as a definite (categorical) "work" of God in Jesus Christ. It relates soteriology rightly not only to theology of the Incarnation or to eschatology, but also to the specific definition of the Christian understanding of God in general, that is, to the theology of the Trinity. Suffering now becomes "suffering between God and God". The non-identity of the human history of suffering is, in the light the *kenosis* of God in the cross of Jesus, taken up into the Trinitarian history of God. There is a great deal which is praiseworthy in these and similar attempts. I would, however, like to formulate a central consideration which is cast in an abridged and extremely formal manner. It is that the non-identity of human suffering cannot be canceled out, in theological dialectics of Trinitarian soteriology, and still keep its historical character. For the painful experience of the non-identity of suffering cannot be identified with that negativity found in a dialectical understanding of the historical process, even that of a Trinitarian history of God. Whenever one tries to relate the history of redemption completed in Jesus Christ to the human history of suffering, not just by juxtaposing them in an ahistorical paradox (so that one is *sub contrario* asserted to be in the other), but to understand the alienation of

---

[37] Jürgen Moltmann, *The Crucified God* and *The Trinity and the Kingdom*, trans. Margaret Kohl (New York: Harper and Row, 1981).

[38] Metz, *Faith in History and society*, p. 55 (52).

the history of suffering itself as within the dialectics of the Trinitarian history of God, what occurs is a confusion between the negativity of suffering and the negativity of a dialectically mediated concept of suffering. A conceptual and argumentative mediation and reconciliation between real and effective redemption, on the one hand, and the human history of suffering on the other, would seem to me to be excluded. It leads either to a dualistic gnostic eternalization of suffering in God or to a condescending reduction of suffering to its concept. *Tertium non datur*.[39]

Does Metz cast his net too wide in criticizing Moltmann? What he objects to is a form of noetic identity whereby there is a reduction of concrete, human suffering and praxis to its concept in its theological (Trinitarian) hypostasis. Human praxis and suffering is comprehended "in advance" and may at best aspire to conform to the divine archetype which it "repeats." History, in its claim to ultimacy as the history of suffering and the place of the advent of the Antichrist, is occluded, made over into the symbol of the eternal being of God. This ontologization of suffering is simultaneously its betrayal.

Yet does Metz's offer a more appropriate resolution? As argued previously, Metz's silence regarding theo-logy threatens to make the *memoria Jesu* empty of content except in its own surreptitious claims to totality. At best, such a theo-logical asceticism is a powerful instrument of critique of existing theological "systems" yet it is constrained to a mathematical point which betrays its own origin from and drive towards "narrative." At worst, it leaves open the back door for an all too facile retrieval of the language of "God's mercy, love, justice, providence" etc.. Metz's polarization of an argumentative versus a narrative-practical soteriology is too broad. *"Tertium non datur"* notwithstanding, the two extremes do not add up to a whole—the one allegedly claiming too much and the other not being able to justify any talk about "God" at all. Without theo-logy, the christological turn is simply an ad hoc gesture.

What Metz objects to in Moltmann's trinitarian theology is its apparent closedness—its totality as a system. Two comments may close this essay—the first about the formal structure of Moltmann's theology bringing it to an end, the other regarding its material content suggesting a beginning. First, Moltmann overlooks what has been called the "confessional proviso" which, in fundamental theology, formally qualifies as provisional and anticipatory all material Christian discourse about God in systematic theology. The practical and narrative core of a turn to

[39] Ibid., p. 132 (118).

the Trinity, even as the capstone of Christian theo-logy and its gesture towards totality, is revealed and, at least, formally preserved with the recognition of the "confessional proviso." Christianity's own claim to identity is made relative to the transmission of tradition in the praxis of discipleship as anticipatory doxology.

Second, Moltmann's retrieval of the "suffering of God" in the Trinitarian dialectics of the cross and resurrection of Jesus occludes a significant point: the silence of the "Father" at the cross. To be sure, Moltmann attempts to come to grips with this through the theme that at the cross, the Father suffers in his loss of the Son because of the Father's self-limitation in relation to the world. Yet it precisely this which occludes the radicality of the suffering of the Son along with that of all other men and women. Why does the Father choose to continue to limit himself before the evil of Golgotha as well as the continuing Golgothas of history? To claim that he cannot do otherwise is to make the resurrection proclamation nonsensical. To claim that this is the way of redemption provokes the question which has long been posed by the victims of evil: "Was there not another, more divine because more humane way, for the Father to show his love for the world?"

Moltmann's Trinitarian theology of the crucified God noetically negates the ultimacy of the claim of suffering because the silence of the Father is presented as always already comprehensible in the cross and resurrection of the Son. "God" is the subject of history, yet Moltmann's theo-logy appears ineluctably to negate the claim to ultimacy of history as a history of suffering. Is Metz's silence then appropriate? I think not. Moltmann is quite correct in locating Christian theo-logy in the dialectic of the cross and resurrection. My suggestion is that construing Christian God-talk from this position must accomplish what Moltmann fails to do, i.e., preserve without attenuation the silence of the Father—both at the cross and the lives of men and women.[40]

"God" is the subject of history as the "Spirit" who conforms men and women to the obedient "Son" at the end of whose life stands the cross and the silence of the Father. God's presence in history as the Holy Spirit *is* at the same time the silence of the Father where the intersection between the two is the Son and his cross.

That the silence of the Father at the cross is not his indifferent abandonment of the Son, that He is finally and ultimately "Abba," is the heart

---

[40] For a expanded version of this argument, see my essay "Christian Theodicy and the Genuineness of Evil," *Journal of Pastoral Counseling* (Forthcoming).

of the resurrection proclamation. In the resurrection proclamation, the living witness of the Son is the pledge that the silence of the Father is not finally and ultimately malevolence even as the Father's vindication of the Son is the pledge that the Son's living witness is not finally and ultimately powerless. The resurrection, however, neither negates the cross as if this were a mere appearance nor makes it "pale into insignificance." The Son who is raised is the Son who is crucified and he still bears the marks of that event in his resurrection. Further, the resurrection does not explain the silence of the Father at the cross. That "God raised him from the dead" represents the vindication of the Son himself who accepted the cross and the silence of the Father and thus also the vindication of the Son's proclamation: that the Father is finally *Abba*. Yet insofar as the resurrection is not an end, but a beginning and the prolepsis of an end, it points away from itself towards an eschatological future when "God is all in all" in the advent of his kingdom. The truth of the resurrection proclamation will only be known retrospectively, from the point of the arrival of the Kingdom or its definitive nonarrival.

Construing "God" as present in history as the Triune God is certainly a wager or risk in a twofold sense. Formally, it is a wager because it stands over and against all other religious and non-religious wagers. Materially, it is a wager because the positive content of how Christianity construes God as present to the world is essentially referenced to and conditional on what is still "not-yet," the Kingdom of God. Whether such a trinitarian theo-logical perspective is possible or whether abiding with the silence of the Father introduces a fatal tension into Christian theology, is clearly a debatable matter which demands further reflection and exposition. And yet I think that the claim of that which is most near to us, the claim to ultimacy of the history of suffering, will tolerate no other position.

SELECT BIBLIOGRAPHY OF PRIMARY SOURCES

-⋅∗⋗═⇥◉⇤═⋖∗⋅-

WORKS BY WOLFHART PANNENBERG

Theology and the Kingdom of God. Edited by Richard John Neuhaus. Philadelphia: Westminster Press, 1969.

Jesus-God and Man. Translated by Lewis Wilkens and Duane Priebe. Philadelphia: Westminster Press, 1968.

Basic Questions in Theology. 2 vols. Translated by George H. Kehm. Philadelphia: Fortress Press, 1970-71.

Grundfragen systematischer Theologie: Gesammelte Aufsatze. 2 vols. Gottingen: Vandenhoeck and Ruprecht, 1970-80.

What is Man? Translated by D. A. Priebe. Philadelphia: Fortress Press, 1970.

The Idea of God and Human Freedom. Translated by R. A. Wilson. Philadelphia: Fortress Press, 1973.

"Weltgeschichte und Heilsgeschichte." In *Geschichte: Ereignis und Erzählung*, pp. 307-23. Edited by R. Kosolleck and W. D. Stempel. Munich: Wilhelm Fink Verlag, 1973.

"Erfordert die Einheit der Geschichte ein Subjekt?" In *Geschichte: Ereignis und Erzählung*, pp. 478-90. Edited by R. Kosolleck and W. D. Stempel. Munich: Wilhelm Fink Verlag, 1973.

Theology and the Philosophy of Science. Translated by F. McDonagh. Philadelphia: Fortress Press, 1976.

Ethik und Ekklesiologie. Gottingen: Vandenhoeck and Ruprecht, 1977.

"Der Gott der Geschichte." *Kerygma und Dogma* 23 (March 1977): 76-92.

Christian Spirituality. Philadelphia: Westminster Press, 1983.

Anthropology in Philosophical Perspective. Translated by Matthew J. O'Connell. Philadelphia: Fortress Press, 1985.

Metaphysics and the Idea of God. Translated by Philip Clayton. Grand Rapids, MI: Eerdmans Publishing Co., 1990.

Pannenberg, Wolfhart; Rendtorff, Rolf; Rendtorff, Trutz and Wilkens, Ulrich. *Revelation as History*. Translated by David Granskou. Edited by Wolfhart Pannenberg. New York: The Macmillan Co., 1968.

WORKS BY MAX HORKHEIMER AND THEODOR ADORNO

Dialectic of Enlightenment. Translated by John Cumming. New York: Seabury Press, 1972.

Adorno, Theodor. "On Popular Music." *Zeitschrift für Sozialforschung* 9 (1941): 17-48.

_____. "A Social Critique of Radio Music." *Kenyon Review* 8 (Spring 1945): 208-17.

_____. "Theses Upon Art and Religion Today." *Kenyon Review* 7 (Fall 1944): 677-82.

_____. "Anti-Semitism and Fascist Propaganda." In *Anti-Semitism: A Social Disease*, pp. 125-37. Edited by Ernst Simmel. New York: International Universities Press, 1946.

_____. "Is Marx Obsolete." *Diogenes* 64 (Winter 1968): 1-16.

_____. "Television and the Patterns of Mass Culture." In *Mass Culture: The Popular Arts in America*, pp. 474-88. Edited by Bernard Rosenberg and David White Manning. New York: Free Press, 1957.

_____. "Sociology and Psychology." *New Left Review* 46/47 (December 1967/January 1968): 79-97, 67-80.

_____, et al. *The Authoritarian Personality*. New York: Norton Library, 1969.

_____. *Aesthetische Theorie*. Edited by Gretel Adorno and Rolf Tiedemann. Frankfurt: Suhrkamp Tauschenbuch, 1970.

_____. "Theses on the Sociology of Art." *Working Papers in Cultural Studies* 2 (Spring 1972): 121-28.

————. *"Die Rividierte Psychoanalyse."* Gesammelte Schriften. Edited by Rolf Tiedemann. Vol. 8: *Soziologische Schriften*, pp. 20-41. Frankfurt: Suhrkamp Verlag, 1975.

————. "The Psychological Technique of Martin Luther Thomas' Radio Addresses." *Gesammelte Schriften*. Edited by Rolf Tiedemann. Vol. 9.1: *Soziologische Schriften*, pp. 12-141. Frankfurt: Suhrkamp Verlag, 1975.

————. *"Die Idee der Naturgeschichte."* Gesammelte Schriften. Edited by Rolf Tiedemann. Vol. 1: *Philosophische Fruhschriften*, pp. 345-65. Frankfurt: Suhrkamp Verlag, 1973.

————. *Negative Dialectics.* Translated by E. B. Ashton. New York: Seabury Press, 1973.

Adorno, Theodor. *"Der Essay als Form."* Gesammelte Schriften. Edited by Rolf Tiedemann. Vol. 11: *Noten zur Literatur*, pp. 9-33. Frankfurt: Suhrkamp Verlag, 1974.

————. *Minima Moralia: Reflections From Damaged Life.* Translated by E. F. N. Jephcott. London: New Left Books, 1974.

————. "Culture Industry Reconsidered." *New German Critique* 6 (Fall 1975): 12-19.

————, et al. *The Positivist Dispute in German Sociology.* Translated by Glyn Adey and David Frisby. New York: Heinemann Educational Books, 1976.

————. "The Stars Down to Earth: The Los Angeles Times Astrology Column." In *Gesammelte Schriften*. Edited by Rolf Tiedemann. Vol. 9.2: *Soziologischen Schriften*, pp. 11-120. Frankfurt: Suhrkamp Verlag, 1976.

————. *Introduction to the Sociology of Music.* Translated by E. B. Ashton. New York: Seabury Press, 1976.

————. "The Actuality of Philosophy." *Telos* 31 (Spring 1977): 120-33.

————. "Commitment." In *Aesthetics and Politics*, pp. 177-95. Translated by Harry Zohn and others. Edited by Ronald Taylor. Afterword by Frederick Jameson. London: New Left Books, 1977.

————. "Adorno-Benjamin Correspondence." In *Aesthetics and Politics*, pp. 110-41. Translated by Harry Zohn and others. Edited by Ronald Taylor. Afterword by Frederick Jameson. London: New Left Books, 1977.

_____. "Reconciliation Under Duress." In *Aesthetics and Politics*, pp. 151-76. Translated by Harry Zohn and others. Edited by Ronald Taylor. Afterword by Frederick Jameson. London: New Left Books, 1977.

_____. "Music and Technique." *Telos* 32 (Summer 1977): 79-86.

_____. "Music and the New Music." *Telos* 32 (Summer 1977): 24-38.

_____. "On the Fetish Character of Music and the Regression of Listening." In *The Essential Frankfurt School Reader*, pp. 270-99. Edited and introductions by Andrew Arato and Eike Gebhardt. New York: Urizen Books, 1978.

Adorno, Theodor. "Freudian Theory and the Pattern of Fascist Propaganda." In *The Essential Frankfurt School Reader*, pp. 118-37. Edited and introductions by Andrew Arato and Eike Gebhardt. New York: Urizen Books, 1978.

_____. "Resignation." *Telos* 35 (Spring 1978): 163-67.

_____. "Culture and Administration." *Telos* 37 (Fall 1978): 93-111.

_____. "*Marginalien ze Theorie und Praxis.*" In *Gesammelte Schriften*. Edited by Rolf Tiedemann. Vol. 10.2: *Kulturkritik und Gesellschaft*, pp. 759-82. Frankfurt: Suhrkamp Verlag, 1978.

_____. *The Philosophy of Modern Music*. Translated by Anne Mitchell and Wes Blomster. New York: Seabury Press, 1980.

_____. *Prisms*. Translated Samuel and Shierry Weber. Cambridge: The MIT Press, 1981.

Horkheimer, Max. *Kritische Theorie: Eine Dokumentation*. 2 vols. Edited by Alfred Schmidt. Frankfurt: S. Fischer Verlag, 1968.

_____. *Critical Theory: Selected Essays*. Translated by Matthew J. O'Connell and others. New York: Seabury Press, 1972.

_____. "Research Project on Anti-Semitism." *Zeitschrift für Sozialforschung* 9 (1941): 124-43.

_____. "The End of Reason." *Zeitschrift für Sozialforschung* 9 (1941): 366-88.

_____. "Sociological Background of the Psychoanalytic Approach." In *Anti-Semitism: A Social Disease*, pp. 1-10. Edited by Ernst Simmel. New York: International Universities Press, 1946.

_____. "The Lessons of Fascism." In *Tensions That Cause War*, pp. 209-42. Edited by Hadley Cantrill. Urbana: University of Illinois Press, 1950.

_____. *Die Sehnsucht nach dem ganz Anderen: Ein Interview mit Kommentar von Hellmut Gumnior*. Hamburg: Furche Verlag, 1970.

_____. *Eclipse of Reason*. New York: Oxford University Press, 1947; reprint ed. New York: Seabury Press, 1974.

_____. "Marx Today-An Address." In *Post-War German Culture: An Anthology*, pp. 128-38. Edited by C. McClelland and S. Scher. New York: E. P. Dutton and Co., 1974.

Horkheimer, Max. "On the Problem of Truth." In *The Essential Frankfurt School Reader*, pp. 407-43. Edited and introductions by Andrew Arato and Eike Gebhardt. New York: Urizen Books, 1978.

_____. "The Authoritarian State." In *The Essential Frankfurt School Reader*, pp. 95-117. Edited and introductions by Andrew Arato and Eike Gebhardt. New York: Urizen Books, 1978.

_____. *Dawn and Decline: Notes 1926-1931 and 1950-1969*. Translated by Michael Shaw. Afterword by Eike Gebhardt. New York: Seabury Press, 1978.

_____. "*Die gegenwartigen Lage der Sozialphilosophie und die Aufgabe eines Instituts für Sozialforschung.*" In *Sozial-philosophische Studien*, pp. 31-46. Frankfurt: Fischer Tauschenbuch Verlag, 1981.

[Frankfurt Institute for Social Research], *Aspects of Sociology*. Translated by John Viertel. Preface by Max Horkheimer and Theodor Adorno. Boston: Beacon Press, 1972.

WORKS BY JOHANN METZ

Christliche Anthropozentrik. Munich: Kosel Verlag, 1962.

"*Gott vor uns: Statt eines theologischen Arguments.*" In *Ernst Bloch zu ehren: Beiträge zu seinem Werk*, pp. 227-41. Edited by Siegfried Unseld. Frankfurt: Suhrkamp Verlag, 1965.

"The Theological World and the Metaphysical World." *Philosophy Today* 10 (1966): 253-63.

"Freedom as a Threshold Problem between Philosophy and Theology." *Philosophy Today* 10 (1966): 264-79.

"The Responsibility of Hope." *Philosophy Today* 10 (1966): 280-88.

Theology of the World. Translated by William Glen-Doepel. New York: Seabury Press, 1969.

"'Politische Theologie' in der Diskussion." In *Diskussion zur politischen Theologie*, pp. 267-301. Edited by Helmut Peukert. Munich: Christian Kaiser Verlag, 1969.

Sacramentum Mundi. S.v. "Apologetics" and "Political Theology."

"Zu einer interdiziplinär orienterten Theologie auf bikonfessionneller Basis: Erste Orientierung anhand eines konkreten Projekts." In *Die Theologie in der interdiziplinären Forschung*, pp. 10-25. Edited by Johann Metz and Trutz Rendtorff. Dusseldorf: Bertelsmann Universitätsverlag, 1971.

"Prophetic Authority." In *Religion and Political Society*, pp. 177-209. Translated and edited in the Institute of Christian Thought. New York: Harper Forum Books, 1974.

Glaube im Geschichte und Gesellschaft. Mainz: Matthias Grunewald, 1977.

Followers of Christ. Translated by Thomas Linton. New York: Paulist Press, 1978.

Faith in History and Society. Translated by David Smith. New York: Crossroad Publishing Co., 1981.

The Emergent Church. Translated by Peter Mann. New York: Crossroad Publishing Co., 1981.

Unterbrechungen. Gutersloh: Gerd Mohn Verlag, 1981.